Unwin Education Books: 1
EDUCATION SINCE 1800

Books by Ivor Morrish

Disciplines of Education
Education Since 1800
The Background of Immigrant Children
The Sociology of Education: an Introduction

Unwin Education Books

Series Editor: Ivor Morrish, B.D., B.A., Dip.Ed. (London), B.A. (Bristol).

1. Education Since 1800 IVOR MORRISH
2. Moral Development WILLIAM KAY
3. Physical Education for Teaching BARBARA CHURCHER
4. The Background of Immigrant Children IVOR MORRISH
5. Organising and Integrating the Infant Day JOY TAYLOR
6. The Philosophy of Education: an Introduction HARRY SCHOFIELD
7. Assessment and Testing: an Introduction HARRY SCHOFIELD
8. Education: Its Nature and Purpose M. V. C. JEFFREYS
9. Learning in the Primary School KENNETH HASLAM
10. The Sociology of Education: an Introduction IVOR MORRISH
11. Fifty Years of Freedom RAY HEMMINGS
12. Developing a Curriculum AUDREY AND HOWARD NICHOLLS
13. Teacher Education and Cultural Change H. DUDLEY PLUNKETT AND JAMES LYNCH
14. Reading and Writing in the First School JOY TAYLOR
15. Approaches to Drama DAVID A. MALE
16. Aspects of Learning BRIAN O'CONNELL
17. Focus on Meaning JOAN TOUGH
18. Moral Education WILLIAM KAY
19. Concepts in Primary Education JOHN E. SADLER
20. Moral Philosophy for Education ROBIN BARROW
21. Beyond Control? PAUL FRANCIS
22. Principles of Classroom Learning and Perception RICHARD J. MUELLER
23. Education and the Community ERIC MIDWINTER

Unwin Education Books: 1

Series Editor: Ivor Morrish

Education Since 1800

IVOR MORRISH

B.D., B.A., Dip.Ed.(London), B.A.(Bristol)

Principal Lecturer in Education
La Sainte Union College of Education
Southampton

London
GEORGE ALLEN AND UNWIN LTD
RUSKIN HOUSE   MUSEUM STREET

First published in 1970
Second impression 1970
Third impression 1973
Fourth impression 1976

© *George Allen & Unwin Ltd, 1970*

ISBN 0 04 370030 6   *Paper*

Printed in Great Britain
in Times Roman type
by Biddles Ltd
Guildford, Surrey

To Marlene

Contents

Part Two: Specific Topics in Education

Author's Preface

Like my *Disciplines of Education* this book was designed chiefly to meet the needs of students who require not so much a detailed critical approach as a brief survey of a rather wide field. This book can, in itself, be little more than a *coup d'œil* of the development of education since 1800; but I have tried to indicate throughout some of the more important primary and secondary sources which are available in one form or another. The book is intended to be a jumping-off ground; and some students will inevitably jump further than others. Part One deals with the general development of popular education; Part Two is concerned with a number of specific topics such as the universities, teacher training and so forth; and Part Three considers several of the more important thinkers in education during the period.

I have to acknowledge my indebtedness to the writers quoted or to whom some reference has been made. In particular I must mention the many reports and circulars published by Her Majesty's Stationery Office, and J. Stuart Maclure's *Educational Documents*, which is a *sine qua non* for every student of education. I am also indebted to my publishers for permitting me to reproduce here a large proportion of my chapter on John Dewey in *Disciplines of Education*: and above all to my wife who has patiently read and typed my manuscript. For the book's defects and omissions I alone am responsible..

Southampton
Hants

IVOR MORRISH

Part One

The General Development of Popular Education

Chapter 1

English
Elementary Education

A ITS ORIGINS
English elementary education in the nineteenth century was the result of
the gradual development and bringing together of a number of organizations basically unrelated in purpose or form. Some were inspired by purely
vested industrial and monetary interests, whilst others were philanthropic
or burning with a religious zeal which saw the education of the poor as a
part of the divine plan for the salvation of souls. Just as it would be facile,
as well as wrong and misconceived, to damn all 'dame' schools, particularly on the basis of some of the contemporary literature, it would be
equally misjudged to think of all 'religious' schools as entirely altruistic
because of the missionary fervour displayed by some of their founders.
Perhaps nothing was more calculated, initially at least, to keep the peasant
in a constant awareness of his 'station' in life than the catechetical indoctrination of some of the church schools, whilst the attempt to teach him
the three Rs frequently did little more than make him increasingly aware
of his ineptitude in the world of literacy. There are ways of keeping people
ignorant other than by simply ignoring their educational needs: they can
be taught enough and in a sufficiently selective manner to make them even
more the mere instruments of political engineering. Today we know only
too well that the 'monitorial' system is not the only way of providing
mass misinformation—although from many points of view it proved
a highly successful one.

It is significant that one of the chief reports of the century, that of the
commissioners appointed to inquire into the state of popular education
in England, supported in 1861 the very limited horizons of elementary
education proposed in the evidence of Rev. James Fraser, an assistant
commissioner who, on the basis of his incredible sagacity no doubt, was
later appointed Bishop of Manchester. He says:

'Even if it were possible, I doubt whether it would be desirable, with a view
to the real interests of the peasant boy, to keep him at school till he
was 14 or 15 years of age. But it is not possible. We must make up
our minds to see the last of him, as far as the day school is concerned,
at 10 or 11. We must frame our system of education upon this

hypothesis; and I venture to maintain that it is quite possible to teach a child soundly and thoroughly, in a way that he shall not forget it, all that is necessary for him to possess in the shape of intellectual attainment, by the time that he is 10 years old' (1).

We shall have a closer look at the Newcastle Report later; it is quoted here merely to indicate that educational sights for the poorer elements in our society were set low even by those who, ostensibly at least, were most concerned with them on humanitarian or religious grounds. There were many, like the assistant commissioner quoted above, who considered that sufficient education had been provided for the peasant if he knew enough of the Scriptures to follow the allusions and arguments 'of a plain Saxon sermon', and had an adequate 'recollection of the truths taught him in his catechism, to know what are the duties required of him towards his Maker and his fellow man' (2).

It is customary to dismiss the 'dame' schools by quoting William Shenstone's piece of Alexandrine doggerel, entitled *The Schoolmistress* and published in 1742. There is perhaps little to be gained at this point in time by defending these schools, if only because 'history' has condemned them. In principle, at least, they provided a service, comparable to that of many contemporary 'baby-minding establishments', which are often equally 'inefficient' when it comes to anything basically educational (3). Dame schools had existed in Shakespeare's England and represented the sole means of education for the masses of poor people, and for a few pence an elderly matron would at least, in the words of George Macaulay Trevelyan, 'half teach' the children to read (4). And just as generalizations about independent primary schools are largely meaningless today, some of which are conducted in poky and inadequate private houses, so it would be equally meaningless to lump together all 'dame' schools of the late eighteenth and early nineteenth centuries and categorize them as bad. H. C. Barnard reminds us that Charles Kingsley had pleasant recollections of at least one village dame school which he must have viewed in Yorkshire in the late fifties (5), and many had good reason to be thankful that they had perhaps learned something from either Shenstone's 'relentless dame' or George Crabbe's 'deaf, poor, patient widow'.

In addition to the 'dame' schools there existed other private venture establishments run, in the main, by men who were both social and academic failures. A few possessed some little learning, enough to put on a pretence of scholarship for unsuspecting or untutored parents, but most were cruel and debased adventurers who saw the possibilities of easy money with a minimum of effort, and whose aims of education were of the Squeers' pragmatic nature at Dotheboys Hall.

The charity school movement really began with the founding of the

Society for Promoting Christian Knowledge (S.P.C.K.) in 1698. This society saw as its prime function the restoration of morals and religion to a country which was becoming increasingly degenerate and irreligious. To this end it proposed a programme of founding schools, the publication and distribution of religious literature, from Bibles to tracts, and the reclamation of the immoral and destitute. The Society was supported by a large number of people who saw it as 'a good thing' for a variety of reasons, not wholly educational. The movement spread rapidly throughout the country and was parish-based; thus there were 'charity sermons' leading to special collections for S.P.C.K. schools; parish clergy taught some children free of charge, and workmen themselves contributed towards the education of their children by these charitable institutions. By the middle of the eighteenth century there were over 2,000 schools connected with the S.P.C.K., dealing with over 50,000 children.

There were naturally those who opposed the whole movement of popular education chiefly on theological grounds, namely that God had created each man's estate and it was the individual's function to fulfil his station in life. Education, however elementary, could do nothing but aggravate discontent and give to the ignoble and ignorant ambitions beyond their rightful destiny. There was an aura of predestination as well as inertia about the whole concept. Others, however, considered that the right selection of material and method within the charity schools could achieve the same end whilst providing a façade of progress. A judicious teaching of the catechism, which formed the basis of religious instruction, could not help but reinforce the concept of 'my station and its duties'. Was the peasant not enjoined to order himself lowly and reverently to all his betters, and to honour and obey the Sovereign and all that were put in authority; and to submit himself to all his governors, teachers, spiritual pastors and masters? If only he were taught these things early enough and often enough, and his appearance in the church gallery every Sunday was a practical demonstration of his religious and moral obedience, the poor peasant would certainly not get ideas above his station.

In addition to religious instruction, reading, writing and arithmetic were provided by different schools in varying quantities. Mostly, however, there was an eye to the industrial function of the pupils—sewing, spinning, knitting, ploughing, gardening: these were the main fare of children destined to become the factory hands, the labourers and the domestic servants in our society.

But it would be wrong to suggest that the whole structure of charity schools was geared to perpetuating the existing class distinctions. We often speak about educating for mobility within the class-system of our society as if there were something specifically modern about the concept. In its early days the S.P.C.K. took considerable interest in the careers of charity school children, and helped many children to gain apprenticeships for which, without even this minimal schooling, they would not be qualified.

If the Church and charitable institutions were interested in the education of the poor, so too was industry itself. This was not perhaps entirely altruistic; the factory owners found that if they were to get the utmost out of their workers they had to provide some initial preparation in mental alertness and physical skill. This included facilities for learning to read and for learning the particular skills of the industry. Thomas Firman was among the pioneers in providing in 1675 such a 'school of industry' in which children of four or five were taught to read and spin. In 1697 Locke had advocated, in *On Education*, that working schools should be set up in every parish, and that children between the ages of three and fourteen should be made to attend. Little came of his suggestion until the latter part of the eighteenth century when, through the development of the factory system, a number of schools of industry were set up.

It was the aim of these schools not simply to give the rudiments of reading and number, but to train boys and girls in industrial occupations such as spinning, printing and sewing and also in such employments as gardening, cobbling and carpentry. The children's products were sold and the proceeds used to pay the costs of their keep; and any surplus was shared among them as a payment for their work. These schools, however, gradually disappeared since they could not compete with the new factory developments in which children proved a valuable source of secondary income to parents, as well as cheap labour for the employers. By the beginning of the nineteenth century only about 20,000 children were left in schools of industry.

As the charity schools became fewer in number and lost their initial zeal and impetus, and as the schools of industry began to close down and children became more fully employed during the working week, the need became apparent for some sort of school that would cater for children during what leisure hours they had. Both Rev. Thomas Stock and Robert Raikes had observed in Gloucester that the thousands of children employed in the local factories had nothing to do on Sundays. They were illiterate and lacking in discipline, and in consequence many of them graduated from mischief and high spirits to delinquency and crime. Stock and Raikes therefore started the sunday school movement in 1780, although work had been done in this direction many years before by such reformers as John Wesley.

A few years after the general movement started a society was formed in 1785, entitled The Society for the Establishment and Support of Sunday Schools. Society at large was developing a feeling that purely individual efforts for social change and the education of the lower classes were not enough; some centrally organized and controlled effort was required.

So there developed in the ensuing era a rash of societies supporting private and sectarian efforts for popular education. In 1803 the powerful Sunday School Union was formed, in which all parties at least made the attempt to sink their denominational interests in order to support the public good. Anglicans and Dissenters alike became involved in a concerted effort to provide a minimum education for all children prepared to attend the school and church. G. M. Trevelyan's judgment on these schools is summed up in his statement that

'The new charity schools and sunday schools had the merit of trying to do something for all, but they had the demerit of too great an anxiety to keep the young scholars in their appointed sphere of life and train up a submissive generation' (6).

Many of the teachers in these sunday schools were at first paid for their services, but in the long run the teaching was done by voluntary workers who, for the main part, were concerned that the Scriptures should be taught and read. For this purpose most of the instruction at first resolved itself into reading and spelling, although some schools were determined to provide as liberal an education as possible within the limits of time and general resources. People such as Hannah and Martha More, and Mrs Sarah Trimmer, were certainly not satisfied with the minimal educational content of the large proportion of sunday schools, and they began to provide special primers and story books for graduated learning.

There were those, such as the poet Southey, who bitterly complained against the sunday schools, although between one and two million children were attending them in Great Britain before 1840. Southey undoubtedly had more than a passing interest in education, but he tended to see exploitation where often none was intended and at other times to become uncritically enthusiastic about methods, such as Dr Andrew Bell's monitorial system, which, to say the least, were educationally dubious. In a letter to Lord Ashley, dated February 7, 1833, Southey suggested that the sunday schools had been made

'subservient to the merciless love of gain. The manufacturers know that a cry would be raised against them if their little white slaves received no instruction; and so they have converted Sunday into a Schoolday' (7).

The rapid expansion of the sunday school movement, exploitation or not, undoubtedly represented the beginnings of popular education in this country, and moreover education that was free to the recipient. It also established that religious leaning which state education has had in this country ever since, despite the many problems and objections on principle that have accompanied it to the present day.

The Welsh 'circulating schools', which began in 1737 on the initiative of Rev. Griffiths Jones of Carmarthen, steadily expanded throughout the eighteenth century and helped establish the principle of peripatetic teachers. Lessons were provided for both children and adults in houses, churches, chapels and embryonic schools, and for up to six months of the year they would take place during the whole of the day and the evening. By the end of the century, however, these schools, which had numbered between six and seven thousand, had almost disappeared and the sunday schools had taken their place.

Of the monitorial, or mutual, system Professor J. W. Adamson has said that

'It made the provision of popular instruction on a national scale feasible, it compensated to a certain degree for the absence of a body of teachers, provided a rough scheme of teachers' training and prepared the way for the pupil-teacher system' (8).

Without entering into the controversy over whether Joseph Lancaster or Andrew Bell was primarily responsible for the inception of the system (and Lancaster certainly acknowledged his own debt to Bell), it seems clear that both hit upon a method of teaching and mass educational production which received acclaim from their contemporaries because of its economy of finance and because of its quasi-efficiency when compared with much of the disorganization and unregimented teaching which was going on in charity, sunday and various other types of school.

Joseph Lancaster (1778–1838) was a Quaker with a missionary enthusiasm to teach but without any sort of business acumen. He attracted a large number of scholars—too many to teach adequately by what were regarded as normal methods at the time. And so he adopted in his schools a system of mutual aid. At his school in Borough Road, Southwark, at the turn of the century, he developed a scheme which he later described in his *Improvements in Education* (1803). The method involved using older pupils to teach younger ones, having first been fully primed on the lesson by Lancaster himself. In this way the latter felt that one teacher could adequately cope with at least 100 pupils, with a hierarchy of monitors including a monitor-in-chief to take charge of all the other monitors. Lancaster found considerable support for his work despite his own financial incompetence, and the work, taken over by the Lancasterian Society in 1810, which was renamed the British and Foreign School Society in 1814, continued to flourish without him after his resignation in 1814.

Dr Andrew Bell (1753–1832) had developed very similar ideas in India, particularly in Madras, where he found himself not only a comparatively rich man but also one with sufficient authority to impose a method which he considered had possibilities. This was substantially the method used by Lancaster, that of employing one instructed boy to teach many others. When he returned to England in 1795 Bell thought more seriously about his 'Madras' method and described it in *An Experiment in Education*, which he published in 1797. Bell was an Anglican clergyman, whilst Lancaster was a Quaker, and at a time of serious religious rivalry the successes of the one quickly upset the other and led to more concerted action. In consequence, in 1811 there was formed the National Society for Promoting the Education of the Poor in the Principles of the Established Church throughout England and Wales. The purpose of this society was to assist church schools whose prime function was to inculcate the Christian catechism of the Church of England, and to ensure that the children regularly attended church.

The method employed by the monitorial schools was almost entirely a mechanical, rote-memory one. There was little or no opportunity to question or investigate the material taught—merely to accept and learn it was enough. It was a long, monotonous, mass-producing drill like the Army process of the 'naming of parts'. But whilst it did not employ the most enlightened methods, the monitorial system did at least highlight the whole question of a popular elementary education which should be free for all. And, again, although the 'religious question' was brought to the fore by the sometimes intense animus displayed by the supporters of the 'national' schools on the one hand and the 'British' schools on the other, at least the competitive element gave rise to a search for better, more universal and more permanent things. There was also a recognition by the sponsors of the monitorial system that there was an urgent need for trained teachers if only to pass on information to 'monitors', and so the National Society founded the College of St Mark's at Chelsea in 1840 (now the College of St Mark and St John). Joseph Lancaster had recognized this need and he had, in fact, established much earlier an institution at Borough Road, where teachers were trained in order to support his school there. The college was moved to Isleworth in 1890 (9).

B EARLY STATE ACTION

It is usual in the context of the history of education to speak of 'State intervention' in a system which had developed from a voluntary outcrop of multiform elementary education. Certainly there were times when the Government appeared to have little or no involvement in popular education until a clash of interests occurred which called for some sort of intervention. 'Intervention' has, however, a negative and at times even pejorative implication, whilst 'State intervention' has the even uglier aspect of a huge, crushing machine set over against the somewhat pathetic efforts of a people struggling to express themselves. State action and participation were, to say the least, sporadic and at times irrational, but historical criticism in retrospect is the most facile of intellectual exercises, whilst to be involved in immediate action is often the most difficult. There were during this period many individuals, both within the political arena and outside it, vitally concerned with the health, wealth and happiness of the common people, and in their view an organized system of education of some sort was involved in this concern. Individuals such as Robert Owen (1771–1858), Samuel Wilderspin (1792–1866) and David Stow (1793–1864) were interested in children for their own sake, and whilst rejecting the all too frequent tendency to ignore their needs, they equally rejected the mechanical, repetitive and impersonal methods of the monitorial system. The school provided by Owen was regarded by all as an attempt to put into practice imaginative insights into the basic principles of education. His view of the purpose of education involved the personal development of each child, and, like Helvétius, the French philosopher who died in the year in which Owen was born, he accepted the dictum that *L'éducation peut tout*. At his school in New Lanark, Scotland, children were encouraged to dance, sing and play.

Whilst Wilderspin was certainly concerned with character development as well as mere instruction, he tended to formalize both in catechismal rhymes and pieces of doggerel. Some of these were set to music and moralized in a mixture of arithmetical tables and somewhat pedestrian aphorism:

> 'Two pints will make one quart,
> Four quarts one gallon, strong;
> Some drink too little, some too much—
> To drink too much is wrong . . . . . .
>
> With gallons fifty-four
> A hogshead I can fill,
> But I hope I never shall drink much—
> Drink much whoever will' (10).

To suggest that this was all that Wilderspin did would be to caricature the efforts of a man who worked out a complete system of infant education at a time when there was a great need in our society to establish aims, matter and method. Much of what Wilderspin developed was based upon either the ideas of Pestalozzi or ideas closely allied to the latter's work, and some of the better infant schools of this period developed a curriculum which was considerably varied and enlightened.

The important features about the work of David Stow were his stresses upon oral work and the impact of the personality of the teacher on the pupil. Stow believed very firmly in the importance of the teacher's influence on the child's development, and this personal contact was to him the most vital element in education. It was the function of the teacher not merely to instruct or purvey information but also to mediate true culture, to stimulate original thinking and to initiate true dialogue on all questions considered within the classroom. Stow made some attempt at a rationally graded system, not only grading children generally according to their chronological age (infant, junior and senior departments), but also streaming them roughly according to their apparent ability.

The mere fact that such private individuals were interested in education and seeking to do something about the general situation throughout the country, by their own example and the propagation of their ideas through publications, was sufficient reason for thinking people, including politicians and social reformers, to look at the whole question from a more national standpoint. Sir Robert Peel, in 1802, produced the first real piece of legislation concerned with the education of the children of the working classes. The Health and Morals of Apprentices Act provided for the teaching of apprentices during the working day and for at least one hour on Sunday. It is true that the educational curriculum provided covered a minimum—namely, the three Rs—but however ineffectual it may have been it at least represented the beginning of government interest and State action in the educational sphere.

Henry Brougham (1778–1868), later Lord Brougham and Vaux, demanded that an enquiry should be instigated into the 'education of the lower orders'. As a result parliamentary committees were set up in 1816 and 1818 which reported on elementary schooling, initially in London and then throughout the rest of the country. By modern standards, no doubt, these reports leave much to be desired as a social or statistical enquiry, but they were at least an attempt to discover something of the national condition of education, both in terms of quality and quantity. Although the reports established that there were grave deficiencies in general provision, accommodation and actual teaching, and much of the evidence produced (such as that provided by Rev. William Gurney, Rector of St Clement Danes) revealed incredible poverty and educational destitution, the total outcome of the report was a general sense of frustration.

In a scheme put forward in a Parish Schools Bill, in 1820, Brougham—who undoubtedly had in mind the organization of a national system—so beclouded the issue with religious prejudice and a demand for Anglican control and teaching that both Dissenters and Roman Catholics opposed the Bill and it was eventually withdrawn. Thus already certain issues became clear in the early nineteenth century. There was an increasing demand for a national system; and there was the depressing prospect of a religious struggle in education which, even over a century later, has not been finally resolved.

There was also the perennial question of costs. In the report of 1816–18

Owen had given some interesting evidence in answer to the question whether the expense of his New Lanark institution was considerable. Owen's reply is interesting, not merely because of his confirmation concerning the costs of education but because he was one of the few people to talk of educational productivity in terms of character formation as well as industrial utility. Owen claimed that the cost per child was apparently considerable,

'. . . but I do not know how any capital can be employed to make such abundant returns, as that which is judiciously expended in forming the character and directing the labour of the lower classes . . . I have made out a short statement of the expense of the instruction of the Institution at Lanark . . . 20s. per year for each child, which if taken under tuition at three years old, and retained to the age of ten would be £7 each, for forming the habits, dispositions and general character, and instructions in the elements of every branch of useful knowledge' (11).

Popular education, and interest in it generally, was accelerated by the various changes in the franchise brought about by the repeal of the Test Acts in 1828–9, which recognized the civil rights of nonconformists and Roman Catholics, and by the Reform Act of 1832 which provided a more realistic form of democratic representation in the House of Commons. Radical changes in one area of public life inevitably effect changes in other areas! The provision of the vote demanded the ability to think about the choices made, and therefore an understanding of the issues involved. It soon became clear to the politicians, at a purely pragmatic level, that if they were to make vote-catching speeches to the populace the latter must have at least a minimal comprehension of their social aims and political purposes. Education was the only answer.

In 1833 John Arthur Roebuck (1801–79) provided Parliament with an outline of 'the universal and national education of the whole people'. Roebuck's Bill was given a long and serious debate in Parliament, but it proved too ambitious as a first attempt and perhaps demonstrated the principle that, short of revolution, reformers need in the first instance to gear their demands to reality and to compromise their ideals in order to realize some part of their vision. At least interest was aroused and in 1833 the first grant of £20,000 was made by Parliament in aid of 'private subscriptions for the erection of school houses'. This money was, in the event, made over to the 'national' and 'British' Societies to assist them in the building of their schools. Thus, the voluntary religious system was supplied by an increasingly paternal government.

The Report of the Parliamentary Committee on the State of Education, produced in 1834, revealed some interesting attitudes towards compulsory,

State-provided education as well as on such questions as the training of teachers, their salaries, and the religious problems. In a discussion of the teaching force the principle of teachers 'rubbing shoulders with the world' before taking up the teaching profession was clearly raised in the evidence of the Clerical Superintendent of the National Society.

'They must all have had some employment before the age of twenty-one, and therefore I should say that they have all tried some profession or calling. The exception is so small that it is not worth mentioning; the greater number have been in some other business than that of keeping school; I think the majority have, certainly' (12).

And to the question of whether a man who was sufficiently skilled in reading, writing and arithmetic could learn the art, indeed the 'difficult' art of teaching, in five months, the sanguine answer was, 'Yes, decidedly; and it may be learnt in three months, if he has tact . . .' (13). The intellectual standards and academic attainments of teachers have been a controversial issue for over a hundred years, and it is interesting to note the evidence given by a member of the Committee of the National Society on the possibilities of better teacher training and its effects on the status of teachers. His view, briefly, was that if the intellectual qualifications of the schoolmaster were raised, without an adequate and corresponding rise in his salary, he would most certainly 'find more profitable occupation with others in another situation' (14).

In 1839 the Committee of Council for Education was set up, and Dr James Philips-Kay (afterwards Sir James Kay-Shuttleworth) became its first secretary. This quasi-education department examined the problems of teacher supply and a number of teacher training colleges were now established, and a modified form of the pupil-teacher system was introduced. Kay-Shuttleworth was himself interested in progressive forms of education, and made a point of becoming acquainted with Pestalozzian principles and practice and the work of Fellenberg. A scheme was developed through his efforts in 1846 for the training of pupil-teachers: syllabuses were drawn up and annual examinations arranged. Moreover, some real attempt was made to provide grants and bursaries for likely students and to boost the salaries of appointed and inspected school teachers depending upon their character and conduct, the satisfactory performance of their duties, and an inspector's report to the effect that their schools were efficiently conducted. In some schools pupil-teachers were appointed at the age of thirteen years on an apprenticeship basis, with a small honorarium; and at the end of their apprenticeship they could compete for the Queen's Scholarship which would provide them with a place at a training college.

The Report of the Commissioners of Inquiry into the State of Education in Wales, published in 1847, revealed a certain lack of scientific objectivity at a time when real social investigation was in its infancy, and data were derived from a particular sample of the populace, notably the local clergy, in a very primitive anecdotal manner. An early distinction was made by one commissioner, J. C. Symons, between the use of the Holy Scriptures as a textbook by which to learn reading, and real scriptural knowledge, of which 'the children have no idea, except in the few superior schools' (15). The commissioner considered that only an improved education could do anything about the general condition of the Welsh society and its religious and moral progress. Indeed, Symons saw in the alleged lack of chastity in women the source of all other immoralities, since each generation derived its moral ethos from the mothers' moral influence.

'When these influences are corrupted at their very source, it is vain to expect virtue in the offspring. The want of chastity results frequently from the practice of "bundling", or courtship on beds, during the night—a practice still widely prevailing. It is also said to be much increased by night prayer-meetings, and the intercourse which ensues in returning home' (16).

But there were others who saw in these accusations another extension of the ever-present and smouldering 'religious difficulty'. Laxity of morals seemed to many the inevitable concomitant of nonconformity in religion: whilst many nonconformists saw the whole report as a baseless and base attempt by the Established Church to discredit the nonconformist element. Perhaps the only judgment one can make is to suggest that 'immorality', whatever its nature, is not the prerogative of any particular group, religious, sectarian or non-religious. And a thorough-going sociological investigation at the time may well have revealed a multiplicity of causes of 'immorality' quite unrelated to the night prayer-meeting—although this might well have provided the occasion.

C THE NEWCASTLE COMMISSION REPORT OF 1861

In 1856 the Privy Council's Committee for Education was replaced by the Education Department, and in 1858 the Newcastle Commission was set up under the chairmanship of Henry Pelham, fifth Duke of Newcastle (1811–64). Its terms of reference were 'to inquire into the present state of Popular Education in England, and to consider and report what measures, if any, are required for the extension of sound and cheap elementary instruction to all classes of the people'. The terms of reference clearly prejudged the nature of the report by the inclusion of the one word 'cheap'. The word 'sound' is open to a variety of interpretations; 'elementary' had no specific overtones—it meant simply an education which provided the rudiments or elements of learning; but the word 'cheap' posed certain limits which stultified any imaginative or even realistic thinking about the necessity and extent of education for all classes of society.

The report of the commission, which appeared in 1861, was the first thorough-going survey of English elementary education. It was a statistical inquiry which revealed, according to the commissioners, that nearly 97 per cent of the children of the poorer classes with which they were concerned were in schools of some kind, although the average school life was between four and six years only and the majority left school at eleven years of age. About 5·4 per cent remained in school after the age of thirteen. But the statistics and estimates provided were of dubious value.

The commission rejected central control of the management of schools and any attempt at interference with denominational interests, although it was perfectly clear that most of the children involved in 'elementary' education received very inadequate education even at the 'sound, cheap' level. Children in the main were left to the mercies of struggling pupil-teachers. Whilst the commission considered that the state grants, which had been provided since 1833, had been ineffectual in providing 'a general diffusion of sound elementary education among all classes of the poor', they nevertheless recommended that grants should be continued. There should, however, be an insistence upon regular attendance at school; buildings should be kept in a good state of repair; there should be a satisfactory report from the inspector.

The role of inspector had become an increasingly important one since the Order in Council on the Inspection of Church Schools in August 1840 and the Instructions to H.M. Inspectors, as set out in the Minutes of the Committee of Council on Education of the same date (17), and in many ways he was to become the villain of the educational scene. The actions of the Education Department after the Newcastle Report were destined to create considerable hostility between teachers and inspectors, who were mistrusted and feared almost as if they were government spies. The word 'inspector' is itself, perhaps, an unfortunate one and hardly conveys the profile of 'guide, counsellor and friend' which is more in keeping with his present role. But the Newcastle Commission recommended payment by results, and results had to be inspected and assessed if they were to be the criterion of grant aid.

In this connection it is salutary to reflect upon the commissioners' views on the character and skill of the teachers employed to educate the children. They felt that a considerable proportion of the children were not satisfactorily taught what they came to school to learn; many of them in some districts did not even learn to read or to write well.

'They work sums, but they learn their arithmetic in such a way as to be of little practical use in common life. Their religious instruction is unintelligent, and to a great extent confined to exercises of merely verbal memory . . . '(18).

This all has a familiar ring about it, and similar complaints are still made. Much of the failure is intrinsic to the process of selection and training of teachers; both then and now the teacher is often a limited, academic animal who has proceeded from school to college, and then back immediately to school.

As Vice-President of the Education Department, Robert Lowe had, in 1860, produced a code which delineated the regulations about grants and procedures in education. In 1862 he undertook the revision of this code in order to align it with the proposals of the Newcastle Commission, at least in relation to payment by results. Lowe was anything and everything but an educationist; he was an administrator with a considerable ability to judge the 'religious' temper of his times, and in consequence he rejected rate aid for schools knowing quite well the religious controversy that would be aroused. He was also a politician who knew precisely how to state things in an epigrammatic, politically propagandist way that would somehow appeal to the majority of his listeners, provided they did not examine his statements too closely from a philosophical or an educational point of view. Lowe informed the House of Commons:

'I cannot promise the House that this system will be an economical one and I cannot promise that it will be an efficient one, but I can promise that it shall be either one or the other. If it is not cheap, it shall be efficient; if it is not efficient, it shall be cheap' (19).

Originally payments were made direct to certified teachers through the Post Office, but now Lowe made them payable to the school managers who were responsible for paying the teachers. The code established six standards which corresponded to six years of school life between the end of the infant stage and the age of twelve. Grants were not made available for children above that age and consequently teachers concentrated their efforts mainly on children below twelve. The code also raised the regulation number of pupils which each teacher was permitted to teach. Children of Standard One were examined, and as with every examination instituted since, the group below—in this case the Infant Department—was affected, and progressive concepts of infant teaching were for some time burked. The code laid down the precise sums which the school managers might claim at the end of each year for each scholar, subject to examination and inspector's report. Certainly Lowe had provided a scheme which was cheap, for within three years government grants dropped by about 22 per cent; if Lowe could not *guarantee* its cheapness he had at least achieved it. He had also ensured that element of decentralization which has been a feature of English education down to our own times, through the distribution of grants to school managers.

Statistics are notably inaccurate, falsifiable and misleading. Both those of the Newcastle Commission and those that followed to demonstrate the defects of the system of payment by results were questionable, but they at least indicated certain trends. In 1867, when Matthew Arnold made his General Report for the year, he claimed that the school legislation of 1862 had struck its 'heaviest possible blow' at pupil-teachers, and that inevitably there resulted the 'slack and languid conditions of our elementary schools'.

'The rate of pupil-teachers to scholars in our elementary schools was, in 1861, one pupil-teacher for every 36 scholars; in 1866 it was only one pupil-teacher for every 54 scholars . . . The performance of the reduced number of candidates is weaker and more inaccurate . . . The mode of teaching in the primary schools has certainly fallen off in intelligence, spirit, and inventiveness during the four or five years which have elapsed since my last report' (20).

Arnold attacked the mechanical processes of teaching as well as the mechanical form of examination which followed, and he appealed for more 'free play' for both inspectors and teachers so that children were not simply crammed for examinations but really knew the subjects they were studying. Behind the mechanical examination system was the ogre of 'payment by results', which Arnold saw as harmful to the whole educational system, but particularly to the 'happy natural movement' of instruction in the primary schools. Arnold also foresaw some of the dangers of trying to make education compulsory, an idea which was becoming increasingly familiar. Whilst he felt that it would not be difficult to pass a law making education compulsory, it would not be quite so simple to make it work. In Prussia, where education was already compulsory, it was not flourishing because it was compulsory, but compulsory because it was flourishing. People in our own society did not prize culture or instruction, but preferred pleasure, politics, business and money-making.

D THE FORSTER ACT OF 1870 AND AFTER

Apart from certain special educational provisions of the Factory Acts during the period 1833–67 and of the Mines Act of 1860, there existed no legal compulsion upon parents to send their children to school. It was the aim of certain bodies, such as the Birmingham Education League, to establish a State secular system of education. In 1868 W. E. Forster became Vice-President of the Education Department when W. E. Gladstone formed his first ministry. Forster was the brother-in-law of Matthew Arnold and a Quaker; he had a great concern both for education and social problems generally. He was quick to see the difficulties of the 'religious question' and to make some attempt to solve them. In the event, his solution was to steer a course somewhere between the Scylla of secularism and the Charybdis of Church control; it provided for the continued existence of voluntary schools and for the establishment of board schools— a compromise usually referred to as the dual system, or the system of dual control.

School boards were to be set up to fill the gaps in those areas lacking schools, and for this purpose the Education Department divided the country into school districts, which corresponded roughly to boroughs and civil parishes. London was considered separately as a school district in its own right. Voluntary schools were to be assisted by a direct grant of 50 per cent from the Education Department, and they had six months only in which to remedy any deficiencies in their district, after which time the newly elected school boards would be empowered to fill any gaps. The latter were further authorized to raise an education rate in order to finance any of their projects.

An accepted compromise was arrived at on the religious question. School boards could decide for themselves whether schools under their jurisdiction should be given religious instruction. If religious instruction were given in such schools then the clause, which was advanced by Mr Cowper-Temple and accepted by Parliament, must apply, namely that 'no catechism or religious formulary which is distinctive of any particular denomination shall be taught'. There was moreover, a clause—a 'conscience clause'—which gave the right to any parent to withdraw his child from religious instruction in public elementary schools, on the grounds of conscience. This applied equally to those voluntary schools which were to receive State aid.

The boards were originally intended, at least ostensibly, to be supplementary to the voluntary denominational schools, but it was soon clear that they were to take the lion's share and that the State was henceforth taking on responsibility for public elementary education. It was not yet a completely national system, nor was it completely free. With respect to the latter the position was a mixed one. Where parents were able to pay fees they were expected to do so, but school boards were empowered to establish special free schools, particularly in large towns where there was extreme poverty. They were also empowered to provide free tickets to parents who they considered could not afford to pay for their children's education. The Act, further, did not in itself establish compulsory education: it simply made it possible. The onus was placed firmly on the school boards to whom power was given to frame by-laws for compulsory attendance of all children, from five to twelve, within their district. Forster summed up the purpose of the Bill in the words:

'What is the purpose in this Bill? Briefly this, to bring elementary education within the reach of every English home, aye, and within the reach of those children who have no homes' (21).

School attendance was enforced by officers appointed by the school boards, and Lord Sandon's Act of 1876 attempted to strengthen school attendance in those areas where no school boards had been established. School attendance committees were set up, and greater pressure was placed upon parents to ensure that their children received efficient elementary instruction in writing, reading and arithmetic, with suitable sanctions where the parents failed to comply. The employment of children below the age of ten was forbidden, and children between the ages of ten and fourteen had to reach the educational levels specified in the First Schedule of the Act before they could be employed.

Arnold was right when he said that the element of compulsion was more easily legislated for than enforced, although even Sandon's Act did not strictly make provision for compulsory education, only for the production of children with certain minimum standards of attainment before they could be certified for employment. But however close these two may seem they certainly were not identical and there were many loopholes.

Mundella's Act of 1880 made the position much clearer, and it became more difficult for both school boards and parents to evade responsibility. Those boards and school attendance committees which had been slow in framing their by-laws to enforce compulsory attendance were now themselves compelled to rectify the situation. Attendance at school was now compulsory between the ages of five and ten; the upper limit was raised to eleven in 1893, and to twelve in 1899. Mundella's Act did not abolish fee-paying, although it was obviously becoming more and more difficult to collect fees as compulsory attendance was increased.

The code of 1882 saw the addition of Standard Seven to the other six, and there was a steady improvement in elementary education generally. The gradual disappearance of 'payment by results', first in the Infant Department and finally throughout the whole of the elementary school system, made for freer progress and for that 'free play' of which Matthew Arnold had spoken in his General Report of 1867. The system finally disappeared in 1897, thirty-five years after the introduction of the revised code in 1862, and thirty years after Arnold's strictures. The abolition of the system was previsioned by the Cross Report which was published in 1888 by the Royal Commission on the Elementary Acts.

The terms of reference of the Cross Commission were 'to enquire into the working of the Elementary Education Acts, England and Wales'. The Church had shown some considerable dissatisfaction with the position of voluntary denominational schools in the 1870 Education Act. The Roman Catholics had a powerful spokesman in Cardinal Manning, and the Anglican Church in Dr Temple, the Bishop of London, both of whom were members of the commission. It was virtually impossible for the commission to have unanimity except on the question of the eventual abolition of payment by results. On all other questions they produced majority and minority reports, and out of the twenty-three members eight wrote a minority report.

With regard to school buildings the majority report, although advocating higher standards in relation to air, light and space, considered nevertheless that the actual demands for school accommodation had been fairly met. The commission felt that there should be more inspectors who had risen from the ranks of the elementary school teachers; the members were obviously very conscious of the ever-increasing hostility and distrust that had developed between teachers and inspectors, and they perhaps felt that the conjunction of the lowest and the highest would result in greater understanding between two elements in the educational system which appeared to be in perpetual opposition.

In a consideration of teachers and their training the majority felt that there should not be any higher level of entry qualification lest both men and women with natural aptitudes and general culture should be excluded. They argued for an improvement in the training of pupil-teachers, and supported an extension of teacher-training in training colleges:

'We are, on the whole, of opinion that an additional year of training would be a great advantage for some students, and only hesitate to recommend it from the doubt whether it is as yet feasible. But, at any rate, we think that picked students from training colleges might even now with advantage be grouped at convenient centres, for a third year's course of instruction' (22).

It has taken almost three-quarters of a century to realize this recommendation of the Cross Commission—as well as its reinforcement by other reports such as the McNair Report of 1944. This topic will be considered in greater detail in later chapters.

The report found that parents were, in the main, in favour of religious training, and it supported Biblical instruction, whilst rejecting any desire to separate the teaching of religion and secular instruction. In fact one witness, Archdeacon Norris, formerly H.M. Inspector of Schools, thought that the moral character of teachers themselves would suffer 'if they were forbidden to impart religious instruction'; whilst Mr Cumin, Secretary of the Committee of Council on Education, protested that many excellent teachers would refuse to be restricted to the teaching of secular subjects. The report concluded that it was of the highest importance that all children should receive moral and religious education and that this could best be done through the medium of elementary schools.

REFERENCES

1 *Vide* Maclure, J. S., *Educational Documents—England and Wales: 1816–1967* (Methuen, 1968), p. 75.
2 Ibid., p. 75.
3 *Vide* Curtis, S. J., *History of Education in Great Britain*, p. 196, where he says that 'Some of these schools attained a certain measure of efficiency, but for the most part they were inefficient baby-minding establishments'.
4 Trevelyan, G. M., *English Social History* (Penguin, 1967), p. 196.
5 Barnard, H. C., *A History of English Education: From 1760*, p. 3.
6 Op. cit., p. 379.
7 Quoted in Barnard, H. C. in op. cit., p. 10, n.1.
8 Adamson, J. W., *English Education: 1789–1902* (C.U.P., 1930, reprinted 1964), p. 25.
9 'The College was founded by Joseph Lancaster in Borough Road, Southwark, about 1798, and is the oldest training college in the country.' *Vide Handbook of Colleges and Departments of Education 1968* (Methuen), p. 186.
10 Wilderspin, S., *The Infant System* (1852), p. 258. Quoted in Barnard, op. cit., p. 61.
11 *Vide* Maclure, J. S., op cit., p. 26.
12 Ibid., p. 29.
13 Ibid., p. 30.
14 Ibid., p. 38.
15 Ibid., p. 59.
16 Ibid., p. 60.
17 Ibid., pp. 46–51.
18 Ibid., p. 78.
19 *Hansard*, vol. 165, 229, dated February 13, 1862 and quoted by Curtis, S. J. and Boultwood, M. E. A., *An Introductory History of English Education Since 1800* (3rd ed. University Tutorial Press, 1964), p. 71.
20 Maclure, J. S., op. cit., p. 81.
21 Ibid., p. 104.
22 Ibid., p. 133.

BIBLIOGRAPHY

Adamson, J. W., *English Education, 1789–1902* (C.U.P., 1930, reprinted 1964).
Barnard, H. C., *A History of English Education: From 1760* (University of London Press, 1961, 2nd ed.).
Birchenough, C., *History of Elementary Education in England and Wales from 1800 to the Present Day* (University Tutorial Press, 1938, 2nd ed.).
Cavenagh, F. A., *James and John Stuart Mill on Education* (C.U.P., 1931).

Connell, W. F., *The Educational Thought and Influence of Matthew Arnold* (Routledge, 1950).

Curtis, S. J., *History of Education in Great Britain* (Chapters VI to IX) (University Tutorial Press, 1963, 5th ed.).

Curtis, S. J. and Boultwood, M. E. A., *An Introductory History of English Education Since 1800* (Chapters I, IV to VII) (University Tutorial Press, 1964, 3rd ed.).

Eaglesham, E. J. R., *The Foundations of 20th-Century Education in England* (Routledge, 1967).

Eaglesham, E. J. R., *From School Board to Local Authority* (Routledge, 1956).

Gregory, R., *Elementary Education* (Nat. Soc., 1905).

Jarman, T. L., *Landmarks in the History of Education* (Chapters XV and XVI) (Murray, 1963, 2nd ed.).

Jones, M. G., *The Charity School Movement in the 18th Century* (C.U.P., 1938).

Maclure, J. S., *Educational Documents: 1816–1967* (Methuen, 1968).

Manning, J., *Dickens on Education* (O.U.P., 1960).

Meiklejohn, J. M. D., *An Old Educational Reformer—Dr. A. Bell* (Edinburgh, 1881).

Owen, R., *The Life of Robert Owen* (Bell, 1920).

Rusk, R. R., *A History of Infant Education* (University of London Press, 1933).

Salmon, D. (ed.), *Lancaster's Improvements and Bell's Experiments* (C.U.P., 1932).

Simon, B., *Studies in the History of Education, 1780–1870* (Lawrence and Wishart, 1960).

Smith, F., *A History of English Elementary Education, 1760–1902* (University of London Press, 1931).

Smith, F., *The Life and Work of Sir James Kay-Shuttleworth* (Murray, 1923).

Stephen, L., *The English Utilitarians* (Duckworth, 1912).

Chapter 2

The Development of
Primary Education

A ORIGINS OF INFANT AND NURSERY SCHOOLS

The work of Robert Owen, of Froebel, the development of Froebelianism, and the original thought of Maria Montessori will be discussed in later chapters. Their general influence upon the methods in both nursery and infant schools has been clearly marked in the history of those departments since the turn of the century. The Forster Act of 1870 emphasized the value and significance of separate infant schools or of infant classes in elementary schools, and infant education was firmly brought into the elementary system with the age of five fixed as the age of admission.

Whilst there was some general acceptance for the need of nursery and infant education, there were those educationists who also saw the desperate need for changes in the environmental conditions of young children. In particular, the sisters Rachel and Margaret McMillan engaged in a campaign not merely to establish nursery schools but also to make adequate provision for the physical care and development of young children. In 1907 the Board of Education had referred the age of admission of young children to school to the Consultative Committee, and their Report in 1908 discussed the general work and influence of nursery schools, expressing the opinion that the age of three should not be regarded as too young for those children for whom such schools were considered necessary. Meanwhile the McMillan sisters were not merely pressing for the provision of school meals, regular medical inspections and health centres for poor children, they were acting upon their convictions. In 1908 they opened their first school clinic at Bow, and in 1911 they developed the first real nursery school at Deptford.

Their concept of a nursery school was in reality a large space of ground where the children could live in the open air and enjoy natural activity and play. It was a garden, a kindergarten, with shelters where the children could go when the weather was inclement and where they could continue their activities without interruption. The sisters believed that the children, both rich and poor, should come under the influence of this environment for as long as possible; and so their school day, which seems perhaps to us rather lengthy, began at 8.00 a.m. and went on to 5.00 or 6.30 p.m. But this was not a day of formal tuition or instruction; it was a day of natural interest and activity, with two and sometimes three meals provided, and an enforced period of rest after lunch. The McMillans had in mind that if you wanted to formulate the character and personality of the child you had to provide the right sort of environment for it during the most impressionable years of its life, and for as long as possible during its active day.

Rachel McMillan died in 1917 but Margaret continued the work until her own death in 1931. In 1918 the local education authorities were employed to make arrangements for supplying or helping the supply of nursery schools and classes for children over two and under five years of age, where such schools and classes were considered to be essential for the healthy physical and mental development of the children concerned. Thus the State, through local authorities, gradually took on the responsibility for the early years of the child's development. And the schools that it began to produce at least had the experimental experience of the efforts of the McMillans, who had emphasized throughout the importance of free movement in play, of the feelings and emotions in personal development, and of the Froebelian principle of education through imagination. Many of the local nursery schools, of course, did not have the basic 'space area' as conceived by the McMillans, nor the gardens, shrubs, lawns and greenhouses. But the Froebelian and Montessorian principles made their impact; the view that the only real form of education is self-education was well entrenched in nursery and infant educational developments.

By 1938 there were 46 nursery schools maintained by L.E.A.s and 57 by voluntary management; in 1946 the number had dropped to a total of 92. It must be remembered, however, that during the war years a very large number of day nurseries and nursery schools had been established by the welfare authorities, and at the end of the war these were handed over to the L.E.A.s. In consequence, in 1947 the total number of nursery schools had risen to 370, 17 of which were now provided by voluntary institutions. In January 1965 the total number of nursery schools under the supervision of the Department of Education and Science reached 639, and the number of pupils in these schools was 27,909 (1). Of these schools 436 were maintained on direct grant.

Whether or not 'Heaven lies about us in our infancy', as Wordsworth insisted, the importance of both nursery and infant education cannot be over-estimated. Of the infant schools in Britain, Martin Mayer has said that they are 'probably the world's most ambitious pattern of beginning instruction' (2). But there is still a great neglect in our society of nursery education; the total number of children actually in nursery *schools* in January 1965 represented only about 7 per cent of the total number of children in the age groups 0–4, i.e. 4,100,000. And when all the children under five in all institutions under the supervision of the Ministry of Health, the Home Office and the L.E.A.s were taken into account, the total number was still only 283,000, i.e. 6·9 per cent of the total number of children under five years of age. The Central Advisory Council for Education (England) recommended in its Report in 1967 that there should be a large expansion of nursery education, and that such education should be available to children at any time after the beginning of the school year after they reach the age of three until they reach the age of compulsory schooling. Over the country as a whole it was considered that provision should be made for 15 per cent of children to attend both a morning and afternoon session (3).

The Advisory Council felt that full-time nursery education for children whose mothers could not satisfy the authorities that they had exceptionally good reasons for working should be given a low priority. It was also recommended that the education of children over three in day nurseries should be the responsibility of the education department rather than of the health department. It went on to say that

'Ideally, all services, including nursery, for the care of young children should be grouped together and placed near the children's homes and the primary schools. The planning of new areas and the rebuilding of old should take account of nursery education' (4).

B LEGISLATION: 1870–1918

We have already mentioned that the Education Act of 1870 did not really introduce free, compulsory elementary education for all, but compulsion was placed upon school boards to provide schools where necessary; the Elementary Education Act of 1876 was the first Act to put compulsion upon parents in order to ensure that their children received education which was efficient at least in reading, writing and arithmetic. The movement was towards free education, for even the 1870 Act restricted fees to 9d per week and gave powers to school boards to pay fees for poorer children.

In 1888 the Cross Commission made it clear that the idea of separate Junior Departments was becoming increasingly more explicit. This was due in the main to the growth of Higher Grade Schools. From the time of the Cross Report to the end of the century many school boards were grading their elementary schools into Junior, Middle and Senior Departments. This is interesting in view of the more recent nomenclature of First, Middle and Third Schools.

The Balfour-Morant Education Act of 1902 abolished the school boards and created in their place the local education authorities. The major L.E.A.s were councils of the counties and county boroughs, whilst the minor L.E.A.s were boroughs with a population of more than 10,000, and urban districts of more than 20,000. These minor L.E.A.s possessed powers over elementary education only. All L.E.A.s were given the duties and powers of the former school boards and attendance committees, and they were obliged to maintain and keep efficient all public elementary schools, whether council or voluntary, and to control all secular education in voluntary elementary schools in the area (Section 7 of the Act).

In 1904 a new elementary code was produced which incorporated the changes proposed by the Balfour-Morant Act. The code has what Professor E. J. R. Eaglesham calls 'a cleverly written preface' which he further claims was a statement of 'training in followership rather than leadership training', and suited more to the working classes than to the middle and upper classes (5). No one would deny that whoever wrote the preface—Sir Robert Morant or Professor J. M. Mackail—it was cleverly composed. Indeed, a detailed examination of its content makes one wonder whether Eaglesham's stigmatization of 'training in followership' is justifiable. After Lowe's revised code of 1862, and its payment by results, one is naturally impressed by the somewhat more philosophical and educational tone of the introduction to the 1904 code. But Morant was cleafly not concerned to develop elementary education by the provision of more resources: in fact Eaglesham suggests that there is evidence to support the conclusion, however cynical, that '*Morant aimed at and achieved a standstill in elementary education*' (6).

But cynicism should not lead us to derogate from the essential educational values made explicit in the introduction to the code, which may well of course have been a philosophical sop to compensate for a lack of practical assistance. But it was an organized attempt to state in straightforward and simple terms the purpose of the public elementary school; this was

'to form and strengthen the character and to develop the intelligence of the children entrusted to it, and to make the best use of the school years available, in assisting both girls and boys according to their different needs, to fit themselves, practically as well as intellectually, for the work of life' (7).

There is here a recognition of the child as a total being who has specific and differing needs within the realms of character and intellect, and additionally the need to be initiated into the world of work and life itself in such a way as to be able to cope practically as well as intellectually. Eaglesham may be right when he comments that whilst there is to be preparation for life there is to be no vocational education. But it is a stage further than the three Rs. The children are to be trained in habits of careful observation and clear reasoning 'so that they may gain an intelligent acquaintance with some of the facts and laws of nature' and this is hardly 'followership'! The school must further arouse in its pupils a lively interest in man's ideals, achievements, literature and history; it must give them 'some power over language as an instrument of thought and expression'—

surely more in keeping with education for leadership! All sound education should make pupils and students aware of the limitations of their knowledge and encourage a due sense of humility within the realms of learning—whether they are leaders or followers. The code consequently adds that, while the school should make pupils conscious of their limitations it should, at the same time, develop in them 'such a taste for good reading and thoughtful study as will enable them to increase that knowledge' when their school career is over, and by their own efforts. This, indeed, is still one of the prime purposes of education—to demonstrate to pupils how to acquire knowledge and learning for themselves.

The influence in practice of the 'sloyd' movement (see Chapter 13) is to be seen in other elements of the introduction which suggests that the school should encourage the natural activities of the child's hand and eye 'by suitable forms of practical work and manual instruction'; and the general, though gradual, movement towards hygiene and health is suggested by the training of pupils in physical exercises, organized games and the simple laws of health.

It is true that the code saw the possibility of discovering 'individual children who show promise of exceptional capacity', and that such children should be qualified to pass at the appropriate age into the secondary schools and there be enabled to derive the maximum benefit from the education offered them. Whilst this was a recognition that some children rather than others were fitted for further education it is worthy of note that there was a clause in parenthesis which had in mind the sort of contention which many educators have put forward in more recent years against the streaming of children in primary schools for the 11+ examination, and the gearing of the whole of the primary curriculum for the benefit of the academic few—

'to develop their special gifts (so far as this can be done without sacrificing the interests of the majority of the children) . . .'

The introduction was not an exhortation to industry, respect and reverence in quite the same sense as that implied in previous codes and reports. There was little or no suggestion of 'followership' subservience in the terminology of the code. It was implied that there was a great responsibility on the part of the teachers to lay the foundations of conduct; and by their influence, example and personal sense of discipline, which should pervade the school, to inculcate in the children 'habits of industry, self-control, and courageous perseverance in the face of difficulties'—training suited, surely, to the middle and upper classes as well as the working classes. Reverence was to be taught, not for the nobility but for what was noble; and children were to be ready for self-sacrifice and to strive to the uttermost for purity and truth. The respect which was to be fostered was not that for 'their betters', but for others, 'which must be the foundation of unselfishness and the true basis of all good manners'. The corporate life of the school was the basis for the development of the instinct for fair play and a sense of loyalty to one another—the very 'germ of a wider sense of honour in later life'. Indeed some of the introduction, for good or ill, reads almost like a public school code.

The introduction concludes that school, parents and home should all unite in an effort to enable the children to reach their fullest development as individuals, and also to become useful and upright citizens in their community. Whether Morant was interested in forwarding elementary education or not, there was a certain liberalizing and humanizing purpose expressed in this introduction. And this was supported by the Blue Book issued by the Board of Education in 1905, which was a handbook of suggestions for teachers involved in the work of public elementary schools. The Blue Book suggested that uniformity of practice throughout such schools was not desirable, but rather that each teacher should think for himself and work out his own methods according to the school's conditions and requirements. Above all the teacher should know and sympathize with the children he was teaching. The entire process of education was viewed as a 'partnership for the acquisition of knowledge'. Facts were not to be dealt with in isolation but in relation to the total experience of the child—

'each lesson must be a renewal and an increase of that connected store of experience which becomes knowledge' (8).

The Blue Book was in line with the introduction to the code in that it insisted that the dignity of knowledge should be impressed upon the pupil, and that the latter should fully realize his duty to use his innate powers to the best advantage. Life must be presented as something at once pleasant and serious, and in consequence the work being pursued in the schools was in a real sense a preparation for life. Moreover, the teacher's influence in all this was a very vital one, however short that period of influence might be.

The Fisher Education Act of 1918 enforced compulsory attendance at school up to the age of fourteen years, and it also underlined the need for a complete re-organization of what today is more specifically referred to as 'primary education', that is, the education of young children below the age of eleven years. All fees were completely abolished in public elementary schools, and all L.E.A.s were required to provide 'practical instruction suitable to the ages, abilities and requirements of the children'. The L.E.A.s were also empowered to supply, or help supply, nursery schools for children over two years of age and under five, 'whose attendance at such schools is necessary for their healthy physical and mental development'. When he introduced the Education Bill, as President of the Board of Education, on August 10, 1917, Mr H. A. L. Fisher concluded by suggesting that the rising generation could be protected against the deleterious effects of industrial pressures only by a further measure of State compulsion. But, he argued, the compulsion proposed in this Bill will be

'no sterilizing restriction of wholesome liberty, but an essential condition of a larger and more enlightened freedom, which will tend to stimulate the civic spirit, to promote general culture and technical knowledge, and to diffuse a steadier judgment and a better-informed opinion through the whole body of the community' (9).

C THE HADOW REPORTS AND AFTER

In 1925 the Board of Education published *Circular 1350* which pointed out that the age of eleven was increasingly recognized as the 'most suitable dividing line between what may be called "Junior" and "Senior" education'. In 1926 the Hadow Report on *The Education of the Adolescent* clearly stated in Section 99 that

'It is desirable that education up to 11+ should be known by the general name of Primary Education, and education after 11 by the general name of Secondary Education . . .' (10).

Thus, the concept of 'primary education' as a distinct area of development was fully established five years before the next report of the Constitution Committee appeared. Certainly the Board did everything it could to keep the concept alive, and after its publication in 1928, *The New Prospect in Education*, L.E.A.s drew up schemes for the full provision of 'post primary' education for children of 11+ along the lines indicated in the Hadow Report.

There can be little doubt that the later Hadow Report of 1931, *The Primary School*, was one of the most important that the Consultative Committee produced. There is a tendency to look upon it as little more than a historical curiosity; certainly beside the Plowden Report of 1967 it appears a very slim and modest volume indeed, and although it took two years to produce its gross cost was minute compared with the cost of Plowden. After a fairly lengthy introduction on general principles, the report provided a historical sketch of the development of the idea of primary education from the beginning of the nineteenth century. It went on to describe the physical and mental development of children between the ages of seven and eleven; and it is interesting to note that, just as

Plowden leans quite heavily upon Piagetian thought, the 1931 report used and quoted Piaget's *Le Langage et la Pensée chez l'Enfant*, published in France in 1923 and translated into English in 1926. Appendix III to the report by Professor Cyril Burt, then psychologist to the London County Council, referred to 'Piaget's brilliant studies' (11). Thus the members of the Consultative Committee were certainly abreast of the psychological developments of their time.

The report then went on to consider the age limits for the upper stage of elementary education, which it felt should be fixed at the age of eleven; that is, the transfer from the primary to the secondary (post-primary) school should take place between the ages of eleven and twelve. It went on to discuss in some detail the arguments against separate 'infant' and 'junior' schools, but finally recommended that, in those areas where it was possible, there should be separate schools for children below the age of seven, and that in all primary schools there ought to be a well-defined line of demarcation between the younger and older children. The report made it pellucidly clear that the primary school should not be regarded merely as a 'preparatory department for the subsequent stage': primary school courses were to be planned and conditioned by the specific needs of the child at that particular phase in his development, both physical and mental. Its attitude towards promotion to the secondary stage was made quite explicit—the 'supposed requirements' of the latter, and 'the exigencies of an examination at the age of eleven', were not to control primary school curricula or activity (12).

The internal organization of primary schools was next discussed, including such problems as the size of classes and co-education at the upper stage of primary education. The report adduced evidence from a variety of sources to establish that classes in junior schools should be kept small, preferably about thirty five, and it further made the point that it would be impossible to put into operation many of its suggestions if large classes were retained in primary schools. The size of primary classes was indeed one of the most urgent problems facing educational administrators. Concerning co-education the conclusion was that there was no valid objection on general or sociological grounds, provided due regard was paid to the differing needs of girls and boys in games and physical activities generally. Problems of mental and educational retardation were considered in detail, and the chief causes, detection, diagnosis and treatment dealt with. Retarded children required special attention between the ages of seven and eleven, and it was recommended that special classes should be organized for this purpose and that they should be small.

The traditional curriculum of the public elementary school was next analyzed, and the general principles on which the upper stages of primary education should be based were elicited. The report considered the complexity of 'modern industrial civilization' and the bearing this had upon the work of the primary school. It emphasized the uselessness, as well as the innate danger, of seeking to inculcate what A. N. Whitehead had termed 'inert ideas'; and it deplored and deprecated the fact that, whilst a great deal of teaching was good in the abstract, too little of it directly assisted children to enlarge and vivify their instinctive hold on the conditions of life by 'enriching, illuminating and giving point to their growing experience'. The report summed up its view of the curriculum and its purpose in the following words:

'The curriculum is to be thought of in terms of activity and experience rather than of knowledge to be acquired and facts to be stored. Its aim should be to develop in a child the fundamental human powers and to awaken him to the fundamental interests of civilized life so far as these powers and interests lie within the compass of childhood, to encourage him to attain gradually to that control and orderly management of his energies, impulses and emotions, which is the essence of moral and intellectual discipline, to help him to discover the idea of duty and to ensue it, and to open out his imagination and his sympathies in such a way that he may be prepared to understand and to follow in later years the highest examples of excellence in life and conduct' (13).

In its further consideration of curriculum detail the report emphasized the desirability of devising new methods in approaching its various branches, and in particular dealt with the project method and 'centres of interest' as set against the traditional practice of treating the curriculum in terms of 'subjects'. It warned, however, against the dangers of such methods when used without due consideration or caution—music and drama were often merely 'dragged in' in order to fulfil what were regarded as the claims of a principle.

The staffing of primary schools and the training of teachers were next considered, and it was argued that teachers with general qualifications rather than specialists were best suited for work in primary schools. A brief survey was made of school premises, equipment, school and class libraries, visual and auditory aids to teaching, school visits and playing-fields. There followed a discussion of examinations in primary schools and it was recommended that, in classifying pupils leaving the infant school, teachers might usefully apply tests and make full use of school records and of consultation between the teachers concerned. Any classification should be merely provisional, and should be subject to frequent revision. The council felt that as the provision of various types of secondary education was extended in the way proposed in the report on *The Education of the Adolescent*, the need for selecting by competition those children who would pass on to grammar and selective modern schools would diminish. It was convinced, however, that some sort of qualifying test or examination would always be required for the purpose of classifying pupils, and argued for the use of written papers in English and arithmetic as a basic test of capacity and attainment of children at the age of eleven, together with carefully devised group intelligence tests.

Throughout the report on *The Primary School* there was a lively sense of the needs of the children themselves. It considered that what any wise and good parent might desire for his own children was precisely what the nation as a whole must desire for all children. The primary school was on the way to becoming what it should be, namely, the common school of the whole population, 'so excellent and so generally esteemed that all parents will desire their children to attend it' (14).

In 1933 the Hadow Report on the *Infant and Nursery School* was published and, like its predecessor, it emphasized the need to build new schools for young children more on an open-air plan. It also made it clear that it really considered that the best place for very young children was in the home; but if this were not possible there was a great deal to be derived from attending nursery classes attached to infant schools, or nursery schools. Officialdom had learned a lot from the less orthodox and more progressive movements already mentioned, but despite all this many of the school buildings were inadequate and unhygienic. And despite the general desire expressed to make the primary school curriculum free from the pressures of selective examinations at the upper end of the school, in practice their classes were geared largely to preparation for secondary school work at the subject level and to some sort of 'scholarship' examination at 11+.

The White Paper on *Educational Reconstruction*, which appeared in 1943, suggested in particular that children of 11+ should not be classified on the basis of a competitive test, but rather upon the assessment of their aptitudes based largely upon school records and intelligence tests. It felt that competitive examinations at the age of eleven were wrong in principle, not only because of the strain to which children were subjected but also because the future schooling and careers of children were largely decided at this one point in time. It argued that at an age when children's minds were nimble and receptive, when their imagination and curiosity were strong and fertile, they were subjected to a cramping and stultifying curriculum in which considerable emphasis was placed upon 'ways and means of defeating the examiners' (15). The White Paper also stated that there should be separate schools for infants and juniors; and, whilst attendance was not compulsory before the age of five, L.E.A.s must make adequate provision for either nursery schools or, where these were considered inexpedient, nursery classes in infant schools.

The Butler Education Act of 1944 gave the primary school statutory authority in this country, and it defined primary education in Section 8 as 'full time education suitable to the requirements of junior pupils', who in turn are defined as children who have not yet attained the age of twelve years. The Act forced a clear break between primary and post-primary education: between primary and secondary schools. We are not here immediately concerned with secondary education, but the new set-up in secondary education, the developing tripartite system, put ever-increasing pressures upon primary schools to act as forcing-grounds for grammar schools. The aims, so clearly expressed in the Hadow Report on *The Primary School*, were very soon forgotten in the cut-throat competition for grammar school places, and the more enlightened development of primary school methods was somewhat delayed. There was a very real sense in which the firm, separate, statutory establishment of primary and post-primary educational institutions postponed the liberation of primary school methods for some years; and the Central Advisory Council for Education was probably not being over-pessimistic when it stated in 1947 that the gap between a reasonable provision of primary schools and the existing provision was formidable: 'half a century's unremitting efforts will be required before we can hope to have good primary schools for all' (16). A lot, of course, depends on the connotation of the word 'good' in this context: the verdict of the Plowden Report, twenty years later, was quite simply expressed in the words, 'the primary schools are giving good value for the inadequate amount of money spent on them' (17). But it made it quite clear that the financial inadequacies had severe educational repercussions, as we shall presently see.

D THE PLOWDEN REPORT 1967

In August 1963 the Central Advisory Council for Education was asked by Sir Edward Boyle, then Minister of Education, 'to consider primary education in all its aspects, and the transition to secondary education'. Their investigations began soon afterwards, in October 1963, under the chairmanship of Lady Plowden, and included among the council's members were Sir John Newsom (Deputy Chairman), Professor A. J. Ayer, Miss M. Brearley, Professor C. E. Gittins, and Brigadier L. L. Thwaytes. Their report was concluded in October 1966 when it was presented to Anthony Crosland, Secretary of State for Education and Science, and it was published in January 1967. Volume I presented the report, and Volume II the statistics derived from a national survey of 20,000 schools. The total cost of the report was slightly over £120,000.

Part One formed an introduction to the whole investigation and referred in particular to the close association between the home background and academic achievement. The importance to the individual of his family and social background was emphasized, and among questions raised in general terms was that of whether 'finding out' had really proved to be better than 'being told'.

Part Two considered in some detail the growth of the child, and stressed the enormously wide variability in physical and intellectual maturity amongst children of the same age, particularly during adolescence, and the tendency for children to mature physically earlier than formerly. It went on to discuss the interaction of heredity and environment, the stages of child development as outlined by Jean Piaget, and the measurement of I.Q. It found a correlation between children's I.Q.s and parental occupations—the children of professional parents have an average I.Q. of 115, whilst those of unskilled workers have an average of 93. The report emphasized that the child was a total personality, and that its emotional, social and intellectual aspects were closely intertwined.

Some of the implications of this section include the fact that individual variations between children of the same age are so great that any class, however apparently homogeneous, must always be treated as a body of children needing individual and different attention. Until a child is ready to take a particular step forward, it is useless to try and teach him to take it. Since any child grows up intellectually, emotionally, and physically at different rates, his teachers need to know and take account of his 'developmental age' in all three respects. The child's physique, personality and capacity to learn will develop as a result of continuous interaction between his genetic inheritance and his environment. Whilst the genetic factors are not as yet under our control, the environmental factors largely are. Part Two of the report, therefore, suggested the need of a very personal approach to the pupil in the primary school, with a special study of each child's 'readiness' for any particular form of learning or operation; and, at the same time, the provision of a sound, healthy, amenable sort of environment in order to present the best learning situations and conditions.

Part Three discussed the home, school and neighbourhood and argued that the differences between parents would explain more of the variations in children than differences between schools: and that there was certainly an association between parental encouragement and educational performance. A minimum programme was suggested for the participation of parents in the education of children—a welcome to the school, meetings with teachers, open days, information for parents via brochures about the organization of the school, and reports for parents. There should be a concerted effort to improve parent-teacher relationships. It was further contended that the primary school should be used as fully as possible, out of ordinary school hours, as a sort of community centre. Community schools should be developed in all areas, but particularly in educational priority areas, where there was need for constant communication between parents and teachers if the schools' aims were to be completely understood. The report emphasized the need for colleges of education to have stronger and more efficient links with such schools and to develop courses to meet the needs of immigrant children in particular.

There was a very strong suggestion that the training of teachers generally should take more account of those social factors which affect school performance, and also of the structure and functions of the school services. It recommended the initiation of experimental schemes in the joint training of teachers and social workers, and already there are colleges of education which are devising courses for social and youth wing work as well as general welfare work. The report made it very clear indeed that the primary school has a social role in the community, as well as an immediate and individual educative role.

Part Four examined the structure of primary education and divided the 20,000 schools surveyed into nine different categories, ranging from Category One ('in most respects a school of outstanding quality') to Category Nine ('a bad school where children suffer from laziness, indifference, gross incompetence and unkindness on the part of the staff'). The report insisted that there ought to be a large expansion of nursery education, and that a start should be made as soon as possible. It went on to suggest that the entry to the infant school should be gradual between the ages of three years and five years via part-time attendance; the existing transition from home to school was too abrupt. There should be *three* years in the infant school and children should not be transferred until the age of 8 years; this would permit both children and teachers to work steadily and without anxiety. The age for admission to a secondary school was suggested as 12+, since this would give a *four*-year course in the junior or middle school, with a median age range from 8 years 6 months to 12 years 6 months. It should be noted here that the definition of primary education provided by Section 8 (1) of the 1944 Education Act was amended by Section 3 of the 1948 Education (Miscellaneous Provisions) Act. Primary education was there defined as 'full time education for children below 10 years 6 months and children above that age but below 12 years whom it is expedient to educate with them'; whilst the 1964 Education Act allowed proposals to be submitted to the Secretary of State for the establishment of new schools with age limits below 10 years 6 months and above 12 years. The report emphasized the need for the fullest possible documentation of each pupil before transfer to the secondary school, and it detailed the type of contents that a folder on each child should contain. A chapter on 'Selection for Secondary Education' suggested that the ill effects upon primary education of selection for secondary schools were lessening, and the council recommended that authorities still employing selection procedures should no longer rely on an externally imposed battery of attainment and intelligence tests.

Part Five dealt with the children in the schools, with curriculum and internal organization. Among a large variety of aims and purposes mooted, and dangers to be avoided, the following aims of primary education were accepted in somewhat general terms, with the proviso that generalities have limited value and can quickly become little more than platitudes; it was agreed that 'a pragmatic approach to the purposes of education was more likely to be fruitful' (18).

(a) Adaptability—to fit children for the society into which they will grow up, and to train them to be capable of adjusting to their changing environment.

(b) The all-round development of the individual child.

(c) The acquisition of the basic skills necessary in contemporary society.

(d) The religious and moral development of the child.

(e) Physical health, intellectual development, emotional and moral health, aesthetic awareness, a valid perspective, practical and social skills, and personal fulfilment (19).

(f) Values and attitudes must be mediated to the children. The school is not merely a teaching shop but a living community in which pupils learn primarily to live as children and not as future adults.

The work of Piaget was emphasized as a sound developmental approach to children's learning, and the importance of children's 'cultural' play was made clear. The report went on to consider certain particular aspects of the curriculum, and throughout there was an enlightened approach to both content and method, and a balanced attitude towards heuristic principles. The council had no doubt that 'children's questions about sex ought to be answered plainly and truthfully whenever they are asked' (20). It gave validity to the modern, both relaxed and friendly, approach within the primary schools as a much better preparation for life in contemporary society than the old authoritative one. Whilst accepting 'discipline', the council were clear that this connoted neither heavy punishment nor soft and flabby relationships: discipline, it felt, was impaired by such elements as disorder, untidiness and slackness—it could flourish only in an ethos of order and purposefulness, in which boredom had been eliminated (21). There must be, in all this, a healthy combination of individual, group, and class work and learning. Due consideration was also given to the education of both handicapped and gifted children.

In Part Six the role of the teacher was discussed, and it was argued that teachers must enlarge their endeavours and enlist to a greater extent parents' interest in their children's education. It was extremely important to diagnose the child's needs and potentialities and there would be increasing demands on the knowledge of the teacher, whether literary, scientific or mathematical. Teachers, said the Report,

'cannot escape the knowledge that children will catch values and attitudes far more from what teachers do than what they say. Unless they are courteous, they cannot expect courtesy from children: when teachers are eager to learn and turn readily to observation and to books, their pupils are likely to do the same' (22).

The report, in effect, asked not only for more teachers but also for better quality ones. It went on to discuss teachers' aides, or trained ancillaries, who might give substantial help to teachers inside and outside the classroom, and who would have equal status with nursery assistants and have comparable training. The council considered that colleges of education, in general, were too remote from the problems of the school; it recommended a full inquiry into the system of training of teachers, and suggested that there should be more joint appointments to college and school staffs. Further, a network of residential teachers' courses should be developed.

Part Seven dealt with independent primary schools, that is those independent schools which do not provide at least a four-year course after the age of eleven. It had some pretty strong recommendations to make about these, as set out on pages 385–6, namely:

'(i) The Department of Education and Science should consider taking steps which would require all independent schools to state on their prospectuses whether the schools were recognized or registered and what this implies. The Department of Education and Science should reconsider the terms "recognized" and "registered" and try to devise more informative ones.

(ii) The Secretary of State's powers to serve Notices of Complaint on independent schools should be based on more stringent criteria. The construction of "objectionable" should be widened to include any conditions, physical or educational, in which children's welfare was not thought to be adequately safeguarded.

(iii) All head teachers of independent schools should be qualified teachers. After a date to be specified, only qualified teachers should be appointed as heads in new schools, or when there is a change of head teacher.

(iv) In-service courses should wherever possible allow some places for teachers from independent schools. The independent schools themselves should take steps through their professional organizations to increase the facilities for in-service training for teachers in independent schools' (23).

In Part Eight the council dealt with problems relating to primary school buildings and equipment, the status and government of primary education, the powers of head teachers, and research, innovation and the dissemination of information. Part Nine summarized the conclusions and the recommendations which the council wished to make to the D.E.S., L.E.A.s, colleges of education, managers, health authorities, institutes of education, the Home Office, the schools, the teachers and their associations, the A.T.O.s, and the Burnham and Pelham Committees.

The report concluded that 'the primary schools were giving good value for the inadequate amount of money spent on them' (24), and went on to state that teachers were too few in number and too unevenly distributed to do the job adequately. The first priority was the establishment of educational priority areas; the recruitment of teachers' aides would be an essential and immediate source of help to the schools everywhere, the essential improvement of bad primary school buildings must be undertaken as soon as possible wherever they existed; and nursery education must be extended through increased accommodation and staff. Planning should begin on changes in the national dates of entry, and also on the ages of transfer between the different stages of primary education (25).

The Plowden Report represents one of the most thorough investigations into any area of education ever produced. Perhaps not least of its achievements was its virtual unanimity, which is a reflection on the goodwill and singleness of purpose of its twenty-five members over a period of three years of intensive work and study. Only after 485 pages do there appear ten pages of notes of reservation, the major ones being as one might expect on the 'religious question'; whilst another note, on the supply and training of teachers, soberly reminds us that a great deal of teacher training for women is, in fact, temporarily rather unproductive higher education—except in the sense that people are probably better people as a result of a further period of education. Out of every 100 women who enter our colleges of education, only 47 will be in the schools after three years of teaching; and after six years of service only 30 will remain. Perhaps the most sanguine way to look at the figures is simply to argue that 70 women out of every 100 so trained have, at least, qualified in a profession to which they may later return, but in any case they have found one way of obtaining higher education, with often a minimum of entry qualifications; and as mothers, in the majority of cases, they will have a better understanding of educational problems. It is certainly not a bad thing for future mothers both to be well educated and to have a professional qualification in reserve.

REFERENCES

1 *Vide Children and their Primary Schools* (Plowden Report) (H.M.S.O., 1967), Table 4, p. 108.
2 Mayer, M., *The Schools* (Bodley Head, 1961).
3 Op cit., pp. 469 f.
4 Ibid., p. 470.
5 Eaglesham, E. J. R., *The Foundations of Twentieth-Century Education in England* (Routledge, 1967), pp. 53–4.
6 Ibid., p. 51. Author's italics.
7 *Vide* Maclure, J. S., *Educational Documents—England and Wales: 1816–1967* (Methuen, 1968, 2nd ed.). This and the following quotations are from pp. 154–5 of this selection.
8 Ibid., pp. 160–1.
9 Ibid., p. 175.
10 Board of Education, *The Education of the Adolescent* (H.M.S.O., 1927, reprinted 1948), p. 95.
11 Board of Education, *The Primary School* (H.M.S.O., 1931, reprinted 1946), p. 271.
12 Ibid., pp. 70–1.
13 Ibid., p. 93.
14 Ibid., p. xxviii.
15 *Vide* Maclure, J. S., op. cit., p. 208.
16 Ministry of Education, *School and Life* (H.M.S.O., 1947, reprinted 1952), p. 11.
17 D.E.S., *Children and their Primary Schools*, p. 431.
18 Ibid., p. 186. The aims will be found on pp. 185–8.
19 Ibid., p. 187. This itemized statement of purposes with further sub-headings was provided by one witness.
20 Ibid., p. 260.
21 Ibid., pp. 271–2.
22 Ibid., p. 312.
23 Ibid., pp. 385–6.
24 Ibid., p. 431.
25 Ibid., p. 441.

BIBLIOGRAPHY

Adamson, J. W., *English Education, 1789–1902* (C.U.P., 1930, reprinted 1964).
Armfelt, R., *The Structure of English Education* (Cohen and West, 1961).
Ayerst, D., *Understanding Schools* (Penguin, 1967).
Barnard, H. C., *A History of English Education from 1760* (University of London Press, 1961, 2nd ed. 1963).
Birchenough, C., *History of Elementary Education in England and Wales from 1800 to the Present Day* (University Tutorial Press, 1938, 2nd ed.).
Blishen, E., *Education Today* (B.B.C., 1964), chapters 1 and 2.
Burgess, T., *A Guide to English Schools* (Penguin, 1964).
Catty, N., *Learning and Teaching in the Junior Schools* (Methuen, 1956).
Curtis, S. J., *History of Education in Great Britain* (University Tutorial Press, 1963, 5th ed.).
Curtis, S. J. and Boultwood, M. E. A., *An Introductory History of English Education Since 1800* (University Tutorial Press, 1964, 3rd ed.).

De Lissa, L., *Life in the Nursery School* (Longmans, 1949).

Dent, H. C., *Growth in English Education, 1946–1952* (Routledge, 1954).

D.E.S., *Primary Education—Suggestions* (H.M.S.O., 1965, 4th Imp.).

D.E.S., *Children and their Primary Schools* (Plowden Report) (H.M.S.O., 1967).

Eaglesham, E. J. R., *From School Board to Local Authority* (Routledge, 1956).

Eaglesham, E. J. R., *The Foundations of Twentieth-Century Education in England* (Routledge, 1967).

Gardner, D. E. M., *The Education of Young Children* (Methuen, 1965).

Isaacs, S., *The Children We Teach* (University of London Press, 1948).

Lowndes, G. A. N., *The Silent Social Revolution* (O.U.P., 1948).

Mansbridge, A., *Margaret McMillan—Prophet and Pioneer* (Dent, 1932).

Mayer, M., *The Schools* (Bodley Head, 1961).

McMillan, M., *The Nursery School* (Dent, 1919, reprinted 1930).

Ministry of Education, *Not Yet Five* (H.M.S.O., 1962).

Ministry of Education, *Seven to Eleven* (Pamphlet 15) (H.M.S.O., 1949).

Ministry of Education, *The Primary School* (Hadow Report) (H.M.S.O., 1931).

Ministry of Education, *Infant and Nursery Schools* (Hadow Report) (H.M.S.O., 1933).

Peterson, A. D. C., *A Hundred Years of Education* (Duckworth, 1952).

Raymont, T., *A History of the Education of Young Children* (Longmans, 1937).

Rusk, R. R., *A History of Infant Education* (University of London Press, 1933).

Chapter 3

English Secondary Education

A THE BEGINNINGS OF POST-PRIMARY EDUCATION TO 1862

It is obvious that one has to go back a long way for the real origins of 'secondary' forms of education in this country—to the endowed 'grammar' schools and the great public schools, many of which still exist outside the state system. We are here, however, concerned with that area of post-primary education which began, in the main, within the elementary education area of development, although this was by no means clear-cut, and certainly cannot be totally divorced from the other 'secondary' developments.

It is perhaps interesting to note, and certainly it is socially significant, that one of the first pieces of educational legislation in the first decade of the nineteenth century was an Act to preserve the health and morals of apprentices and others similarly employed in cotton and other mills and factories. In 1802 Peel's Factory Act required employers to make provision for adequate instruction in reading, writing and arithmetic during at least the first four years of a seven years' apprenticeship. Such instruction in the three Rs had to be included within the twelve hours which made up the working day of these unfortunate apprentices, and it was laid down that such a working day could not begin before 6.00 a.m. nor end later than 9.00 p.m.

We have already looked at the work and influence of such educators as Lancaster and Bell, and for the first half of the nineteenth century a great deal of the work done in post-primary education was supported by voluntary contributions and voluntary workers, as well as by school fees for those who could afford to pay them in some of the more select schools. But post-primary education was really simply an extension of elementary education into the early years of adolescence.

In 1833, when the government provided a grant of £20,000 for the erection of schools, one of the first bids for a national system of education was made in Parliament. On July 30, 1833 Mr J. A. Roebuck in a speech in the House of Commons asked the House to consider making it obligatory, by law, for every child from about the age of six to twelve years to attend a school regularly. If parents were able to give their children sufficient education in a school other than a 'national' one, then no compulsion needed to be applied to make such children attend State-provided schools. If parents were unable or unwilling to give their children such education, then the State would compel them to send their children to State schools. Such schools were to be confined to the education of the poor, and were to be classified as (a) infants' schools; (b) schools of industry for children between the ages of seven and fourteen; and (c) normal schools for the training of teachers (1).

Much of the early legislation in the realm of education displayed a very noble interest in the plight of the very poor, but very often provision for the children of the not-so-poor was ignored. Many of the parents in this class found it difficult to get State help in the education of their children, whilst they themselves were too indigent to pay fees at the private industry schools or the costly public schools. In consequence, they were often worse off than the very poor. It was such people that thinkers like Francis Place and Jeremy Bentham had in mind when they began to suggest the establishment of higher grade elementary schools using systems similar to those of Lancaster and Bell. But Bentham received little encouragement. His *Chrestomathia* propounded a scheme of learning for children between the ages of seven and fourteen years which was encyclopedic but quite incapable of implementation in the contemporary climate. There can be little doubt, however, that his 'chrestomathic' scheme helped other thinkers and educators to visualize a more extensive, as well as realistic, curriculum for higher grade elementary schools; so that, before 1925, there were schools in Britain which had introduced at least one modern foreign language, French, and developments towards more serious mathematics for older boys, such as geometry and trigonometry as well as linear drawing.

Before 1850 various types of school for dealing with vocational interests in commerce, as well as industry, were developing fast, and the Manchester Church Education Society had opened schools in which the curriculum was extended to include more than one modern foreign language, and certain liberal arts studies as well as the essentials of accounts and book-keeping. The Wesleyans, in particular, became interested in post-primary education for the children of the not-so-poor; indeed, many of their pupils came from quite prosperous families, where the parents were beginning to see the value of an education which was becoming increasingly aligned to the social and economic developments of the age. Matthew Arnold, who took his inspection duties very seriously and sought to get an overall picture of the education of his time, reported that the Wesleyan schools which he had viewed existed 'for the sake of the children of tradesmen, of farmers, and of mechanics of the higher class, rather than for the sake of the children of the poor' (2). The needs of different areas were also recognized by the Wesleyan schools, and the curricula of urban schools were different from those of rural ones, where some study of agriculture was made and some instruction given in land surveying and mensuration.

The terms of reference of the Newcastle Commission, set up in 1858, are outlined in Section C of the first chapter of this book (3). The commission was critical of the poor standard of attendance of children at the schools provided by the various bodies, and in particular of the early age at which children left school to take up some form of employment. There were complaints by the commissioners that some teachers neglected their duties with regard to the younger children and 'early leavers', and concentrated too exclusively on the older and brighter pupils. Apparently the accuracy of these complaints was questioned by Matthew Arnold (4), but the report of the commission revealed a certain ambivalence of attitude towards 'post-primary' education, at once deprecating the early leaving age and supporting the evidence of Rev. James Fraser, an assistant commissioner, who was quoted in Chapter 1 as doubting 'whether it would be desirable, with a view to the real interests of the peasant boy, to keep him at school till he was fourteen or fifteen years of age' (5). In the event, neither the Newcastle Commission nor Lowe's Revised Code of 1862 did much to assist the development of 'secondary' education. Indeed, for some time higher primary school work was positively discouraged; it was a general move back to the three Rs, with some needlework thrown in for the girls.

The need, however, for further education for selected pupils in the elementary schools was still recognized by the educators and teachers, if not by the administrators. In consequence, many of the schools outside the State system persisted in a broader curriculum, and taught older children. Some of these schools in rural areas, and others in industrial works, developed what were known as 'higher tops', that is, classes at the top of the schools specifically for older and more clever children.

B THE TAUNTON COMMISSION 1864–8

In 1864 the Schools Inquiry Commission was set up to inquire into the education provided by schools not dealt with by the Newcastle and the Clarendon Reports; it was asked also, within its terms of reference, to consider what measures might be required for the improvement of such education. This investigation was an exhaustive one into all types of existing secondary education, including 'private', 'proprietary' and 'endowed'. Both written and oral evidence was taken, and questionnaires were issued. Proprietary schools were those promoted by companies, and not many of these were investigated; private schools, of which there were a large number, were organized for private, individual profit; endowed schools were represented by the large number (nearly 3,000) of grammar schools.

When the commission reported in 1868 it recommended three main grades of higher or secondary schools which it considered ought to be established according to the leaving age of the pupils and the level in the social scale at which their parents were situated. Grade One schools existed for the sons of parents with ample means who wished their children to continue their schooling until the age of eighteen or over. These schools could pursue curricula which included classics, mathematics, modern languages and science. Grade Two schools were for the sons of parents who could well afford to keep their children at school for another two years after sixteen but who intended to place them in employments which demanded special preparation at that age. Other parents were financially unable to keep their children at school for another two years in any case. In most of these schools some attempt was made to retain Latin, and the curricula usually included English, arithmetic, natural science and modern languages; and for some there was a development of mathematical studies. According to the report some of the parents who came within this category were 'not insensible to the value of culture itself, nor to the advantage of sharing the education of the cultivated classes' (6). The Grade Three schools, whose education ceased when the child was about fourteen, belonged to a class which was lower in the social scale, but so numerous as to be quite as important as the other two. These existed for the children of smaller tenant farmers, the small tradesmen, and superior artisans. It was felt that the needs of this group were not technical or vocational, but restricted mainly to a sound training in reading, writing and arithmetic.

The 'tripartite' system described in this report was clearly based on social and class distinctions, and general economic factors. It was also obvious from the exhaustive enquiries of the commission that not only was there social inequality but an inadequate supply of schools to meet demands, and an uneven distribution of schools. Throughout the whole country it appeared that there were only thirteen secondary schools for girls. A large proportion of those children whose parents could afford to send them to one of the three grades of school, were nevertheless ill-taught.

Although it is true to say that little notice was immediately taken of the commission's report, its general tone and ethos affected educational thinking and prepared public opinion generally for the changes that were to be effected in secondary education during the ensuing decades. The Endowed Schools Act of 1869 'gutted the Report', as H. C. Barnard puts it; the recommendations of the commission were given scant attention, and only endowed schools were dealt with (7).

c 1870–1894

In 1870 the Forster Elementary Education Act was passed, and the newly-formed school boards were empowered to frame by-laws making attendance at school compulsory for children between the ages of five and thirteen. It should be noted that this was permissive only and numerous exemptions were made for a large variety of reasons. The Act was concerned with the development of elementary education, mostly at the primary stage; and most of the schools which kept any large numbers of older children were of a voluntary nature. The Hadow Report gives an interesting brief account of two such voluntary schools at Lancaster and Oswestry where there were no school boards in the early 1870s (8).

At Lancaster there was a top class comprising boys drawn from a large catchment area. The course was a highly competitive one, and any boy seeking entry was subjected to a pretty rigorous oral test which was designed to discover the most brilliant of the candidates. At the end of the course, which included some Latin, mathematics, science and drawing, most of the pupils entered industry and commerce as clerks, whilst some became assistant teachers. At Oswestry the pupils in the 'higher top' (as the top class was termed) were largely farmers' sons from small village schools. Although it was not apparently too difficult to get into this course, pupils were expected to remain until they were at least sixteen. From the school, where there was emphasis on clear, accurate speech, they entered merchants' offices in such cities as Liverpool. Their curriculum included Latin, English literature and grammar, mathematics, mechanics, mensuration and practical drawing.

In 1876 the Lord Sandon Education Act was passed. This provided for the awarding of Honour Certificates to pupils who were ten years of age, and had passed the Standard Four examination, and who possessed a certificate of regular attendance at school for a period of five years. Possession of such a certificate meant the provision of free education for a further three years. This was obviously an inducement to remain at school for a longer period, and the scheme, which remained in operation until 1881, helped the development of 'higher tops' in many elementary schools. Further provisions in the Education Acts of 1876 and 1880, relating to the enforcement of school attendance through by-laws, helped to keep a large number of children on at school until the age of thirteen or fourteen.

The addition of a seventh standard in elementary schools, by the Education Department in 1882, and the drafting of classes in this standard into one central school covering a particular area, led to the gradual development of higher grade schools, some of which were later to be referred to as 'central schools' and others as 'secondary schools'. References are made to some of these schools in statistical returns to the House of Commons in June 1898. There was a great deal of 'administrative muddle' at this time (9), in which the Education Department, the Charity Commission, and the Science and Art Department all had some say in the control and organization of secondary education; and altogether there were some 2,568 school boards responsible for higher grade schools and the 'higher tops' of elementary schools.

Sheffield had established what it called a 'higher central school' for sixth and seventh standards only, to which pupils were admitted by competition. It had a very broad curriculum of physics, chemistry, mechanics, machine drawing and construction, as well as the three Rs and English literature; Manchester and ·Birmingham also developed central schools. Both the Education Department and the Science and Art Department shared the costs of providing this secondary education. Many of these schools—higher grade, central, higher tops, secondary and so forth—not only developed further subjects but also organized full science courses for their pupils.

A Royal Commission on Technical Instruction was set up in 1881, and it produced its report during the years 1882–4. The gaps in secondary education were particularly mentioned in Part IV of the report, and the commissioners were clearly impressed with the work of the higher elementary schools like those of Sheffield and Manchester. They considered that more of these schools should be established so that the more advanced pupils of the primary schools could be transferred to them, if their parents were willing to keep them at such schools until they reached the age of fourteen or fifteen. The commissioners clearly wanted a more marked distinction between elementary and secondary education, and the tenor of their report helped to strengthen the whole position of the 'higher grade schools', whatever name they went by. Thus, the commissioners argued:

'The best preparation for technical study is a good modern secondary school of the types of the Manchester Grammar School, the Bedford Modern School, and the Allan Glen's Institution at Glasgow. Unfortunately our middle classes are at a great disadvantage compared with those of the Continent for want of a sufficient number of such schools . . . Power should be given to important local bodies . . . to originate and support secondary and technical schools' (10).

The Report of the Royal Commission on the Elementary Education Acts, namely the Cross Report, appeared in 1888 after two years of investigation. The commission was obviously divided as to the value and function of higher grade schools. There were arguments on both sides, some of them not unlike the arguments currently for and against such institutions as the sixth form college. Some argued that the withdrawal of all the children in the higher standards of the elementary schools could have the effect only of destroying incentives for both teachers and pupils. The teachers would be deprived of scholars at a time when they were becoming most interesting from an intellectual point of view, and when they would, for the first time perhaps, begin to stretch their educators mentally. The pupils who remained in the ordinary elementary schools would lack models of higher industry and ability, and so much of their source of ambition would be destroyed. Others, the majority, argued that the advantages of a distinctive secondary education outweighed any disadvantages advanced by the minority. Moreover, they considered that separate higher grade schools, which centralized the cleverest pupils in the upper standards, were in fact a more efficient and economic way of using the teaching force.

D THE BRYCE COMMISSION 1895

The Royal Commission on Secondary Education was appointed in 1894 'to consider what are the best methods of establishing a well-organized system of secondary education in England' (11). It had to take into account the deficiencies which already existed in the country, and had to pay due regard to any local sources of revenue for endowments which might be available. For the first time in our history there were women on the Royal Commission—three out of the seventeen members, namely, Lady Frederick Cavendish, Dr Sophie Bryant and Mrs E. M. Sidgwick. It was one of the purposes of the commission to clear up the 'administrative muddle' and to make recommendations for the simplification of the 'hydra-headed administrative structure' (12).

The report tried to clarify the situation regarding higher grade schools and those elementary schools which were, in fact, giving some form of education beyond the seventh standard. The nomenclature of such schools had become multiform as well as confusing, but the report pinpointed at least three main types of school to which the term 'higher grade elementary school' had been attached. The first type was the school which taught from the fifth standard upwards, and gave an education after the seventh standard for at least two years, so that the age of a pupil leaving such a school would be fifteen years of age at least. Some of these schools rejoiced in such names as 'higher grade school', 'higher central school', 'higher elementary school', and 'higher standard school'. The second type ranged from Standard One to Standard Seven plus a course of two to four years, which would again bring the leaving age up to at least fifteen years. Many of these schools had an organized science course under the aegis of the Science and Art Department. The third type is referred to by the report as the pseudo 'higher grade school'. This was a school which charged fees; and, although it was supposed to be more select, curriculum-wise it was almost entirely elementary.

The Bryce Commission regretted the discontinuous and incoherent growth of secondary education; it also regretted the lack of co-ordination of effort between the Charity Commissioners, the Education Department, and the Science and Art Department. Even the borough councils had often acted independently of the school boards so that there was further confusion in the administration of grants. There was needless competition between the various agencies of education and a consequent uneconomic dispersal and overlapping of effort. Through the administrative muddle there had resulted 'waste of money, of time, and of labour'.

The commissioners recommended, as the only reasonable solution, that the schools of the third grade (see above, Section B) should be classified as 'secondary schools', and that they should be placed under the jurisdiction of local authorities. In order to avoid unnecessary and wasteful competition between secondary schools they should all be co-ordinated within any particular district, and brought into some organic relationship so that they might co-operate as 'places of preparation for advanced instruction'. The commissioners spoke out strongly against the lack of coherence and correlation, and blamed vested interests which stood in the way of badly-needed reforms.

The report recommended the establishment of one central education authority under a Minister of Education, which would merge the functions and powers of the Education Department, the Science and Art Department, and the Charity Commission in respect of educational trusts and endowments. The Minister was to be assisted by an Educational Council whose function it was to help him in certain judicial activities. The Board of Education Act of 1899 set up the Board of Education 'to superintend matters relating to education in England and Wales'. The President of the Board was appointed by the Crown, and the remainder of the Board comprised the Lord President of the Council, the Principal Secretaries of State, the First Commissioner of the Treasury, and the Chancellor of the Exchequer. From 1899 to 1944—the period during which the Board existed—it never met; its work, however, was carried on by the President and certain senior administrative officials. A Consultative Committee was established to advise the Board when the latter referred any matter to it, but it had to wait for the President to request such help.

But the really vital legislation had yet to come in the Education Acts of the twentieth century. The conclusion of the Bryce Report had said:

'Thus it is not merely in the interest of the material prosperity and intellectual activity of the nation, but no less in that of its happiness and its moral strength, that the extension and reorganization of secondary education seem entitled to a place among the first subjects with which social legislation ought to deal' (13).

It was the Education Act of 1902 which eventually gave reality to the vision of the Bryce Commissioners.

REFERENCES

1 *Hansard*, 1833, Vol. xx. See columns 153–61.
2 Arnold, M., *Reports on Elementary Schools, 1852–1882* (H.M.S.O., 1910).
3 Maclure, J.S., *Educational Documents—England and Wales, 1816–1967* (Methuen, 1968, 2nd ed.), p. 70.
4 *Vide* Board of Education, *The Education of the Adolescent* (H.M.S.O., 1927, reprinted 1948), p. 11, n.1.
5 Maclure, J. S., op. cit., p. 75.
6 Ibid., p. 94.
7 Barnard, H. C., *A History of English Education from 1760* (University of London Press, 1961, 2nd ed., 1963 Imp.), p. 133.
8 Op. cit., p. 15.
9 *Vide* Adamson, J. W., *English Education: 1789–1902* (Methuen, 1930, reprinted 1964), Chapter XVI; and the excellent chapter in Eaglesham, E. J. R., *The Foundations of Twentieth-Century Education in England* (Routledge, 1967), Chapter 2.
10 Maclure, J. S., op. cit., p. 125.
11 Ibid., p. 140.
12 Ibid., p. 140.
13 Ibid., p. 148.

BIBLIOGRAPHY

Adamson, J. W., *English Education, 1789–1902* (C.U.P., 1930, reprinted 1964).
Archer, R. L., *Secondary Education in the Nineteenth Century* (C.U.P., 1932).
Curtis, S. J., *History of Education in Great Britain* (University Tutorial Press, 1963).
Curtis, S.J. and Boultwood, M. E. A., *An Introductory History of English Education Since 1800* (University Tutorial Press, 1964).
Eaglesham, E. J. R., *The Foundations of Twentieth-Century Education in England* (Routledge, 1967).
Maclure, J. S., *Educational Documents—England and Wales: 1816–1967* (Methuen, 1968).
Meyer, A. E., *An Educational History of the Western World* (McGraw-Hill, 1965).
Ministry of Education, *The Education of the Adolescent* (Hadow Report) (H.M.S.O., 1926).

Chapter 4

The Development and Organization of Secondary Education

A 1900–1918

The importance of 'secondary' education as represented by the higher grade schools was gradually being forced on the attention of politicians and administrators. In his *Special Reports on Educational Subjects* in 1898, Robert Morant, then Assistant Director of the Office of Special Inquiries and Reports of the Education Department, concluded by saying,

'Surely it is not too much to hope that England may yet learn to value and to create for herself a true and complete organization of her schools, not merely of her primary education, but also of that most valuable asset of the national welfare—her middle and higher schools . . . Thus, and thus only, can each and every school, and each and every grade of education, have its due share of national interest and assistance, and be enabled to pay its due part in national development' (1).

A crisis was reached in 1899 when an obscure Local Government Board district auditor, Mr T. B. Cockerton, disallowed the expenditure of the London School Board for certain continuation classes, and surcharged them. The auditor argued that the Board had gone beyond its terms of reference in teaching adults, and also in teaching certain areas of art and science. The whole matter resulted in actions in Court and Cockerton's ruling was supported by the judgment of the Court of Queen's Bench towards the end of 1900. When the London School Board appealed the judgment was further upheld by the Court of Appeal in 1901 (2).

One of the chief results of the 1902 Balfour Education Act was the provision of county secondary schools, many of them resulting from a conversion of the higher grade elementary schools and pupil-teacher centres. When the Prime Minister, Mr A. J. Balfour, introduced the Bill in the House of Commons he underlined the insufficiency of the supply of secondary education; and he also pointed out that the higher technical instruction, which was becoming increasingly in demand, could be truly effective only when based upon a 'sound general secondary education'.

The addition of 'higher tops' to elementary schools was not the ultimate solution to the problem. Balfour saw no future in the *ad hoc* school boards and he expected the newly created L.E.A.s to provide new secondary schools.

In the *Regulations for Secondary Schools*, which Mr Robert Morant, who was now Permanent Secretary of the Board of Education, devised in 1904, the term 'secondary school' was at last defined. It was held to include

'Any day or boarding school which offers to each of its scholars, up to and beyond the age of 16, a general education, physical, mental and moral, given through a complete graded course of instruction of wider scope and more advanced degree than that in elementary schools' (3).

The Board of Education gave priority to a general education in these secondary schools—specialization and vocational training came only after this sound initial basis had been established. Emphasis was laid upon training the pupil to use all his faculties, to understand the laws and structure of the physical world, to be able to use thought and language in an accurate manner, and to show some competence in dealing with affairs.

But the course had also to be complete, that is, there was to be no superficial introduction to the various areas of instruction—there was to be depth as well as breadth. The regulations envisaged the possibility of entering the secondary school as early as 8, and of continuing up to the age of 19, but generally the point of entry would be about 12+, and most pupils would probably leave at 16 or 17. Whatever the length of the course provided, however, it should be systematic and complete. Whilst a fair amount of freedom was given to schools to plan their own curriculum according to their needs and local conditions, the regulations provided general guidance concerning subjects, or groups of subjects, which should be taught. A certain minimum time had to be given to English language and English literature, geography and history; to languages, ancient and modern; and to mathematics and science. Other subjects should include drawing, singing, manual training and physical exercises; and for girls there should be at least the elements of housewifery. The pattern followed very much that of the typical grammar school, and the regulations concluded with the requirement that

'when two languages other than English are taken, and Latin is not one of them, the Board will be required to be satisfied that the omission of Latin is for the advantage of the school' (4).

In 1907 *Supplementary Regulations for Secondary Schools in England* were published whereby any secondary school that was receiving a grant from the Board of Education had to provide a proportion of school places free. This would 'ordinarily be 25 per cent of the scholars admitted'. These regulations gave a full legal position to the scholarship system which was already working to a partial extent. By 1927 there were something like 150,000 free places in secondary schools. Despite this fact, however, thousands of candidates for free places were being rejected each year, and the qualifying examination for them—which was not originally intended to be competitive—soon became fiercely contended.

In the absence of an adequate number of secondary school places, it is not surprising that the higher grade schools reappeared under the title of 'central schools'. These date in London from the educational year commencing April 1, 1911. The chief purpose of the central school (5) was to prepare pupils for immediate employment on leaving school; the curriculum was, therefore, generally of a practical nature, geared to prepare the children to go into business or the workshop on completing the course without any intermediate or special training. The training given in these schools was thus eminently practical without being too narrowly vocational in the sense that the trade school, or junior technical school, was. *The Report of the Board of Education for 1911–12* revealed that similar developments were also taking place in Manchester where six district central schools had been established along lines similar to those already found in London. The day trade schools and junior technical schools will be considered in greater detail elsewhere: suffice it to say here that these represented another development along post-primary lines.

In 1911 the Consultative Committee of the Board of Education published its *Report on Examinations in Secondary Schools*. The committee argued very well, in Chapter IV, some of the more important effects of examinations on both the pupil and the teacher; and, despite the dangers involved, they had no hesitation in stating their conviction that 'external examinations are not only necessary but desirable in secondary schools' (6). They were equally convinced, however, that in order to minimize the dangers involved stringent measures had to be taken to regulate the number of examinations, their general nature, and the age at which they were taken. They recommended that an Examinations Council should be set up comprising representatives of the L.E.A.s and of the universities, and in 1917 such an advisory council was set up, and a new scheme of secondary school examinations was devised, namely the Secondary School Certificate.

The Fisher Education Act of 1918 attempted to make up for that 'lack of scientific correlation between the different parts of our educational machinery' (7) referred to by H. A. L. Fisher when he introduced the Bill. He recognized that there were populous areas which lacked any secondary school whatsoever, whilst other areas existed, 'older and less important', with as many as four secondary schools. The solution seemed to be to give a new general direction to post-primary education through the existing elementary schools—in some ways a retrogressive step. However, all exemptions from the school-leaving age of fourteen were abolished, and it became the duty of local education authorities, which were responsible for elementary education, to make provision by means of special classes and central schools for advanced practical, general instruction. Practical instruction was later defined, in an Education Act in 1921, to include such instruction as cookery, laundry-work, housewifery, dairy-work, handicrafts and gardening.

B THE HADOW REPORT 1926

The Consultative Committee of the Board of Education was given the task, in February 1924, of considering and reporting on the organization, aims and curricula of courses designed for children who would remain at schools, other than secondary schools, for full-time courses up to the age of fifteen. They were asked to bear in mind the basic requirements of a good, general education as well as a practical one, suitable for children of varying talents and abilities, whilst weighing also the probable occupations of these pupils in ndustry, commerce and agriculture. 'Incidentally', they were asked also to advise upon suitable arrangements for testing such pupils at the end of their course, and for facilitating, where suitable, the transfer of individual pupils to secondary schools at an age above the normal age of entry. This was no mean task to set any committee, but it possessed members, such as R. H. Tawney and Ernest Barker, who had done some deep thinking on the problem already; and the report, completed in 1926 and entitled *The Education of the Adolescent*, clearly bore the stamp of these thinkers.

It will always be remembered for its introductory remarks about the 'tide which begins to rise in the veins of youth at the age of eleven or twelve', and its conclusions from this fact in relation to taking the tide at the flood and embarking on a new voyage in the strength and along the flow of its current, eventually arriving at fortune (8). Piaget might have provided the committee with better reasons for transferring children at the age of eleven or twelve, but it is generally agreed today that administrative considerations were of greater importance than psychological ones in giving their conclusions.

The committee recognized that at every stage of the development of elementary education in this country there had been a tendency to throw up all sorts of experiments in post-primary education. From this fact it was deduced that, despite all attempts at curtailment of such experiments, there was a sort of 'half-conscious striving' of our highly industrialized society to evolve a type of school which was distinct from the more traditional and orthodox secondary grammar school, and yet which was analogous to it, making provision for an education calculated to fit pupils for the various branches of commerce, industry and agriculture at the age of fifteen.

The report made it clear that it envisaged two main stages of education, 'primary' and 'post-primary'. Primary education should be regarded as ending at about 11+ (taking into account the pupil's mental as well as chronological age). The post-primary stage should then begin. Here there was room for a great variety of education, but it would, in fact, be some form of 'secondary education for all'. For the majority it would go on to about 14+ or 15+, for many it would continue to 16+, and for some it would end at eighteen or nineteen. The aim of all the various types of education at this 'post-primary' level would be to provide for the needs of children passing through the stage of adolescence.

The committee made the important point that 'equality . . . is not identity' (9), and that the educational system should not attempt to press different types of children into an identical mould. It should seek to provide a wide range of educational opportunity, appealing to the varied interests and abilities of a large number of children. The report concluded in this respect that the secondary stage of education should include junior technical schools; the trade schools; the then existing 'secondary' type schools which were following a predominantly literary or scientific curriculum; the selective central schools, with a realistic or practical trend in the last two years of a four-year course; the non-selective central schools, and senior classes, central departments or 'higher tops', which provided advanced instruction for pupils over the age of 11+, and for whom no other local provision could be made. The committee recognized that it would be some time before post-primary schools could be created in sufficient numbers for all children to be transferred to one or another type, but in the meantime the organization of post-primary education must take place in the elementary school itself, and the minimum leaving age must be raised to fifteen, thus providing six years of primary education and at least another four years of post-primary education.

The committee also concluded that the post-primary schools, in providing a humane and liberal education, should not be concerned with one mediated only through books, but rather one which involved children in practical work and living interests. This was not to be conceived in any narrowly vocational, or technical, sense but rather in the sense that 'realistic' studies often formed the best basis and instrument for a sound education.

One of the principles supported throughout the report was that of the case for transfer of a pupil from one type of school to another. This obviously involved knowing individual pupils well, but it was always in the minds of those who conceived different types of school for different sorts of pupil that mistakes would inevitably be made; and there should therefore be adequate machinery for rectifying such mistakes.

There was a concerted effort to regularize the classification and nomen-clature of the various types of post-primary school (10). Schools normally pursuing a predominantly literary or scientific curriculum should be known as grammar schools. The selective central schools, which gave at least a four-years' course from the age of 11+, as well as non-selective central schools, should be known henceforth as modern schools. Those depart-ments or classes within the existing public elementary schools, which provided post-primary education for children who would not go to any of the aforementioned schools, should be known as senior classes.

The curriculum of the modern school should be planned as a whole to avoid overcrowding the timetable, with a view to arousing the interest of the children, with due regard to accuracy of material and local conditions and possibilities, and so as to stimulate the pupils' capacities with a liberal provision of practical work. It was important that these new modern schools should neither become nor be regarded as inferior secondary schools, nor offer a fare which was merely a vague continuation of primary education, lacking liberality and depth. The report emphasized repeatedly that the modern school was not 'an inferior species', and hence its equip-ment and accommodation should in no way be inferior. Selection pro-cedures for such schools were discussed, and it is interesting to note that, as early as 1926, whilst it was suggested that cramming might be combated by using individual psychological tests of intelligence in order to arrive at a 'comparatively accurate estimate of the candidate's capacity', it was equally recognized that such tests had to be used with care since children specifically prepared for them could develop test sophistication (11).

C THE SPENS REPORT 1938

In 1933 the Consultative Committee of the Board of Education on second-ary education, with special reference to grammar schools and technical high schools, was appointed. Out of the twenty-two members selected six had been members of the 1926 Hadow Committee. Their terms of reference were

'To consider and report upon the organization and inter-relation of schools, other than those administered under the Elementary Code, which provided education for pupils beyond the age of 11+; regard being had in particular to the framework and content of the education of pupils who do not remain at school beyond the age of about 16' (12).

The committee sat during the next five years, and, after examining 150 witnesses, produced its report in November 1939. In addition to the main report there were some very useful appendixes supplied by Dr R. F. Young (on 'The Conception of General Liberal Education'), Dr I. L. Kandel (on 'The Secondary School Curriculum'), Dr (later Sir) Cyril Burt (on 'Faculty Psychology'), and Dr H. R. Hamley ('The Cognitive Aspects of Transfer of Training').

The report discussed, in the introduction, the possibility of multilateral schools, later termed comprehensive. It outlined the characteristics of this type of school as the provision of a good, general education for two or three years for all pupils over the age of 11+ in a given area, and the organization of a number of 'streams' (say, four or five), so that pupils of thirteen or fourteen years and over might pursue courses suited to their particular individual abilities and capacities. Such multilateral schools would cover the curricula of existing grammar, modern and junior technical schools, and pupils would be provided with the particular courses they needed, and moreover could transfer more easily from one course, or one 'stream', to another. The committee found the policy 'very attractive' and certainly were aware of the considerable advantages of the close association of pupils of widely varied ability, interests and objectives. They were also conscious of the possibility of transferring pupils without great administrative difficulty, from an academic to a less academic course, and vice versa.

Despite such advantages, and with some reluctance, the committee felt that it could not advocate multilateralism as a general policy. The reasons which they felt weighed against such a policy are clearly stated in the introduction, and supported later in Chapter IX where some administrative problems were dealt with. In an age of 'comprehensiveness', some of the statements read somewhat amusingly today, for example 'the size of the school would have to be very considerable, say, 800 or possibly larger' (13). The average size of comprehensive schools in 1966 was over 900 pupils, but many had over 1,000 and some over 2,000 pupils. The committee took evidence from Dr I. L. Kandel, Professor of Education, Columbia University, who stated that the problem was not simplified even in such a country as the United States, where the single comprehensive school was organized end-on with the elementary school. It had to meet the needs of all the adolescent population and to provide courses which were suited to the capacities of each individual child. Professor Kandel stated:

'It is beginning at last to be admitted that the single school may cater to the average but it does justice neither to the bright nor to the dull pupils, that the attempt to provide general cultural and vocational courses side by side in the same institution tends to militate against the success of both . . .' (14).

The committee still felt, however, that 'the multilateral idea' should permeate the system of secondary education as they conceived it. And their concept of secondary education was its further development in separate grammar, technical and modern schools. They recognized that parents themselves were influenced in their preferences between modern schools and grammar schools—and parents have not changed very much—not only by educational and vocational considerations but by the greater prestige grammar schools had always enjoyed. In our own time we are solving the problem largely by getting rid of the object of such prestige. The solution of the Spens Committee was somewhat different—to give equal prestige to all secondary schools. They recommended a new code of regulations for secondary schools, including the adoption of similar standards for the size of classes and for planning of school buildings, and the parity of staffing. The committee was also clearly in favour of the abolition of all fees in both grammar schools and technical high schools 'as soon as the national finances permit'.

The committee recommended the adoption of a minimum leaving-age of sixteen years, which however unattainable it might be at the time of the report was to be regarded as eventually inevitable. It was the prime duty of any school which provided secondary education to cater for the needs of children who were passing through adolescence. It had to provide a curriculum which, in the words of *The Primary School Report* of 1931, should be thought of in terms of 'activity and experience rather than of knowledge to be acquired and facts to be stored'. It was felt that both the creative and conservative elements in the activities of the community ought to be represented in the curriculum, with a larger emphasis on creativity and the practical affairs of life. It was suggested that a 'tutorial system' should be widely tried in all types of secondary school, and careers masters should be appointed. The committee strongly opposed the formation of what today would be termed a sixth form college. The sixth form, it was held, was the most valuable as well as the most characteristic feature in the grammar school in developing a sense of responsibility and in training the character. To 'behead' the grammar school by centralizing the sixth form work would destroy the grammar school as such. Provision for entry into the grammar schools of about 15 per cent of the 'secondary school age-group' in the public elementary schools should be regarded as a working annual figure.

The Spens Report was a very workmanlike effort, covering a vast area of material, and making a total of nearly 170 suggestions and recommendations. We shall have another look at its content when we come to consider technical and technological education.

D THE NORWOOD REPORT 1943
The Norwood Committee of the Secondary School Examinations Council on Curriculum and Examinations in Secondary Schools was appointed by

the Board of Education in October 1941. Its terms of reference were to consider the suggested changes in the secondary school curriculum and the related question of school examinations. The committee made its general philosophical position clear in the introduction to its report, which was published in 1943, a philosophy which became quite explicit in such chapters as those on religious education and classics. The committee believed that education could not but recognize the ideals of truth, beauty and goodness as absolutes, 'final and binding for all times and in all places'. The committee further held that the recognition of such values 'implies, for most people at least, a religious interpretation of life which for us must mean the Christian interpretation of life' (15). Its values were independent of time or any particular environment, so that no education which ignored such ultimates and operated merely in the realm of relative ends was acceptable. Science and scientific method were important as means to an end—the realization of the 'good life', i.e. the Christian life.

The report accepted the view that secondary education is the stage which follows that of primary education. In the secondary stage the attempt was made to provide for special interests and aptitudes the kind of education most suited to them. The committee considered that rough groupings, whatever might be their ground, had in fact established themselves in general educational experience. Three main groups of pupils could, apparently, be distinguished, and in consequence the report proposed that at the age of 11+ pupils should pass into the type of school which seemed to meet their needs. There should be three main types of secondary school—grammar, technical and modern. This was a clear statement of the 'tripartite' system. It considered, however, that children should follow practically the same course of study during the first two years, which was to be a diagnostic period. At 13+ the selection of children should be reconsidered and where necessary children should be transferred to another type of school. The division of children into three broad psychological types was criticized then and has been criticized since.

Whilst accepting that each type of school should have such parity as amenities and general conditions could bestow, parity of esteem, in the committee's view, could not be magically conferred by some administrative decree, nor indeed by the equality of cost per pupil; it could be won only by the schools themselves. It was the particular and primary function of the secondary school to provide a training for entry into industry and commerce at the age of 16+ in order to meet the requirements of local industrial conditions. Wherever possible these schools should also provide facilities for more advanced work to children from sixteen to eighteen years of age. It was the task of the secondary modern school to provide a general education for the majority of the nation's boys and girls up to school-leaving age. The curricula of such schools should be related closely to the immediate interests and environment of their pupils. Methods should be practical and concrete. The report looked for fruitful growth and experimental approaches in this particular area of education. The distinguishing feature of the secondary grammar school was 'the intellectual ideal which it upholds as best suited to a particular group of pupils' (16). And that particular group of pupils apparently was interested in learning for its own sake, in connected reasoning, in causes, in proofs and precise demonstrations, in relationships, structures, development and a coherent corpus of knowledge.

Finally, the difficult problem of differentiation and selection at 11+ was carefully considered by the committee who stressed the value and importance of effective school record cards, the judgment of the teachers in the primary schools, and suitably selected intelligence, performance, and other tests.

During the same year (1943) the Government issued a White Paper on *Educational Reconstruction* in which they stated that they intended to recast the national education service. A war, particularly a total war, is a wonderful opportunity for assessing a country's potential, and the Government was now ready to admit that its greatest national asset was its Youth. At last it was clearly heeding the various reports that had been produced since the Education Act of 1918, and it presaged the Butler Education Act of 1944. Education, it averred, was to be a continuous process conducted in successive stages, which were clearly marked as nursery, primary and secondary. The period of compulsory school attendance would be, without any exemption, extended to 15, and then to 16 as soon as circumstances permitted. The White Paper accepted the tripartite principle of secondary grammar, secondary modern and secondary technical schools, but whilst these would be 'of diversified types' they would, nevertheless, be of equal standing. Moreover, they would not always be 'separate and apart'; different types might well be combined in one building or upon one site, and in any case there must be the facilitation of free transfer from one type of education to another.

The White Paper was strongly opposed to any emphasis upon examination subjects in junior departments, and felt that nothing could be said in favour of a system which subjected children of 11+ to the strain of competitive examinations, particularly when the whole of their careers might well depend upon the result. Children should be classified on the basis of their individual aptitudes which could best be adjudged by their school records and, if necessary, intelligence tests, 'due regard being had to their parents' wishes, and the careers they have in mind' (17). The White Paper must have escaped the notice of a large number of directors of education and headmasters, for its instructions were almost completely ignored with regard to the 'non-competitiveness' of 11+ selection. But this was inevitable in the nature of things, and in the event the Government withdrew from the tripartite position before the 1944 Education Act was introduced.

E THE BUTLER EDUCATION ACT 1944

It is not our purpose here to discuss all the clauses of the 1944 Education Act—only those which were in some way related to the further development of secondary education. The main changes in this direction were, firstly, the raising of the school-leaving age to fifteen. This had been recommended by the Hadow Report in 1926, whilst the Spens Report had suggested raising it to sixteen. Even now special power was given to the Minister in the 1944 Act to delay the raising of the school-leaving age for two years, partly because of the inadequate school accommodation, but also because of a palpable lack of trained teachers. The leaving age was raised to fifteen in April 1947. The Act gave the Minister power to raise it to sixteen by an Order in Council, as soon as he was satisfied that this was practicable.

Secondly, the Act clearly distinguished three stages of education, namely, primary, secondary and further. Secondary now meant post-primary education, and secondary schools had to exist in buildings separate from the primary schools. Secondary schools were defined as those schools which provided secondary education; and this in turn was defined by Section (1) (b) as education suitable to the requirements of senior pupils, that is, pupils who had attained the age of twelve years but had not yet reached the age of nineteen years. This did not, of course, include such full-time education as might be provided for senior pupils under separate provisions relating to further education, for example technical education. L.E.A.s were given the duty of securing adequate provision of both primary and secondary education for their pupils, and all tuition fees in maintained schools were abolished. A duty was laid also upon the parent to ensure that his child received 'efficient full-time education suitable to his age, aptitude and ability either by regular attendance at school or otherwise' (18). Subject to conscience-clauses, children were to be provided with opportunities for collective worship and religious instruction within all primary and secondary schools. The religious instruction was to be developed in county schools according to syllabuses which were agreed upon by representatives of local authorities, the schools and religious denominations. The dual system in English education persisted—there were schools provided by the L.E.A.s and those provided by the various Church voluntary bodies, some of which were aided and others controlled.

In 1947 the Government produced *Circular 144/1947*, entitled *The Organization of Secondary Education*. In it the Minister showed that he was fully aware of the problems involved in a too rigid tripartite system, which had in fact never been the subject of precise legislation. He did not accept that all children fell within the three distinct groups of the 'Norwood Myth', nor did he consider that only three types of secondary education were possible. Since the publication of the Hadow Reports there had been a fair amount of experimentation—and successful experimentation—in various forms of secondary education; and there was the possibility of further development of bilateral, multilateral and comprehensive forms of education.

The Ministry felt that a pamphlet on the whole question of secondary education would be the most useful way of getting across some of the new concepts, and so in 1947, largely under the direction and stimulus of Ellen Wilkinson, *The New Secondary Education*, Ministry of Education Pamphlet 9, appeared. Again, the keynote was variety to suit different children with, at the same time, parity of esteem between the different types of school. Miss Wilkinson felt that this could be little more than a phrase unless there were some parity of social esteem for the avocations in society to which children would go from the schools themselves. Emphasis was laid upon education through interest, co-operation between the schools and the home, and vocational guidance. But again it was stressed that the Ministry was not seeking any rigid structure:

'The Minister desires to lay down no set guides for organization but to encourage local authorities to plan as best suits their local needs. In some places where conditions are favourable the best way of carrying out the new plan may be to combine two, or three, types of secondary education in one school . . . There is, indeed, no end to the possible varieties of organization; the system must be flexible and experiments of many kinds are to be welcomed. The only proviso that must always be observed is that the real interests of the children must come first' (19).

The one thing that it was necessary to avoid, according to this pamphlet, was rigidity and stereotypy in secondary education.

There was something a trifle pathetic about the pious hope expressed by the authors of the pamphlet that, as the secondary modern schools developed, parents would see that they were good, and it would become an increasingly common thing for them to retain their children at the school beyond the upper compulsory limit. They would even begin to *select* the secondary modern school as the one best suited to their children's needs unhindered by considerations of prestige (20). Not many parents have in the intervening years been convinced by this sort of argument, even when they really have been asked whether they would like their child to go to a secondary modern or a secondary grammar school. Certainly few parents have argued, after their child has been selected for a grammar school, that in fact they really felt their child was more suited to a modern school. And one wonders how many parents have been convinced by argument, once their child has reached the grammar school and has proved himself quite inadequate to the task as well as thoroughly unhappy, that he is really more suited to the modern school and ought to be transferred. The pamphlet was certainly well written and well produced with most attractive photographs, but somewhat unconvincing.

F THE CROWTHER REPORT 1959
In March 1956, the Minister of Education asked the Central Advisory Council for Education (England) to advise him on the education of boys and girls between the ages of fifteen and eighteen; the Chairman of the Council, Sir Geoffrey Crowther, presented the report in July 1959. Part One of the report on *'Education in a Changing World'* was concerned to paint the broad educational picture, within the given terms of reference, and to give the background to what followed. It made the very important and significant point that the majority of children whose full-time education extended beyond the age of fifteen were the first generation in their families to attend a grammar school. It emphasized that, despite the fact that there had been much discussion of the 'tripartite system of education', there was not, and never had been, a tripartite system. In fact, technical schools as a group were slightly less numerous in 1959 than they had been in 1947; there were four times as many grammar schools as technical schools, and six grammar school pupils to every technical school pupil. New types of secondary school were being developed in many areas—the comprehensive school, the bilateral school and the two-tier organization of secondary education. Five points were noted in relation to all these variants:

(1) All aimed at giving each pupil a better chance of an education suited to his needs.
(2) All levels of ability were represented in the same school.
(3) Not all levels of ability were represented in the same class.
(4) All the variants attempted to provide a common social life.
(5) None of them provided a uniform curriculum.

Part Two dealt in particular with *'The Development of the Modern School'*. By 1965 the council thought that it was possible that extended courses would be needed for half the fifteen-year-olds, averaged over the country as a whole. Moreover, these courses should, as far as possible, take place in the schools which pupils had attended since they were eleven years of age. In the examinable minority there were two distinguishable groups—one comprised those who had the capacity to attempt some subjects in G.C.E. 'O' Level, the other was composed of about one-third of the pupils in modern schools over the age of fifteen, for whom some form of external examination below the level of the G.C.E. might serve a useful purpose. After a detailed discussion of the case for and against an examination at a lower level, the report went on to consider the consequences of extended courses, with or without an examination. These were far-reaching since not only the clever child was affected, but also the backward child and the child of below-average ability who were too immature to go out into the world at the age of fifteen.

Part Three bore the familiar title '*Secondary Education for All*' and was concerned with those who left school at fifteen or thereabouts. It set out at some length the arguments for extending the period of compulsory full-time attendance to the age of sixteen. As early as 1938 the Spens Report had maintained that the leaving age of sixteen 'must now be envisaged as inevitable', and the Crowther Report, twenty-one years later, stated that there was now sufficient experience to justify the argument that 'the ordinary boy or girl' could benefit by staying on at school until sixteen. The age of fifteen was not sufficiently mature to be exposed to the pressure of the world of commerce and industry; moreover, their sexual maturity preceded by some years their emotional and social maturity. The report was emphatic that the extra year should not be simply a continuation of what had gone before, but that the schools should be able to offer new and challenging courses, devised in such a way as to satisfy the developing child's interest in the larger world of society and his own need for independence. He should be able to see the purpose of what he was doing in school and its relevance to the world outside. The raising of the school-leaving age would also be in the national interest, since the demand for more and better educated workers was growing at almost all levels in industry. Whilst the council raised the question of county colleges in Part Four, it felt, nevertheless, that the raising of the school-leaving age had priority over their development.

Part Five dealt with the sixth form, assessing the forces which were causing its remarkable development since the Second World War, and considering the closely interwoven problems of specialization and university entrance. The council expressed its anxiety to preserve the English system of education in depth, or specialization, and also to see greater attention paid to the use of 'minority' time, that is, the time in school which was devoted to subjects other than specialist ones. The unsatisfactory elements in the situation of the late fifties seemed to arise fundamentally from the fact that demand for university education exceeded supply. The council felt that the pressures in schools could not be removed until there existed a better balance between the supply of places in universities and other institutions of higher education and the demand for them. Chapter

21 summarized what the council considered to be 'The Marks of a Sixth Form'. They were ideally:

(a) A close link with the university, even though not all the sixth formers are going there.
(b) Concentration on the study in depth of a relatively restricted range of subjects (i.e. specialization).
(c) Provision for a greatly increased amount of independent work.
(d) An intimate relationship between pupil and teacher, best described as 'intellectual discipleship'.
(e) The growth of social responsibility (21).

It was felt that in the use of minority time the main common elements which should be taken by arts and science specialists together could be summarized under three heads—religious education and everything that went towards the formation of moral standards; art and music; and physical education. The complementary elements should be designed to ensure the literacy of the science specialists and the numeracy of arts specialists. The council rejected proposals to make good the deficiencies either by a general course or by making it the normal thing for an arts specialist to take one science subject at Advanced Level, and a science specialist one arts subject.

G THE NEWSOM REPORT 1963

The terms of reference of the Central Advisory Council, which began its work in March 1961, were:

'To consider the education between the ages of 13 and 16 of pupils of average or less than average ability who are or will be following full-time courses either at school or in establishments of further education. The education shall be understood to include extra-curricular activities' (22).

We can deal here only with the main recommendations of this report which has led to the use of the unfortunate appellation, 'the Newsom child'. These recommendations were made with one object in mind: that the children who came within their terms of reference might have an effective secondary education. It supported the plea made by the previous Central Advisory Council (four members of which were in the reconstituted council) that the school-leaving age should be raised to sixteen. The Newsom Report set a date when this should become effective—September 1965. Whilst it felt that full-time education to the age of sixteen should be school-based, this did not necessarily preclude some work in the final year being pursued in, for example, a college of further education. It was felt that social and environmental handicaps could be more damaging than genetic influences, and the Advisory Council recommended the institution of a programme of research into techniques of teaching designed specifically to help those pupils who had abilities but whose capacity was artificially depressed by their environment and social conditions, and who, in consequence, suffered linguistic handicaps. It was this sort of recommendation that Sir Edward Boyle, no doubt, had in mind when he said in his foreword to the report that the potentialities of the pupils under investigation were

'no less real, and of no less importance, because they do not readily lend themselves to measurement by the conventional criteria of academic achievement. The essential point is that all children should have an equal opportunity of acquiring intelligence, and of developing their talents and abilities to the full' (23).

The council recommended that attention should be given to the functional deficiencies of many schools. Needless to say these were not the schools that featured in the 1947 pamphlet on *The New Secondary Education*, but they nevertheless represented something like 80 per cent of the school buildings in which the average and below-average children were being taught (24). There were children in slum areas who desperately needed access to the countryside, and therefore some priority in relation to school journeys, visits overseas and adventure courses. In order to deal with some of these general social and educational problems it was felt that an interdepartmental working party should be set up; and in particular certain incentives should be devised in order to ensure stability of staffing in such areas where the staff mobility was very high indeed.

In discussing objectives some of the more platitudinous generalizations were reiterated—such as a sense of responsibility which children should develop towards others and for their own work, and an understanding of the world and society in which they lived. But the report went a little more deeply into some of the current changes in society, in the number of hours of work, and in the status and economic role of women. What our pupils needed most was training in discrimination, improvement in their powers of speech, a general extension of their vocabulary, and a general strengthening of their critical powers. The schools needed greater imagination in finding approaches and providing purpose and coherence for their courses. The pupils themselves should have some choice in the subjects and sort of programme they wished to follow; many of the courses should be related in a broad way to occupational interests.

The council proposed an extended day for pupils aged fourteen to sixteen for further educational activities, including the extra-curricular, which should be regarded as an intrinsic part of the educational programme. In the development of this particular theme, the possibilities of a third session in the late afternoon or early evening should not be ignored, and there should be more experiments in joint appointments of the teacher/ youth leader type. In consideration of the problems of spiritual and moral development a realistic approach was adopted. It was recognized that the simple moral teaching of the past could no longer be applied in the secondary schools; but the council were agreed that religious instruction had a part to play in assisting to discover a firm basis for 'sexual morality based on chastity before marriage and fidelity within it' (25). Local education authorities were asked to review and revise their agreed syllabuses for religious instruction in order to make adequate provision for the needs of older boys and girls of average and below-average ability, bearing in mind that the important thing was to begin with the actual problem that pupils had to face. There was an urgent need to provide positive and realistic guidance to adolescents on sexual behaviour; guidance which should include biological, moral, social and personal aspects.

In the last school year the pupil's programme should be deliberately outgoing—it should be an initiation into society, into the adult world of work and leisure. To this end every attempt should be made by the schools to link up with the social and youth employment services and to give information about them so that the pupil would always feel at home and have connections in the larger society. To achieve this the report emphasized the need for schemes which would augment the personal advisory and welfare services to the school leavers. Whilst all sixteen-year-old leavers should be provided with some sort of internal leaving certificate, all external pressures to extend public examinations to pupils for whom they were entirely inappropriate should be resisted. Finally, there should be an experimental building programme in order to improve facilities in conjunction with modern teaching methods.

H COMPREHENSIVE SCHOOLS

The comprehensive school has political and social as well as educational origins. Forms of this type of school were developing before the end of the Second World War in various parts of the British Isles; in particular the Isle of Man has had a complete system of such schools since 1948, and Anglesey since a few years later. In its analysis of comprehensive schools the Crowther Report stated that in 1957-8 in England there were 61 comprehensive schools with 15,027 pupils and 45 bilateral schools with 7,423 pupils of the same age; that is about 3·3 per cent of the pupils aged thirteen in England were in either comprehensive or bilateral schools (26). By 1965 there were some 289 comprehensives in England and Wales, of which 80 were in London and 216 were co-educational (27).

At its 1950 Margate conference the British Labour Party passed a resolution calling upon the Government to implement the party's policy on comprehensive schools, and to provide assistance to L.E.A.s prepared to plan such schools. In 1951 a sub-committee of the National Executive of the Labour Party produced a pamphlet entitled *A Policy for Secondary Education*, which was essentially a brief for the comprehensive school. It considered that the first two years of comprehensive schooling should be mainly diagnostic, and the remaining years should seek to provide each pupil with a course adapted to specific aptitudes and capacities. In *Challenge to Britain*, which the party published in 1953, it further defined the political and social purposes behind their policy. The chief aim envisaged was to break down the existing class distinctions in our society, which they felt were being perpetuated by the existence of separate types of school under the tripartite system. There could never exist parity of esteem between such schools so long as buildings and general amenities were different, and the qualifications and quality of the staffs were considerably different. With the comprehensive system all courses and teachers in the same type of school could not but enjoy that parity of esteem to which so much lip-service had been given but which had never effectively materialized. The Labour Party felt that such an organization was more democratic, would eliminate any real or imagined distinctions of status and would contribute more than separate types of secondary school could to the development of common social understanding. In particular, it was argued that class and intellectual distinction would be eliminated and there would be no *élite* of either fee-payers or the intelligent.

Apart from these more doctrinaire political assumptions there have long existed more educational arguments in favour of comprehensive schools. It had been felt for some time that the common entrance examination at the end of the junior school course, which was intended as a process for the *allocation* of pupils to the type of school best suited to their abilities and aptitudes, had in fact become a highly and artificially competitive examination for entrance to the grammar school. The comprehensive school was intended, educationally, as an experiment in dispensing with such tests and examinations except for purely diagnostic purposes within the school itself. It was claimed that the junior school would be liberated to work out its own curriculum in terms of activity and experience if all its leavers were admitted to one large comprehensive school covering a whole area; and that there courses could be organized which were currently found in secondary grammar, secondary modern and secondary technical schools. It would also help to overcome the well-founded objection that parents attached more value to one type of school than to another—whether mistakenly or not—instead of accepting that the best type of school for their particular child was that which could provide a course of study most closely correlated to the latter's aptitude and ability. It would also ensure that no pupil of high intelligence and capacity, or with a developed flair for a particular group of studies, fell by the wayside because he got into the wrong stream at 11+, or because of the poverty of his home background. In addition, it was also clear that the transfer of pupils from courses ill-suited to their abilities to others more appropriate would be facilitated at any time during their secondary school course, and thus would help to reduce the number of maladjusted children or outright failures.

The Crowther Report presented very clearly and concisely a description of the specialized functions of the comprehensive school, namely its educational and its social functions. Through the medium of the comprehensive school there would be less waste of time or talent, and a large range of options could be provided—there ought to be something for nearly everybody. It would also act as a socially unifying force, bringing pupils together at an age when they would otherwise begin to draw apart. In such a school the range of pupils' backgrounds would closely correspond with the national pattern of different social strata of employment. The report concluded that

'At present, then, the only sensible attitude to comprehensive schools seems to us to be a non-dogmatic one that neither condemns them unheard nor regards them as a prescription for universal application' (28).

It is always dangerous to compare the system of education in one country with that in another without a very detailed examination of the social, economic and philosophical history of the countries concerned, or without a close look at variables which are not always amenable to any sort of statistical analysis or judgment. Professor I. L. Kandel, who worked as an educationist both in this country and in America, sounded a warning note in his *The New Era in Education: A Comparative Study*. He attacked some of the assumptions of those who supported the comprehensive school, and suggested that many of the arguments in its favour were inspired by political and social motives as well as doctrinaire assumptions based on information about American high schools which was unverifiable. Kandel argued that both the choice of courses in such high schools, whether such courses were general, vocational or academic, as well as student participation in extra-curricular activities, were frequently influenced and determined by social status; and he felt very strongly that such social stratification was in fact perpetuated in the high school despite the artificially-contrived identity of environment within it. Kandel argued that

'The failure of these high schools to achieve any of the results from the single school whether in promoting understanding between different social groups or in providing a preparation for an *élite* is ignored. There is no reference to the studies that show how strongly the activities of the high schools are affected by the social origins of the pupils. Finally, the influences that determine social, political and economic attitudes after school days are over are omitted from consideration. Whether the effects of subsequent social stratification can be offset by educating all the children of all classes in the same school is doubtful, but that the attempt would be made at a sacrifice of the right education for the right pupil is indicated by American experience' (29).

How far Kandel was justified in his comments with regard to America the reader must be left to judge or investigate for himself. The fact is that our society is currently almost totally committed to the comprehensive type of education, which Kandel regarded as a system which catered for the average only and was 'too fast for the slow and too slow for the fast'. The D.E.S. report for 1968 (30) stated that by the end of the year the great majority of local education authorities had completed the preparation of their schemes. Out of 163 L.E.A.s, 92 had schemes implemented or approved for the whole or greater part of their areas; a further 27 authorities had schemes covering parts of their areas implemented or approved; 13 authorities had submitted schemes which were being considered by the Department; 7 authorities had been requested by the Secretary of State to reconsider their submitted schemes; whilst of the remaining 24 authorities most were preparing schemes, but there were 8 authorities which had formally declined to do so. Apparently the most popular form of organization continued to be the orthodox comprehensive school, with pupils aged from eleven to eighteen. Other schemes which were well represented were middle schools which linked, or 'straddled', the primary and secondary stages, and five-year comprehensive schools with separate sixth-form colleges. By January 1968 there were 748 comprehensive schools, representing 13·4 per cent of the total number of maintained secondary schools, and claiming 20·9 per cent of the total number of pupils in these schools. And so the conversion in education to a 'comprehensive' society proceeds.

REFERENCES

1 Morant, R., *Special Reports on Education Subjects*, Vol. III, p. 47 (H.M.S.O., 1898). Quoted in Curtis, S. J., *History of Education in Great Britain*, p. 314, n.1.
2 R. v. Cockerton (1901), 1.Q.B. 322, and Rex v. Cockerton C. A. (1901), 1.K.B. 726. For a more detailed account see Eaglesham, E. J. R., *The Foundations of Twentieth-Century Education in England* (Routledge, 1967), Chapter 2, entitled 'Administrative Muddle'.

3 Maclure, J. S., *Educational Documents—England and Wales, 1816–1967* (Methuen, 1968, 2nd ed.), p. 157.
4 Ibid., p. 159.
5 *Vide L.C.C. Elementary Schools Handbook* (1933), pp. 118 ff.
6 Quoted in the Beloe Report, *Secondary School Examinations Other than the G.C.E.* (H.M.S.O., 1960), p. 51.
7 Maclure, J. S., op cit., p. 173.
8 *The Education of the Adolescent*, p. xix.
9 Ibid., pp. 78–9.
10 Ibid., pp. 93–100.
11 Ibid., p. 137.
12 Board of Education, *Secondary Education* (Spens Report) (H.M.S.O., 1938, reprinted 1959), p. iv.
13 Ibid., p. xx.
14 Ibid., p. 291, n.1.
15 Board of Education, *Curriculum and Examinations in Secondary Schools* (H.M.S.O., 1943, reprinted 1944), p. viii.
16 Ibid., p. 6.
17 Maclure, J. S., op cit., p. 208.
18 *The 1944 Education Act*, Part II, Clause 36.
19 Ministry of Education, *The New Secondary Education* (Pamphlet 9) (H.M.S.O., 1947, reprinted 1958), p. 24.
20 Ibid., p. 47.
21 Ministry of Education, *15 to 18* (Crowther Report) (H.M.S.O., 1959, reprinted 1962), Vol. I, pp. 222–5, 458.
22 Ministry of Education, *Half Our Future* (Newsom Report) (H.M.S.O., 1963), p. xv.
23 Ibid., p. iv.
24 Ibid., pp. 258–9.
25 Ibid., p. 58.
26 Op. cit., pp. 23–4.
27 *Vide* Pedley, R., *The Comprehensive School* (Penguin, 1966, rev. ed.), Appendix.
28 Op. cit., p. 420.
29 Kandel, I.L., *The New Era in Education, A Comparative Study* (Harrap, 1955), p. 112. *Vide* also pp. 110–14, 260–4, 304–6.
30 D.E.S., *Education and Science in 1968* (Cmnd. 3950) (H.M.S.O., 1969), pp. 36–8.

BIBLIOGRAPHY

Armfelt, R., *The Structure of English Education* (Cohen and West, 1961).
Banks, O., *Parity and Prestige in English Secondary Education* (Routledge, 1955).
Board of Education, *The Education of the Adolescent* (Hadow Report) (H.M.S.O., 1926, reprinted 1948).
Chapman, J. V., *Your Secondary Modern Schools* (College of Preceptors, 1959).
Cheshire Education Committee, *The Secondary Modern School* (University of London Press, 1958).
Chetwynd, N. R., *Comprehensive School* (Routledge, 1960).

Curtis, S. J., *History of Education in Great Britain* (University Tutorial Press, 1963).

Curtis, S. J. and Boultwood, M. E. A., *An Introductory History of English Education since 1800* (University Tutorial Press, 1964).

Davis, R., *The Grammar School* (Penguin, 1967).

Dempster, J. J. B., *Education in the Secondary Modern School* (Pilot Press, 1946).

Dent, H. C., *Secondary Education for All* (Routledge, 1949).

Dent, H. C., *Growth in English Education, 1946–52* (Routledge, 1954).

D.E.S., *The Organization of Secondary Education* (Circular 10/65) (H.M.S.O., 1965).

Eaglesham, E. J. R., *The Foundations of Twentieth-Century Education in England* (Routledge, 1967).

Eaglesham, E. J. R., *From School Board to Local Authority* (Routledge, 1956).

Gould, R. (ed.), *Inside the Comprehensive School* (Schoolmaster Publishing Co., 1958).

Jeffery, G. B. (ed.), *External Examinations in Secondary Schools* (Harrap, 1958).

Kandel, I. L., *A New Era in Education* (Harrap, 1955).

Loukes, H., *Secondary Modern* (Harrap, 1956).

Lowndes, G. A. N., *The Silent Social Revolution* (O.U.P., 1941).

Maclure, J. S., *Educational Documents—England and Wales: 1816–1967* (Methuen, 1968, 2nd ed.).

Miller, T. W. G., *Values in the Comprehensive School* (Oliver and Boyd, 1961).

Ministry of Education, *Secondary Education* (Spens Report) (H.M.S.O., 1938).

Ministry of Education, *Curriculum and Examinations in Secondary Schools* (Norwood Report) (H.M.S.O., 1943).

Ministry of Education, *School and Life* (H.M.S.O., 1947, reprinted 1952).

Ministry of Education, *The New Secondary Education* (Pamphlet 9) (H.M.S.O., 1947).

Ministry of Education, *15 to 18* (Crowther Report) (H.M.S.O., 1959).

Ministry of Education, *Secondary School Examinations Other than the G.C.E.* (Beloe Report) (H.M.S.O., 1960).

Ministry of Education, *Certificate of Secondary Education* (Lockwood Report) (H.M.S.O., 1961).

Ministry of Education, *Half Our Future* (Newsom Report) (H.M.S.O., 1963).

N.A.S., *The Secondary Modern School—An Interim Inquiry* (N.A.S., 1956).

N.A.S., *The Comprehensive School—An Appraisal from Within* (N.A.S., 1964).

Partridge, J., *Life in a Secondary Modern School* (Penguin, 1968).

Pedley, R., *The Comprehensive School* (Penguin, 1966, revised ed.).

Rée, H., *The Essential Grammar School* (Harrap, 1956).

Reese Edwards, K. H. R., *The Secondary Technical School* (University of London Press, 1960).

Rowe, A. W., *The Education of the Average Child* (Harrap, 1960).

Simon, B., *The Common Secondary School* (Lawrence and Wishart, 1955).

Simon, B., *New Trends in Education* (MacGibbon and Kee, 1957).

Tawney, R. H., *Secondary Education for All* (Allen and Unwin, 1922).

Taylor, W., *The Secondary Modern School* (Faber, 1963).

Vernon, P. E., *Selection for Secondary Education* (Longmans, 1957).

Young, M., *The Rise of the Meritocracy* (Penguin, 1961).

Part Two

Specific Topics
in Education

Chapter 5

Independent, Private and Public Schools

A BEFORE 1800

Our nomenclature for different types of school is both confused and confusing to the extent that terms such as 'voluntary', 'maintained', 'independent', 'private' and 'public' have lost their more popularly accepted significance, and have now acquired a specific educational and administrative connotation. The meaning of these terms will be elicited as far as possible as we look at the history of the process, but no one in England, at least, needs to be told that some of the most 'private' schools in our society have been for many years those termed 'public'. Moreover, there are schools, which have been termed 'grammar', that today may be state, independent, controlled, voluntary aided, special agreement, public or even private.

During the fourth century A.D. there were, throughout Europe, a class of 'public' schools which taught rhetoric and grammar, but by the end of the sixth century they were practically non-existent. During the seventh and eighth centuries there developed the bishops' schools, which initially were actually run by bishops but which, later, were taken over by their vicars. During the Middle Ages there gradually developed Church schools which sought to mediate the Seven Liberal Arts of the *trivium* and *quadrivium*: these schools were usually referred to as grammar schools, and later as collegiate schools or colleges. By the later Middle Ages there were something of the order of 300 grammar schools in England, some with as few as five pupils and others with nearly 200. In many of these schools there were certainly poor children of serfs as well as sons of merchants and land-owners. The Statute of Artificers of 1406 stated that

'every man or woman, of what state or condition that he be, shall be free to set their son or daughter to take learning at any school that pleaseth them within the realm' (1).

In 1382 Winchester College was founded by the Bishop of Winchester, William of Wykeham; moreover, it existed to provide a means of education for seventy 'poor and needy' scholars who were to live in a community (*collegium*). Up to ten sons of 'noble and influential persons, special friends of the said college', were also permitted to become pupils. William linked this collegiate school very closely with New College, Oxford, which was also his foundation. Winchester College itself became a model for future foundations of this type; Eton College, which was founded by Henry VI in 1440, was clearly imitative of Winchester and was to provide education for seventy poor scholars and up to twenty sons of noblemen and special friends of the college.

During the sixteenth and seventeenth centuries the number of grammar schools and colleges increased; and many merchants and others who had made their fortunes out of the commercial and political expansion of the times endowed schools to perpetuate their names, and in some instances to salve their consciences. How far the 'common people' and the really poor, in the long run, really benefited is a matter of some dispute. Cranmer certainly argued very forcefully in 1540 that,

'Poor men's children are many times endued with more singular gifts of nature, which are also gifts of God, as with eloquence, memory, apt pronunciation, sobriety, and such like, and also commonly more apt to apply their study than is the gentleman's son delicately nurtured' (2).

Cranmer made this claim in reply to the commissioners under the chairmanship of Lord Rich, who in discussing the future of the Canterbury Grammar School had maintained that the children of husbandmen were more fit for the plough, or to be artificers, than to occupy the place of the more learned, such as gentlemen's children, in the grammar school.

The eighteenth century saw Harrow School and Rugby School well established in the company of the great public schools such as Winchester, Eton, Westminster, Canterbury and others. Rugby really came to the fore through Thomas James, who became headmaster in 1777; James reorganized and rebuilt it on the pattern of Eton, where he had been a pupil. Both Harrow and Rugby were now in permanent demand as public schools suitable for the sons of the upper classes; and instead of being a day school for local boys Harrow became a successful boarding school for boys from all over the country.

B THE ROYAL COMMISSIONS

The majority of grammar schools and colleges had been originally founded, both during the Middle Ages and later, in order to prepare boys for the Church or the Law. In consequence the curriculum was devised with these professions in mind, and little was done over the years to modify the curriculum in any radical sort of way. Schools of this sort were little affected by changes and new ideas in educational theory. As a result both the public schools of the 'great' variety and a large number of the less renowned grammar schools, proved to be inadequate for the demands of the time. They were heavily criticized and suffered considerable unpopularity during the early decades of the nineteenth century. There was a great resistance among these schools to any sort of change, particularly to any alteration of the curriculum which was by now quite outmoded. It was also noticeable that during a time of improving standards of living, these schools remained thoroughly archaic in accommodation and amenities generally. The schools were, in general, also criticized for their general lack of discipline; and such indiscipline was out of harmony with the tenor of the time.

There were two headmasters during the first half of the nineteenth century who saw precisely where change was needed. Samuel Butler (1774–1839) became headmaster of Shrewsbury in 1798, at the age of twenty-four, and during the next forty-one years he introduced many innovations there. Firstly, he had a look at the curriculum, and decided on a much more liberal approach to culture. Mathematics, geography and history were adopted, and the detailed study of classical grammar was considerably modified. As an incentive to learning and general development, Butler introduced also the spirit of keen competition enforced by a system of marks. His system of promotion developed, so it was argued, a sense of fulfilment and intellectual self-confidence. Finally, he adopted a method within the school of self-government through a prefect system. In these various ways Butler sought to meet the criticisms of the public schools and the demand for change. Similarly, at Rugby, Thomas Arnold (1795–1842) was appointed headmaster at the age of thirty-three and he remained there until he died at the somewhat early age of forty-seven years. Like Butler he adopted the prefect system and developed a voluntary code of behaviour, in which the members of his sixth form were considered as gentlemen. Again, with Butler, he rejected the somewhat inflexible grammatical and linguistic approach to the classics; he put more emphasis on the literary qualities of the texts as well as upon their moral and philosophical implications. He also saw the potential of history as a medium for the discussion of ideas and social developments. As a keen evangelical Arnold made the school chapel the centre of community life.

Largely through the efforts of such great figures as Butler, Arnold and Thring of Uppingham, the public schools began to enjoy a somewhat better public image. In 1864 Her Majesty's Commissioners, under the chairmanship of the fourth Earl of Clarendon, produced their report on the revenues and management of certain schools and colleges. Their terms of reference asked them to inquire into the endowments, funds and revenues of Eton, Winchester, Westminster, Charterhouse, St Paul's, Merchant Taylors', Harrow, Rugby and Shrewsbury. They were also required to look into the system and course of studies pursued by these schools, as well as into their methods, subjects and extent of instruction (3). Many of the recommendations of the commission were very much in line with what had already been initiated by Shrewsbury and Rugby. They considered that classical languages and literature should still hold pride of place in the general curriculum, but all pupils should also be taught mathematics, a modern foreign language, natural science and drawing or music. The usages of history and geography at the schools already mentioned convinced them of the value of those two subjects, whilst specialization in the sixth form was to be encouraged.

It was clear from the Clarendon Report that the classics were certainly not going to be ousted. The study of classical languages and literature occupied a central position in the great English public schools:

'It has . . . the advantage of long possession, an advantage so great that we should certainly hesitate to advise the dethronement of it, even if we were prepared to recommend a successor' (4).

Composition, translation, grammar and etymology were regarded by the report as essential elements in the development of common speech, and there were few educated men who were insensible to the advantages gained from their steady practice in school. The study of literature was a study of the deeper levels of life, of the intellectual and moral world in which we live. A study of the lives, the thoughts, and the characters of outstanding men of history was a worthwhile pursuit. The report also underlined the perfection and grace of the classical languages which had been preserved, without 'degeneration and decay'; they provided suitable models for young minds and would leave a lasting impression on them.

The commissioners, however, were not so starry-eyed that they did not see the negative possibilities, and realities, of the classical situation. If after four or five years spent in studying the classics a youth of nineteen were unable to construe a simple piece of Latin or Greek without the aid of a lexicon, and were to be virtually ignorant of his own country's geography and history, then 'his intellectual education must certainly be accounted a failure' (5). And still a failure, even though the youth be faultless in manners, principles and character. The commissioners felt that whilst this was not to be regarded as typical of the ordinary product of English public school education, it was a much more common type than it ought to be. The very strong arguments they put forward in support of introducing natural science sound interesting today. Its exclusion from public school education was a plain defect, in fact an evil, for this was injurious to mental training. The faculty of observation would be directly quickened and cultivated by its study, and it would accelerate the power of accurate and swift generalization. Its introduction was, in fact, both desirable and practicable; indeed, the great difficulty with public school life was its sheer idleness, and there was no problem from the point of view of available time—there was plenty of time for the introduction of natural science into the timetable.

The commissioners were, in the main, pleased with some other developments and improvements in the public schools. More actual work was being done than formerly even if it were still insufficient. Religious and moral training had also shown some advance—in fact it had more than kept pace with advances in intellectual discipline. A great deal of the old roughness of manners had now disappeared, and much of the former cruelty which appeared to be intrinsic to public school life. Moreover, more attention was paid to the health, comfort and accommodation of the boys. The report contained a eulogy of public schools, referring explicitly to their system of government, discipline, and their universally accepted excellence; the schools had been 'the chief nurseries of our statesmen'; in them, it claimed, men of all classes in English society, destined for every type of career and profession, 'have been brought up on a footing of social equality' (6).

The Clarendon Report was followed in 1868 by the passing of the Public School Act, which reformed the governing bodies of all the schools which had been inquired into by the commission, with the exception of St Paul's and Merchant Taylors'.

In 1864 another commission, under the chairmanship of the first Baron Taunton, was set up to inquire into the education which schools not comprised within the terms of reference of the Newcastle and Clarendon Commissions gave. It considered 782 grammar schools, some proprietary and private schools, and the secondary education of girls. It called for written and oral evidence from schools, examining bodies, charities and religious organizations. It estimated that there were more than 10,000 schools run for private profit by individuals; these were referred to as private schools. It also investigated some proprietary schools, that is, schools run by private companies. The commission recommended more inspection of schools, more examination of pupils and improved girls' education. In 1869 there followed the Endowed Schools Act, and the majority of the commission's recommendations were either rejected or ignored. The charitable trusts of the endowed schools were to be supervised, and in some instances reorganized, by three appointed commissioners. There was recognition, in the Act, of the freedom of conscience with relation to religious observances; parents were to have the right to withdraw their children in endowed schools from denominational religious worship or instruction.

The Bryce Commission was set up in 1894 to consider the best methods of establishing a well-organized system of secondary education in England. Its report in 1895 noted a great improvement in the condition of endowed grammar schools since the Taunton Commission of 1864 and the Endowed Schools Act of 1869. It found that, in seven counties specially selected for the inquiry, the population had increased from about six millions to nearly nine millions, but the number of pupils had more than doubled. The commission, however, found that the position was not satisfactory, particularly in many of the smaller schools, and that the total provision of secondary education was quite inadequate. Whilst the Taunton Commission had discovered a sort of 'tripartite' division of secondary education, roughly corresponding to the social classes, the Bryce Commission argued that such a classification required modifying. The Endowed Schools Act of 1869 had already helped to open those schools which led directly to the universities to the sons of the poor and uneducated (7). The report, finally, recommended that a central education authority should be established, and in 1899 an Act brought the Board of Education into being. This Board took over the educational work of the Charity Commission.

C THE PRIVATE SCHOOLS

The private schools were referred to in the nineteenth century as 'private adventure schools', and today they are schools which are run for a profit by either a company or a private individual. In 1861 the Newcastle Commission adversely criticized many of them at a time when there were no laws which prevented any person from opening a school in his own house, whether he possessed any teaching qualifications or not. Not only were such proprietors not required to have experience or qualifications in teaching—their schools were not open to inspection, unless they themselves requested it. The commissioners described some of the shocking schools that they encountered on their inspection tours, but in the end they recommended that there should be no central control over the management of schools, and no interference with the private sector of education, except to provide grants to those schools which, after inspection, were considered to be run satisfactorily, and which had reasonably adequate accommodation.

Private schools were certainly popular, and have remained so despite the often high fees involved. The desire to keep one's children away from the *hoi polloi* has undoubtedly been one of the reasons for this, and this was largely the case put forward by the Newcastle Report. But it is by no means the whole truth. Many parents have sincerely believed that large, unwieldy and frequently unruly classes militated against the sound education and development of their children. For this reason they preferred the smaller and more closely-knit community of the private school. In general they may have been wrong in their choice, from a purely educational point of view, but they may sometimes have been right that their children had more individual attention in the smaller, 'private' school and were occasionally taught better manners. The commission, at least, brought to the attention of the public the fact that they were frequently not getting value for money, and gradually the most inefficient of the private schools began to disappear. The Education Act of 1902 sought to eradicate some of their worst features by placing upon parents the onus of ensuring that their children were adequately instructed in the three Rs; but summonses had to be issued against particular parents, not against the school, and the inspectors had to prove in Court that the instruction received was inadequate. This could be a lengthy and costly business, but once a case was proved against a school its closure was largely a matter of time, since the stigma of inadequacy and inefficiency was now upon it.

Both the Education Act of 1918 and the Consolidating Act of 1921 helped to make it a little more difficult for inefficient private schools to persist. By the 1918 Act any school which was not in receipt of a grant from the Board of Education was compelled by law to register, that is, to send to the Board its name and address and a short description of the school. Any violation of this law was liable to prosecution. The Consolidating Act of 1921 made the inspection of such schools a criterion in law of proficient elementary instruction. Such inspection might be undertaken by the central authority, i.e. the Board, or by the local education authority, free of cost at the request of the school. Some schools, notably those that were conscious of their own efficiency, were happy to request such an inspection, and to have their brochures headed 'Inspected by the Board of Education'; but when the private schools were more closely scrutinized in 1944 it was found that very few had in fact availed themselves of this opportunity.

Part Two of the 1944 Education Act states that:

'The Minister shall appoint one of his officers to be Registrar of Independent Schools; and it shall be the duty of the Registrar of Independent Schools to keep a register of all independent schools, which shall be open to public inspection at all reasonable times, and, subject as hereinafter provided, to register therein any independent school of which the proprietor makes application for the purpose in the prescribed manner and furnishes the prescribed particulars' (8).

There follow certain provisions relating to disqualifications and complaints, and the acceptance that certain schools which had already been recognized as efficient secondary schools, and some preparatory and private schools which had already been inspected, were exempt from registration. Owing to the lack of teachers, H.M.I.s and building materials the Act could not be stringently enforced until about April 1949 when the inspection of independent schools began in earnest. By 1957 the Ministry of Education had recognized 1,450 independent schools as efficient, whilst during that year 145 schools were closed, of which 138 had only recently opened. On September 30, 1957 Sections 70–75 of the 1944 Education Act became fully operative (9).

Despite the increased facilities for free State education after the 1944 Education Act, there was no decrease in the number of private schools. In fact, for a variety of reasons, there was an increase. A large number of parents did not accept the tripartite system of education as a satisfactory system of selecting children for the type of education suitable to their age, ability and aptitude. Many felt, as did many educators, that the so-called '11+ selection test' not only came too early, and so stigmatized a child for the rest of his school career as well as probably for life, but also was inadequate, invalid and unreliable for the purposes of selection. Many also felt that the secondary modern school was a very poor third best rather than a third acceptable alternative. Parents still thought in terms of their children 'failing' to get to a grammar school, rather than (as the authorities would have it) being 'selected' for a certain type of education other than that provided by the grammar school. In consequence, a number of new and private grammar schools came into existence to meet the demands of parents who refused to send their children to the secondary modern schools. These new grammar schools were registered, inspected and regarded as efficient: many of them were staffed by schoolmasters in retirement. There was also an increase in the numbers of private primary schools; this was mainly because many State-controlled schools were overcrowded, and because many parents felt that their children might stand a better chance of being prepared for the dreaded selection test if they were in small classes and in receipt of more individual attention. Some children, of course, were crammed for the 11+ in both State and private primary schools.

D PREPARATORY SCHOOLS

The chief aim of the preparatory school is to prepare pupils for entrance to the public schools. At one time such schools were not considered necessary, and small boys of eight frequently found themselves in the larger public schools, very often the butt of the older boys for amusement, ridicule and often sadistic cruelty. About the middle of the nineteenth century, however, there was a development of the preparatory school as a sort of 'breaking-in' establishment for the public school. Social conditions generally made it increasingly possible, with the aid of transport advances, for the more wealthy to become more mobile; and so children were sent away to boarding schools at quite an early age. Today, most of these preparatory schools are privately owned, some are junior departments of the public schools, and others belong to grammar schools not yet completely within the State system.

In 1903 a special examination was inaugurated called the Public Schools Common Entrance Examination, and pupils preparing for it, between the ages of eight and fourteen, either attend a preparatory school or have a private tutor or 'crammer'. Such schools are specially geared to this examination, and in the main this has been a one-pointed objective; success at this entrance examination is the key to the public school with, of course, the parents' ability in most cases to pay the fees. Since they are preparing for the public schools, right from the earliest age of eight or nine the preparatory schools provide as their staple diet a study of the classics, mathematics, science, a modern foreign language, and frequently scripture.

Such schools are undoubtedly, in the main, adequate to their task of preparing their pupils for the public school type of education. They have in the past been regarded as efficient, as judged by their purpose at any rate; and their situation is usually healthy, providing either country or seaside life for their pupils. More recently the First Report of the Public Schools Commission, when referring to the public and private sectors of education, has said that,

'Each sector can point to its centres of excellence and its pioneers in the secondary field, while in the opinion of most judges the maintained schools, and not the preparatory schools, are the leaders in primary education' (10).

Whilst the report does not explicitly state who these judges are, it would undoubtedly appear to express the opinion of the members of the commission, including their chairman, Sir John Newsom, J. E. Dancy, the Master of Marlborough College, and T. E. B. Howarth, High Master of St Paul's School, although the last-named signed a Note of Dissent from the order of priorities and recommendations for the selection of pupils advanced by the majority.

E THE 1944 ACT AND ITS CLASSIFICATION OF SCHOOLS

The 1944 Education Act sought to establish, among other things, a clear nomenclature and classification of the various types of school existing in the country. A local education authority has power, under the Act, to establish both primary and secondary schools and to maintain them; and these schools are known as *county schools*. Primary and secondary schools maintained by local education authorities, but not established by them, are known as *voluntary schools*. The L.E.A. normally appoints and dismisses teachers in the county schools, unless some article in the government of such schools makes other provision. The local authority is responsible ultimately for the religious and secular instruction given in such schools, although it must, with regard to any religious instruction, observe Sections 25 and 26 of the Act. The local authority is also responsible for the provision, improvement, and development of the accommodation of its schools.

Voluntary schools are divided into three categories, namely controlled, aided and special agreement schools. After the publication of the Act voluntary schools had to decide, within a certain time, which category they wished to choose; and by the end of 1959 it had been decided that 4,549 schools should be 'controlled', out of a total of 9,453 voluntary schools. Those voluntary schools whose managers or governors were unable or unwilling to meet half the cost of alterations or necessary repair of buildings became *controlled*, and the local education authorities were obliged to meet all costs and other expenditure. Two-thirds of the managers/governors were appointed by the L.E.A.s, and one-third were foundation managers/governors. The L.E.A.s were responsible for the appointment of all staff, but they consulted the managers/governors when appointing head teachers or teachers 'reserved' for religious instruction. All secular instruction was to be under the control of the L.E.A.s, whilst religious instruction was to be given in accordance with the trust deed or the particular practice in force before the school became a controlled school, and for not more than two periods per week; or else in accordance with an 'agreed syllabus', that is a syllabus agreed upon by a conference representative of the various denominations, the teachers and the authority.

Managers/governors of a voluntary school which wished to become *aided* had to satisfy the Minister that they were able and willing to defray any expenses incurred in the day-to-day running of the school and in effecting those alterations to the school buildings which the L.E.A. required in order to ensure that the school premises conformed to the prescribed standards of the Schools Building Regulations. The managers/governors originally had to agree, by the 1944 Act, to contribute one-half of the costs, but this was modified by the Education Act of 1959 (Chapter 60) to one-quarter; the Ministry was then made responsible for a maintenance grant of three-quarters of any sums so expended (11). The local education authorities were responsible for appointing one-third of the managers/governors, the remaining two-thirds being foundation appointments. Whilst the managers/governors were responsible for the appointment of staff, in each case the local authority regulated the number of teachers to be employed. The secular instruction of the school, if primary, was under the control of the L.E.A.; if secondary, it was under the control of the governors unless other provisions were made in the rules of management or the articles of government. Religious instruction was normally to be given in accordance with the trust deed or previous practice of the school; but where parents so desired provision was to be made for instruction to be given in accordance with an agreed syllabus.

Local education authorities were empowered, by the Education Act of 1936, to help financially towards the erection of 'non-provided' schools; that is, schools not provided by the State. By this Act L.E.A.s could pay grants ranging from 50 to 75 per cent of the cost of providing new senior schools of this type. Altogether 519 proposals for development were made, of which 289 were from Roman Catholic sources, but only a few of these had actually materialized by the outbreak of war. The Education Act of 1944 allowed these proposals to be revived, and in 1959 there were eighty-seven such voluntary schools, termed *special agreement schools*. In such schools the appointment of teachers was under L.E.A. control, and this included any reserved teachers for whom the special agreement provided. However, the authority had to consult foundation managers/governors in making the appointment of any reserved teacher. Two-thirds of the managers/governors were foundation managers/governors and one-third were appointed by the L.E.A. Secular and religious instruction followed the same provisions as for aided schools.

Thus, both county and voluntary schools, as defined above, became maintained in various ways through the 1944 Education Act and subsequent Education Acts making miscellaneous and specific provisions. There still remained outside these categories, however, a number of schools which had under previous Education Acts received grants from either local or central authority. In return for this assistance a certain proportion of pupil places in the schools were made either free or partially free. Schools receiving grants from L.E.A.s were usually required to keep a minimum of 25 per cent of their places for non-paying pupils; and those receiving grants from the central authority provided free places for 10 per cent of their admissions. Those schools which did not desire to become *voluntary aided* could temporarily become *assisted*, but had, eventually, to decide either to become *independent* or to apply for a *direct grant* from the Ministry. Any school accepted for direct grant by the Direct Grant Schools Regulations of 1959 had to offer not less than 25 per cent free places to pupils who had been in attendance for two years at a maintained or grant-aided primary school. Up to another 25 per cent free places might be reserved for the L.E.A. if they found that the number of places already offered was insufficient. These reserved places were open to any pupils whether they had been educated in a grant-aided primary school or not. Any remaining places might be filled by the governors whose duty it was to ensure that preference in admission should be given to candidates who were considered most likely to profit by such an education. Whilst fees could be charged for these pupils parents were entitled to apply for remission of fees. The central authority would make a grant to the governors on a capitation basis, and would also encourage local authorities to make special arrangements for nominated pupils to be admitted to independent boarding schools, if this form of education were thought to be desirable for them.

Finally, the Minister, or since April 1, 1964 the Secretary of State, was declared responsible for seeing that no child was prevented through the poverty of parents from pursuing the type of education suited to his age, ability and aptitude, and this included education at a costly independent boarding school—if that were really the best type of education for him. Any fees and expenses incurred should be paid by the central authority, which was also responsible for inspections of independent schools and of the registers of pupils at such schools. Such inspections, by H.M. Inspectorate, could take place at any time; if any independent school were not up to the required standard it could be struck off the register, and there were heavy penalties for running a school not so registered (12). The clause in the 1944 Act was not specifically aimed at public schools, but rather at the private schools which often outlasted their educational value and their efficiency. An *independent* school was defined by Section 114 of the 1944 Education Act as

'Any school at which full-time education is provided for five or more pupils of compulsory school age (whether or not such education is also provided for pupils over that age), not being a school maintained by a local education authority or a school in respect of which grants are made by the Minister to the proprietor of the school.'

F THE LATER DEVELOPMENT OF THE PUBLIC SCHOOLS

When R. A. Butler (later Lord Butler) was asked in the House of Commons in 1942 to define a public school he replied that it was a school 'in membership of the Governing Bodies' Association or Headmasters' Conference'. But it is clear that among the schools in membership of the Headmasters' Conference there are certain aided and maintained grammar schools, as well as some direct grant schools. If these are public schools, then not all public schools are independent schools (13).

It is important to note that the public schools have developed and used the same type of examination system as the maintained schools, beginning in 1917 with the School and Higher School Certificates, and then taking on the 'O' and 'A' Level G.C.E. examinations; and they have inevitably vied with the secondary schools for university places and open scholarships.

The Fleming Committee on Public Schools was asked, in July 1942, to consider means by which the association between the public schools and the general educational system of the country could be developed and extended. From the report itself, which appeared in 1944, it is evident that the public schools were anxious to align themselves with the rapid social changes of the time, and that they felt that the class differences and divisions in our society could be aggravated or mitigated by the particular form of educational system in operation. They also felt that there were many children who could benefit from the boarding system, but that they were prevented from doing so by the insurmountable financial barrier. They said,

'We are convinced that this most important of all educational choices ought not to depend, as it does now, on financial considerations and that the issue ought not to be confused by the social distinctions, real or imaginary, which divide the two types of school' (14).

The Fleming Committee, in consequence, put forward two schemes both of which were to apply to boys' and girls' schools. *Scheme A* was concerned with the direct grant schools, most of which were day schools. These schools would have to abolish tuition fees altogether or grade them according to a sliding income scale; boarding charges would be similarly graded, and the only criterion for admission to such schools would be the pupil's capacity to profit by the education provided in them. It was within the power of a local education authority, under this scheme, to reserve a number of places; the precise number would be a matter of agreement between the governors and the authority. The authority would pay tuition and boarding fees, and would recover the appropriate amount from the parents, according to the sliding scale. In such schools a minimum of one-third of the governing body would be appointed by the L.E.A. Scheme A applied only to those schools which were not recognized as independent according to the definition of the 1944 Education Act.

Scheme B was concerned with boarding schools only, recognized by the Board as being efficient and not conducted for private profit. The Board was to grant bursaries to qualified pupils who had attended for at least two years at a grant-aided primary school. Such bursaries should include tuition and boarding fees, and once more these bursaries would depend upon parental income. Those schools which accepted Scheme B would be required to offer at least 25 per cent of their annual admissions to pupils from primary schools. The local authorities would be able to reserve places for their pupils at particular schools, and parents would make applications for bursaries through the local authorities. They could apply to any school or schools which accepted the scheme, indicating the order of their preference. It was suggested that the bursary holder, or 'bursar', who was only eleven years of age might spend two years in the preparatory department of a public school, or in a preparatory school, in order to be prepared in such subjects as classics, modern languages, science, and so forth, before transfer at the age of thirteen to the public school. Bursars who had already reached the age of thirteen would be transferred immediately (15).

The report, interesting and in many ways revolutionary as it was, did not gain full acceptance by the newly-formed Ministry of Education. The selection procedure alone was never fully developed or established; there were many public schools which were suspicious of the scheme and unwilling to surrender their autonomy or near-autonomy; the general public were by no means geared to the acceptance of a boarding school education as a viable alternative, and parents hesitated long to make their children guinea-pigs in a somewhat uncomfortable social class-contact situation; finally, the local education authorities were loth to push a scheme which, in the long run, could only prove costly to themselves. Although a Central Advisory Committee was set up in 1947, in accordance with the report's recommendations, it existed for only four years and came to an end in 1951.

In December 1965, the Department of Education and Science appointed a Public Schools Commission under the chairmanship of Sir John Newsom, who, when Chief Education Officer for Hertfordshire, was interested in the Fleming Report proposals and made use of bursaries at Winchester, Eton and Rugby. The First Report of the Public Schools Commission appeared in April 1968, and it dealt with boarding schools only; the future of public day schools was left for the Second Report. The terms of reference stated that it was the main function of the commission

'to advise on the best way of integrating the public schools with the state system of education. For the immediate purpose of the Commission public schools are defined as those independent schools now in membership of the Headmasters' Conference, Governing Bodies' Association or Governing Bodies of Girls' Schools Association' (16).

The commission was expected to collate information concerning public schools and the need and provision for boarding education; to assess information concerning the collaboration between the public schools and the maintained system; to work out the role which individual schools might play in national and local schemes of integration; to recommend some national plan for integrating the public schools with the maintained sector; and to recommend what action might be needed in respect of other independent schools, whether secondary or primary. In addition, the commissioners were asked to bear in mind certain objectives: they were to ensure a maximization of the contribution of public schools to the national educational needs, in particular to any unsatisfied needs for boarding education; they were to create a socially-mixed entry into the schools so as to reduce any divisive influence they might at the present exert; they were to develop a progressively wider range of academic attainment amongst public school pupils in order that 'the public school sector may increasingly conform with the national policy for the maintained sector'; they were to co-operate closely with L.E.A.s in seeking to match provision with need for boarding education; and they were to ensure the progressive application of the principle that the public schools should be open to children irrespective of their parents' income.

In making its recommendations the commission argued that any suitable independent boarding schools which were willing to enter an integrated sector should be given every encouragement to do so. A school must, however, admit assisted pupils from maintained schools to at least a half of its places, by the end of a period of about seven years. It recommended that most schools, especially boys' schools, should admit pupils of a wide range of ability, and should cater for pupils whose ability level corresponded to that required for courses leading to C.S.E. If, however, there were children who needed boarding education, schools should be encouraged to admit them even if their ability level were below that of C.S.E. Low academic ability should not be a criterion in itself for excluding a child from a place at an integrated school. Where schools were too small to admit children of widely differing ability over the whole age range, they should as far as possible adapt to the comprehensive system and adjust their ages of admission. The commissioners argued that a group of schools which had a common foundation or religious bond might cover, between them, the whole secondary age range, and also a very wide span of ability.

Some schools should be enabled to reorganize themselves to cater mainly or wholly for pupils at the sixth-form level. Several schools might become 'academies' which would cater for children with special skills or aptitudes in ballet or music. Independent boarding schools should be encouraged to work closely with one another, and with certain maintained day schools with which they might share teaching resources and other facilities, and whose boarding needs they might help to meet. The report recommended that L.E.A.s, in consultation with governing bodies, should plan new comprehensive schools to work in close co-operation with integrated boarding schools. It noted that most girls' schools were less geared for integration than boys' schools; schools, however, which were small but otherwise suitable for integration ought to be encouraged to make 'tiering' or similar arrangements with other schools.

The commissioners showed a strong acceptance of the principle of co-education, and they recommended that there should be more co-educational boarding schools. This would help to meet the wishes and convenience of the parents of both girls and boys, and would help to extend the opportunities of boarding education for girls. The commissioners recommended that there should be no discrimination against immigrants in allocating places in boarding schools. There should be an interflow of teachers between maintained and independent sectors; governing bodies of integrating schools should include one-third of members representing bodies or interests other than the foundation. Schools which were Christian foundations should be encouraged to accept pupils from denominations other than their own, as well as pupils of other religions or of no religion. In the whole process of integrating, schools would have to reconsider their life-style; in particular there should be more men on the staffs of girls' schools, and there should be more women on the staffs of boys' schools; there should be greater provision for pupils to pursue their personal interests in their leisure time; there should be more variety and choice in games and other activities; weekly boarding should be encouraged wherever possible in order to increase contacts with home; there should be greater freedom in forms of dress and eccentric school uniforms should be avoided; pupils should not wield excessive authority either as prefects with powers to beat other boys or by using other boys for fagging.

The report estimated that by 1980 boarding need in schools of all kinds would reach the level of 80,000 children in England and Wales, and recommended that places for 45,000 of these pupils should be sought in independent schools. A further addition of 2,000 places for Scotland would make a total of 47,000 assisted boarding pupils in independent schools. 20,000 places were already taken up wholly or partly at public expense in independent schools; the commissioners were proposing that a further 27,000 pupils should be assisted, and that all assisted pupils should attend schools approved for integration. All assisted pupils would be entitled to free tuition equivalent to the average cost of education in maintained day schools—whatever their parents' means. Parental contributions should be made, according to means, towards the remaining cost of an assisted place. In this respect the report recommended a scale of contributions identical in the lower ranges of income to the existing university awards scale, but graduated more steeply at income levels exceeding £2,000 a year: It estimated that the take-up of 38,000 secondary and 9,000 preparatory places would cost £18,400,000 annually, and recommended that the cost of assisted places (subject to parental contributions) should be met by L.E.A.s on a pooled basis. The pooled expenditure should qualify for grant from the Exchequer.

Finally, there should be an Education Act enabling an integrated sector to develop under the guidance of a Boarding Schools Corporation, and schools should be invited to submit development plans as a basis for negotiation. No school, however, would have any prescriptive right to be accepted for integration. In the last resort, the D.E.S. should have the power to compel a school to enter into a scheme of integration if all efforts at persuasion and negotiation had failed, and if a school's refusal to enter the scheme would prejudice a successful integration policy (17).

REFERENCES

1 7 Henry IV, c. 17.
2 Quoted from Strype, *Memorials of Thomas Cranmer*, Book 1, Chapter 22, in Board of Education, *The Public Schools* (Fleming Report) (H.M.S.O., 1944), p. 10.
3 *Vide* J. S. Maclure, *Educational Documents—England and Wales: 1816–1967* (Methuen, 1958, 2nd ed.), p. 83.
4 Ibid., p. 84.
5 Ibid., p. 85.
6 Ibid., p. 87.
7 *Report of the Royal Commission on Secondary Education* (Bryce Report), 1, 133.
8 *Education Act, 1944* (7 and 8 Geo. 6, Ch. 31) (H.M.S.O., 1944), Sections 70–75.
9 *Vide* Taylor, G. and Saunders, J. B., *The New Law of Education* (Butterworth, 1965, 6th ed.), p. 188 (Notes).
10 Public Schools Commission, *First Report*, Volume 1: Report (H.M.S.O., 1968), p. 62, para. 101.
11 *Education Act, 1959* (7 and 8 Eliz. 2, Ch. 60) (H.M.S.O., 1959), p. 1, para. 1(1).
12 *Education Act, 1944*, Section 73, p. 31.
13 *Vide* Board of Education, *The Public Schools*, p. 34, paras. 84–92.
14 Ibid., p. 50, para. 137.
15 Ibid., pp. 62–70, paras. 172–185.
16 Public Schools Commission: *First Report*, Volume I, p. vii.
17 Ibid., pp. 8–14, para. 29.

BIBLIOGRAPHY

Ayerst, D., *Understanding Schools* (Penguin Books, 1967).
Badger, A. B., *The Public Schools and the Nation* (Hale, 1944).
Badley, J. H., *Bedales, a Pioneer School* (Methuen, 1923).
Blishen, E., *Education Today* (B.B.C., 1964).
Board of Education, *The Public Schools and the National System* (Fleming Report) (H.M.S.O., 1944).
Child, H. A. T. (ed.), *The Independent Progressive School* (Hutchinson, 1962).
Crump, G., *Bedales since the War* (Chapman and Hall, 1936).
Curtis, S. J., *et al.*, *An Introductory History of English Education Since 1800*, Ch. XIII (University Tutorial Press, 1964).
Gilkes, A. N., *Independent Education* (Gollancz, 1957).
Hughes, D., *The Public Schools and the Future* (C.U.P., 1942).
Kalton, G., *The Public Schools: A Factual Survey* (Longmans, 1966).
Kamm, J., *How Different from Us (Miss Beale and Miss Buss)* (Bodley Head, 1964).
Kamm, J., *Hope Deferred* (Bodley Head, 1964).
Lambert, Royston, *The State and Boarding Education* (Methuen, 1966).
Leeson, Spencer, *The Public Schools Question* (Longmans, 1948).
Mack, E. C., *Public Schools and British Opinion*, Vols. I and II (Columbia University Press, 1938/41).
Neill, A. S., *Summerhill: A Radical Approach to Education* (Gollancz, 1962).
Ogilvie, V., *The English Public School* (Batsford, 1957).

Partridge, E. H., *Freedom in Education* (Faber, 1943).
Pekin, L. B., *Progressive Schools: Their Principles and Practice* (Hogarth, 1934).
Public Schools Commission: *First Report*, Volumes I and II (H.M.S.O., 1968).
Rodgers, J., *Old Public Schools of England* (Batsford, 1938).
Snow, G., *The Public Schools in the New Age* (Bles, 1959).
Waugh, A., *Public School Life* (Collins, 1922).
Webster, F. A. M., *Our Great Public Schools* (Ward Lock, 1937).
Williams, R., *Whose Public Schools?* (Bow Group, 1957).
Wilson, J., *Public Schools and Private Practice* (Allen and Unwin, 1961).
Wolfenden, J. F., *The Public Schools Today* (University of London Press, 1948).
Worsley, T. C., *The End of the Old School Tie* (Secker, 1941).
Worsley, T. C., *Barbarians and Philistines* (Hale, n.d.).

Chapter 6

Technical and Technological Education

A BEGINNINGS OF TECHNICAL AND SCIENTIFIC EDUCATION

It is quite impossible to separate education in any particular era from the political, economic, industrial, commercial and social developments in that age and in any particular country. During the nineteenth century scientific and technical education gradually evolved and increased in importance, largely as a result of the political and industrial revolutions which had spread throughout Europe. Life and philosophy can change society: and society can change life and philosophy. Steam and electrical power did more than revolutionize modes of transport: they changed men's minds, the way they thought and believed. Mechanical devices in turn led to mechanistic forms of thinking; biological discoveries and theories led to theological revision and uncertainty. The concept of evolution gradually led to concepts of control of evolution, control of life and death, increased control in agriculture, and control of disease.

In 1754 the Society for the Encouragement of Arts, Manufactures and Commerce in Great Britain was founded, and in 1851, largely through the patronage of its President, Prince Albert, it helped to establish the Great Exhibition. Whilst this was acclaimed as a success for Britain and her industrial developments, on the more technical and scientific side it was clear that Europe was ahead. The lesson was, however, being learned slowly. In 1848 Cambridge University established a Natural Science Tripos; in 1853 the Oxford Honour School of Natural Science was founded, and six years later, in 1859, London University created a new faculty— that of Science. New departments were also being set up in order to encourage more education in science for people generally. The Science and Art Department was formed in 1853 and in 1856 became associated with the Education Department. The Literary and Mechanics' Institutes had also been developing since the turn of the century when Birkbeck left Glasgow to work in London, where he founded a Mechanics' Institute in 1823.

It was the comparative failure of British production in 1867, at the Paris Exhibition, that led to a Royal Commission on Scientific Instruction and the Advancement of Science. T. H. Huxley (1825–95), who was a member of it, made a serious plea for science in the elementary school, emphasizing its educational value. Herbert Spencer (1820–1903) provided strong pragmatic arguments for science as not only a necessary element of education, but virtually the essence of education. The Royal Commission, which reported between 1872 and 1875, and whose Chairman was the Duke of Devonshire, was asked to enquire into the state of scientific instruction and the advancement of science in the country, as well as the measures being taken for providing grants for this purpose. The report made a detailed survey of the scientific education provided, mainly at the universities and in higher education generally, but also in elementary schools, training colleges, grammar and secondary schools. It was obvious that, if more science were to be taught in the schools, more teachers had to be trained with scientific knowledge, and that the curricula of the training colleges had to be drastically revised.

The Devonshire Report found it necessary to insist that for every 200 boys there should be at least one science master. It felt, in discussing the aims of science teaching, that the real value of such teaching consisted

'not merely in imparting the facts of Science, but in habituating the pupil to observe for himself, to reason for himself on what he observes, and to check the conclusions at which he arrives by further observation or experiment' (1).

It also considered that it was doubtful whether any other form of educational study offered the same advantages for 'training and developing the mental faculties'. However wrong the commissioners might have been in supporting the teaching of science on the basis of transfer of training and a faculty-psychology, they were right on more utilitarian grounds concerning the need for developing scientific and technical instruction. They thought it highly important to introduce science into education at a very early stage; they argued that it was no more difficult to young pupils than grammar or arithmetic, and certainly more interesting. They considered, further, that, in public schools during a thirty-five-hour week of study, at least six hours should be given over to science, and another six to mathematics; and they would not concede to the pupil the right to choose between literary and scientific culture before going up to the university.

The Devonshire Commission did not mince matters when it came to a final judgment on the national position concerning the teaching of science. They felt compelled to express the opinion that the general position was extremely unsatisfactory, a matter for serious regret; and considering the increasing importance of science to the country from an industrial and economic point of view, in the context of expanding European economics, they felt that its exclusion from the education of the middle and upper classes was 'little less than a national misfortune' (2). Professor Huxley, in the special evidence he gave to questions raised by the rest of the commission, argued that the separation of the teaching of science from education was like 'cutting education in half'.

The obvious concern felt by the Devonshire Commission was sustained both at the educational and the industrial level. Without educational interest in technical education it became increasingly clear that industry would suffer, and so there began a mushroom growth of all sorts of institutions with pretensions to giving some form of technical instruction. This created further anxiety that such instruction might not be properly controlled nor, in fact, be adequate to deal with the actual industrial and social problems. It was largely with these questions in mind that a Royal Commission on Technical Instruction was appointed in 1881, under the chairmanship of Bernhard Samuelson who had served on the Devonshire Commission. Samuelson was well qualified for the task; he had been a merchant and engineer, and a Liberal M.P.; he was a man of wide culture with interests in modern languages, music, mathematics, science, and technical education. At the age of forty-seven he made a study of technical education in many European countries, and had already made comparisons with our own. He was a Fellow of the Royal Society and was later to serve on the Cross Commission.

The Samuelson Commission was to inquire into the technical and other instruction provided for the industrial classes of certain foreign countries, and then to compare such provisions with that made for the corresponding classes in this country. The commission was also asked to consider the influence of this instruction upon manufacturing and other industries at home and abroad. It was, in itself, a considerable and searching exercise to set any commission, and without the spadework and know-how of the chairman over the previous fourteen years it seems impossible that six men could have performed the task.

The report itself appeared in several volumes during the years 1882–4; it felt, optimistically, that despite the progress of other countries Britain still held its position at the head of the industrial world; but

'In two very important respects . . . the education of a certain proportion of persons employed in industry abroad, is superior to that of the English workmen; first, as regards the systematic instruction in drawing given to adult artizans, more especially in France, Belgium and Italy; and secondly, as to the general diffusion of elementary education in Switzerland and Germany . . .' (3).

As a result of these contentions the report recommended that writing and rudimentary drawing should be developed as a single elementary subject, and that there should be less part-time employment and more full-time education for children. The work of the Mechanics' Institutes came in for special mention, as well as a hint that many of them had fallen behind in their development of technical instruction. Many of them, however, had clearly seen that their teaching, both in content and method, was outmoded and unsuited to the needs and requirements of expanding industry. They were, therefore, revising their constitutions and their curricula. The co-operative societies were particularly praised for taking the initiative in providing facilities for artizans to obtain instruction in art and science, whilst there was more than a suggestion that the trades' unions had a duty 'to promote the technical education of their members' (4).

The commission strongly supported the further development of technical instruction in this country, but it felt equally strongly that the 'Imperial budget' was providing enough. There should be greater expenditure by local authorities on this type of education, and they should be empowered to establish more secondary and technical schools. There should exist opportunities for intelligent young artizans to gain scholarships to such schools. Also, it was important that the great mass of the working class should be given those basic elements of the sciences which had some bearing upon industry. The use of the rule and the compass was essential to all, as well as geography taught as a branch of elementary science, more object lessons from nature, more simple agriculture and more craft work. The commissioners took the view that men selected as foremen in industry should not be entirely ignorant of the more theoretical side of their work; and since they were drawn from the working classes the latter, as a whole, must be better educated in technical matters as well as in general knowledge. Similarly, when it came to the education of the leaders of industry, the commissioners believed that no part of the national expenditure on education was more important than that spent on their scientific culture and technical training.

Other recommendations of the report included the provision of works schools in which young workers might be trained in the shops and factories themselves. They cited as an example the workshop school of Messrs Mather and Platt, which was a private evening school providing technical education for the firm's apprentices. The firm worked on the basis that the school must be brought to the workshop and not the workshop to the school (5); not only was this a simple and inexpensive way of training workers, it also had the advantage of providing the work atmosphere and brought home the immediate utility of the technical theory. Another recommendation concerned the training of teachers. If the children in elementary schools were to receive adequate tuition in technical subjects then teachers themselves also had to be taught more science and more art; this would mean changes in the curricula of the training colleges.

From their general tone, as well as from more specific recommendations, it was clear that the commissioners were in favour of modifying the more generally accepted curriculum of the secondary grammar-type school. They were not opposed to a broad culture, but they were opposed to what they considered the dead wood of a great deal of secondary education. They were in favour of dropping Latin and Greek and putting in their place more study of modern languages, mathematics, science and technical drawing. This sort of educational programme reflected very much the interests of the chairman and the general trend of educational thinking at this time.

A number of Parliamentary Acts as well as grants now began to assist technical education, in however small a way. The setting up of county and county borough councils by the Local Government Act of 1888 delineated certain areas of responsibility for the development of scientific education, and the onus for the further organization and establishment of technical secondary schools was firmly laid on local authorities. In 1889 the Technical Instruction Act was passed whereby the new organs of local government were empowered to spend a certain proportion of the rates on technical education and manual instruction. The local rates were further subsidized by grants from the Science and Art Department, as well as by the somewhat odd diversion of customs and excise 'whiskey money' to aid higher technical education. It was chiefly through such grants, and through the somewhat *laissez-faire* attitude which inevitably arises when authorities are 'empowered' but not 'compelled' to do certain things, that the Science and Art Department appeared to be gaining more and more control of technical education, whilst the Education Department seemed to be getting less and less. It was for this reason that the Cross Report of 1888 had recommended that the responsibility for institutions which provided technical instruction should be transferred to the Education Department. The Education Act of 1899 finally created the Board of Education, which became a central authority taking over the educational functions of the Charity Commission and the Science and Art Department.

It is interesting to note, in passing, that despite the desire of the Samuelson Commission to see the gradual extinction of Latin and Greek, the Bryce Report of 1895 boldly stated that

'The classical languages are taught more extensively than ever, but less as if they were dead, and more as if they still lived, rich in all those humanities by virtue of which they have been supreme instruments of the higher culture' (6).

This report, most enlightened in many respects, saw no reason why classical and modern languages should not be taught together; and it applauded the growth in scientific and technical as well as manual instruction. It saw technical instruction as a means 'for the formation of citizens capable of producing or distributing wealth', and felt that an 'enlarged education' would result (7).

Whilst the 1902 Education Act represents a landmark in many ways in the history of the development and organization of education, it in fact paid very little attention to the pressing need to organize further technical education along sound lines. The science schools which had developed through the grants of the Science and Art Department were being gradually absorbed into the secondary system, or continued as higher elementary schools. Once the Board began to function it produced some regulations for the running of schools of art, art classes and technical institutions. These regulations, which appeared in 1903 and 1904, made provision for day instruction for suitably qualified students who might profit from more advanced education. These students were being prepared specifically for work in industry and commerce, and therefore such day instruction as they received would naturally be geared to the work of life. This was a theme taken up by the *Introduction to the Elementary Code* of 1904, where it was claimed that the purpose of public elementary education was to assist the pupils to fit themselves both practically and intellectually for the work of life.

The *Regulations for Secondary Schools* of 1904 sought to distinguish very clearly secondary schools from technical institutes and classes which gave, almost exclusively, instruction and training in certain subjects to both adults and young people who had already completed a general education. Thus it was inevitable that the technical school should eventually emerge as a different breed of educational institution.

B JUNIOR TECHNICAL SCHOOLS

The junior technical schools had been under consideration, and developing in a disorganized way, for a number of years. In 1905 they became a reality and had an immediate success, associated as they were with further education generally and with technical colleges in particular. The accommodation and equipment, as well as the staffing, of the further education institutions were profitably used by the junior technical schools; whilst, starting as they did with virtually no tradition, they were able to diverge considerably in curricula from both the orthodox higher elementary school and the tradition-bound secondary grammar school. Employers became immediately interested in these schools because of their vitally practical nature, and because they would obviously begin to supply a superior type of youth for apprenticeship—one already trained in certain skills as well as possessing clear aptitude for the practical work of the factory or workshop. The various industries became sufficiently interested in this new educational project to make substantial grants towards their foundation and development, as well as providing staff to teach and train the pupils, and industrial equipment of every nature to give a sense of realism to technical education.

In 1912–13 the Board of Education published *A Report and Regulations for Junior Technical Schools* whereby such schools were officially recognized as a separate category which in future would 'receive aid from the state to a degree more commensurate with their importance'. This was double-edged. It was obviously an attempt to gain a greater control over the proliferation of educational institutions through the outside efforts of industry and commerce; it was not a declaration of the supreme importance nationally and economically of the expansion of technical education (8). The regulations established two main types of technical school at this time:

(a) those which prepared pupils for particular trades and occupations (i.e. trade schools);
(b) those which provided an education to pupils who wished to enter a particular industry, but not a specific occupation in that industry (i.e. pre-apprenticeship schools).

In 1926 in the Hadow Report, on *The Education of the Adolescent*, there was the first organized attempt to define the origin, aim and province of the junior technical schools. Their chief purpose was to provide a course of instruction, extending over two or three years, for pupils who previously had attended elementary schools and had there received a general education. The curriculum of the junior technical school was designed to continue and expand this general education, whilst making provision for a special type of training for entry into some particular occupation or group of occupations. The committee felt that it was inadvisable to place a pupil of the age of 11+ in a school planned specifically to provide a course of definitely vocational education, and so the normal age of entry to such schools was fixed at 13+. They argued, as many have argued since about the whole question of the 11+ selection procedure, that the arrangement whereby pupils were given admission to junior technical schools at the age of 13+ considerably reduced the risk of committing a pupil to a course of study and training which might ultimately prove to be completely unsuitable.

From 1924 to 1928 Lord Eustace Percy, who was then President of the Board of Education, produced a number of surveys and reports on technical education, education for industry and commerce, and further education generally. A very thorough investigator, Lord Percy examined the problem from the side of industry and commerce as well as from the side of education. In the process he consulted something like 500 firms, and opened up enquiries into the field of special education for industry and commerce. He reported in 1928 that about 80–90 per cent of those undertaking further education in industry and commerce attended evening classes, and he argued that it was of great importance to develop day courses for such students, both full-time and part-time.

In 1929 the Clerk Committee on Engineering Industries strongly commended the work done by junior technical schools, and underlined the importance of recruiting for the engineering industry those who had received full-time education in them. By then there were 108 officially recognized junior technical schools with something in the region of 18,000 pupils, including 4,600 girls. The next year the Board of Education published its report, *The Junior Technical School*. In this it was stated that the growth and progress of this type of school was steady, although not considerable. Each school had less than 200 pupils, whilst some had even less than 100; this was uneconomical, particularly when one considered the costly equipment used and the problems of staffing. Nevertheless, the report emphasized the serious-mindedness of the pupils under instruction, and the fact that their concentration derived from a sense of the relevance and practicality of their work. They were learning for life and this provided the necessary motivation to tackle their studies.

The 1930 report highlighted the real problem. The growth of these schools, like many before and since, had not in any way been planned; and lack of planning in any sphere can lead to considerable wastage. The Board realized that local authorities had to be encouraged to work together in the establishing of more technical schools, and so it issued in 1936 its *Circular 1444*, in which it stressed the need for co-operation between neighbouring authorities when planning such provision. During the same year the Board published *A Review of Junior Technical Schools in England*, a systematic survey of the way in which these schools were organized and distributed, the nature of their curricula, and their classification. Trade schools were included in junior technical schools, which now totalled 220; there were 41 junior art departments and 6 nautical schools. In 1937 there were 26,513 pupils in the junior technical schools; 2,366 pupils in the junior art departments; and 882 pupils in the schools of nautical training—a total of nearly 30,000 pupils in all schools which came under the general heading of 'junior technical schools'. During that year there appeared a Board of Education conference report on *Co-operation in Technical Education*. The purpose of this again was to impress upon local authorities the need to co-operate in order to pool their technical resources and prevent unnecessary duplication. The Board was determined to accomplish three things: the expansion of technical education; strict economy in this expansion; and the maximum of co-operation between industry, the staffs of technical schools and colleges, and board inspectors. It was suggested that joint advisory committees should be formed.

C SECONDARY TECHNICAL AND TECHNICAL HIGH SCHOOLS

The Spens Consultative Committee received its terms of reference in 1933 and published its report in 1938, which contained a number of recommendations about technical schools. It was felt that the word 'junior' in the name 'junior technical school' had misleading associations; and so it recommended that the expression 'technical school' should in future be used as a general term for all technical schools which recruited pupils at the age of 13+ and provided courses lasting for two or three years. The committee urged the establishment of a 'new type of higher school of technical character quite distinct from the traditional academic grammar school' (9). To effect this it was suggested that a number of the already existing junior technical schools should be converted into technical high schools, and should be given in all respects equality of status with grammar schools. They would recruit their pupils at 11+, by means of the general selective examination, and provide a five-year course up to the leaving age of 16+.

The committee felt that the curriculum for pupils between the ages of 11+ and 13+ in such schools should be, in general, the same as that in other secondary schools of equal status, such as the grammar school. After thirteen there should be a liberal education informed by the spirit and practice of science. Subjects in the curriculum would include English, mathematics, history, geography, engineering drawing, practical crafts in the workshops, physical education and aesthetic subjects. In addition, some pupils would continue with a modern foreign language if they showed some capacity for profiting from it. Wherever possible these schools should be housed in the premises of technical colleges or technical institutes in order to make full use of the equipment and staff which these had. The technical high school would be organized as a department of the college or institute; and the head of this department would be the headmaster of the school (10).

The committee recommended that there should be a new type of school-leaving certificate for pupils in technical high schools on the basis of internal examinations. These would be founded on the curriculum of the school, but there would be external assessors, appointed by the Board of Education, who would ensure a uniform minimum standard of certification in technical high schools throughout the country. The certificates would have an equal standing with the existing school certificates as fulfilling the first conditions for matriculation. Finally, the report recommended that there should be close relations between the newly-created technical high schools and grammar schools, so that there might be ease of transfer at 13+ for those pupils whose later development made it clear that they were more suited to an alternative form of education.

The terms of reference supplied, in October 1941, to the Norwood Committee asked them to consider any changes they might suggest in the curricula of the secondary schools, and also the question of any school examinations relating to them. The Norwood Report of 1943 largely supported the recommendations of the Spens Report, rather on the basis of a faculty-psychology which Dr Cyril Burt had already rejected in an appendix to that report (11). It argued that the relationship between local industry and the technical high school was an essential one which could not be maintained unless the school could freely control its own destiny. The report accepted a tripartite division of secondary schools, namely, secondary grammar, secondary technical and secondary modern, and opposed multilateralism as a general policy although it did not reject the possibility, or even desirability in some instances, of bilateralism. The technical high school, or secondary technical school, should give a general education, orientated from 13+ onwards towards special technical courses. Its chief function should be to provide a training for entry to industry and commerce at 16+, a training which met, at the same time, the demands of local industrial conditions. Facilities for more advanced work should also be offered from the ages of sixteen to eighteen.

In 1943 it was discovered, in the throes of a life and death struggle with Germany and her allies, that 'in the youth of the nation we have our greatest asset' (12). The White Paper on *Educational Reconstruction*, published in that year, recognized the need for some positive action if the country were to recruit more youths into industry and commerce through the technical schools, which it claimed held out great opportunities for pupils with a practical bent. It accepted the principle of the tripartite system laid down in the Norwood Report and set the general tone for further secondary development. The 1944 Education Act made it clear in Section 8 that it was the duty of every local education authority to make schools available sufficient in number, character and equipment so that all pupils, whatever their age, ability or aptitude, would have the most desirable form if instruction and education, including practical instruction.

The parity of esteem and equality of status, which had been sought so long for all forms of 'secondary' education, were at least recognized in law by the 1944 Education Act, even if they did not exist in fact. A great deal of hard work was put into establishing in the public mind this equality of status, but parents remained, and remain, strangely unconvinced. The Ministry Pamphlet 9, *The New Secondary Education*, which appeared in 1947, maintained that the technical high school had become an integral part of the secondary school system by the passing of the 1944 Act. Because of this it had, at least in theory, equality of status with the grammar school; and, moreover, it came under the aegis of the new Building Regulations.

With the invaluable help of the 'Ninth Body', i.e. the Associated Examining Board, which was formed in 1953, the secondary technical schools have developed a whole range of G.C.E. and other courses. Provision at the sixth-form level has developed with demand, and a greater degree of vocational specialization has now become available.

D HIGHER TECHNOLOGICAL EDUCATION

In 1945 a Special Committee on Higher Technological Education, under the chairmanship of Lord Eustace Percy, reported on the needs of higher technical education in England and Wales, with regard to the requirements of industry and the contributions made by the universities and technical colleges. One of the committee's main considerations was the lack of liaison between the major technical colleges and the technological departments of the universities. Its chief recommendations included the establishment of Regional Advisory Councils whose main purpose was to co-ordinate the technological studies and investigations in the colleges of technology, the universities and all other technical institutes. Coupled with the recommendation was the suggestion that the Ministry of Education should establish a standing organization known as the National Council of Technology (N.C.T.), which should give advice on national aspects of all regional policy.

It was further recommended that each Regional Advisory Council should establish an Academic Board to ensure that there existed co-ordination at the teaching level. At the same time adequate arrangements should be made for the representation of industry on both the Council and the Board, and for full consultation. The committee recommended that a selected number of colleges of technology should provide full-time courses of a university standard, as well as facilities for post-graduate work. Links with industry could be strengthened if industry released some of its more articulate specialists as part-time teachers. It was also envisaged that in the future both technical colleges and universities should educate students with a view to becoming senior administrators and managers in industry rather than concentrating upon the production of science teachers, research workers and pure scientists by the universities, and upon the training of technical assistants and craftsmen by the technical colleges.

The Percy Report further recommended that colleges of technology should conduct their own examinations and award their own qualifications. Courses of study would be approved and moderated by the N.C.T. through the Academic Board, who would also advise on equipment, accommodation and staffing. It was the function of the Board to ensure some parity of standards throughout the country and to select external examiners. There was some disagreement over the actual title of the qualification provided by the major institutions, but none concerning its nature. It was to be the equivalent of a university first degree, awarded with classified honours. But it was felt that the institutions involved should not be granted a charter to confer degrees, and the award was therefore to be called a diploma in technology. The Chairman, however, had reservations about this:

'If higher technological education is to be developed on the scale and with the intensity which we have been convinced are necessary to the well-being of the nation, it is natural to propose that such higher studies, wherever pursued, should lead to a Bachelor's degree' (13).

The Barlow Report, which appeared in 1946, was concerned with the nature and organization of the country's scientific manpower. It pointed out in general terms that only about 20 per cent of those capable of reaching universities, based on the level of their intelligence as shown by tests, actually went there. It underlined some of the conclusions of the Percy Report, in particular that university-type institutes of technology should be encouraged. Thus the number of universities should be increased and the output of scientists should be doubled. In the same year the Ministry of Education published *Circular 87/46* which accepted the main recommendations of the Percy Report and adopted a scheme for the reorganization of further education on a regional basis. In this way a close and effective contact between industry and education could be ensured, courses and curricula could be continually reviewed, new developments could be mooted and planned, and existing facilities could be expanded.

In 1948 the National Advisory Council on Education for Industry and Commerce (N.A.C.E.I.C.) was established. The Carr-Saunders Report of 1949 suggested that several defects existed in education for commerce. It was not based on a sufficiently broad study of the subject; it started vocational training, as distinct from vocational education, too early; and too much of the study took place in the evenings—there should be longer periods of full-time day study. With this in mind it recommended sandwich-courses leading to new qualifications of degree standard.

The first report of the N.A.C.E.I.C. on *The Future Development of Higher Technological Education* appeared in 1950, and discussed technological education of first degree standard (i.e. Dip. Tech.). The report recommended that there should be improvements in the financing of those colleges which provided such courses, and an improvement in their accommodation and equipment. It also proposed that a Royal College of Technologists should be established, which would award associateships, memberships, and fellowships. In 1951 the Advisory Council produced a White Paper (Cmnd. 8357), which was a brief statement of the Government's policy for the development of *Higher Technological Education in Great Britain*. It stressed that in the university field the numbers of full-time students in technology had increased from 5,288 in 1938–9 to 10,933 in 1949–50; and similarly the numbers of post-graduate students had more than doubled from 662 to 1,539. New building was in process. The University Grants Committee was encouraging some universities to institute post-graduate courses in particular fields of technology, including mechanical, electrical, chemical, agricultural and civil engineering, metallurgy, mining and textiles (14). The committee was also considering the possibility of establishing a university of technology for two or three thousand students, but the Government was satisfied that it would not be in the national interest to proceed with such a project at that particular point in time. The proposal to arrange for the establishment of a College of Technologists was later reversed. The Ministry of Education's *Circular 255* of 1952, however, provided for a special grant at the rate of 75 per cent in respect of approved advanced technological courses.

In 1956 the White Paper (Cmnd. 9703) entitled *Technical Education*, stated that the aim of the Ministry of Education was to increase by 50 per cent the output of students from advanced courses at technical colleges, and to double the number of part-time release students during the day, thereby raising the number to 700,000. It clearly distinguished three grades of workers—technologists, technicians, and craftsmen; and it stated that the main road to the highest technological qualifications would be sandwich courses lasting four or five years with alternate periods in industry and technical colleges. It was expected that the scheme would attract pupils leaving school at eighteen, most of whom would be concentrated in colleges of advanced technology (C.A.T.s) which would be developed from existing technical colleges.

In 1956 the Ministry also published *Circular 305, The Organization of Technical Colleges*, which delineated four main types. *Local colleges* provided, on the vocational side, courses which were mainly part-time and up to the level of Ordinary National Certificate or its equivalent. *Area colleges* provided, in addition to these courses, varying amounts of advanced work, mainly of a part-time nature and above Ordinary National Certificate and Diploma level. *Regional colleges* were those which did a substantial amount of full-time and sandwich courses involving advanced work. The standard of staff and equipment made it unrealistic to spread this work over too many colleges. Finally, *colleges of advanced technology* (C.A.T.s) would provide a broad range and substantial volume of ex-clusively advanced work, including post-graduate work.

The terms of reference given to the Central Advisory Council for Education in 1956 were quite simply to advise the Minister on 'the educa-tion of boys and girls between the ages of fifteen and eighteen'. Part Six of the Crowther Report, which was eventually published in 1959, was entitled 'Technical Challenge and Educational Response'. This section remarked on the need to produce far larger numbers of technicians and craftsmen. Among a number of recommendations made was the desirability of a greater degree of integration between schools and further education, and the need to transform what was then a varied collection of plans for vocational training into a coherent national system of practical education (15). Whereas only about 12 per cent of fifteen to eighteen year-olds were in full-time education, it was suggested that 50 per cent at least should be the aim. There was a lack of integration between school and college education, and it was argued that there should be expanded provision for 'college based' sandwich courses for young people aged sixteen to eighteen, provided satisfactory arrangements could be made for training in industry.

The White Paper (Cmnd. 1254) entitled *Better Opportunities in Technical Education* was published in 1961 and made some far-reaching proposals for a major reconstruction in the system of courses for technicians, craftsmen and operatives in technical colleges. The Government looked for a large increase in the number of students attending technical courses. It suggested a wider range of courses, an improvement in the methods of selecting students for courses, and more time for students to cover the necessary ground. There was an explicit desire expressed for more students to succeed, and for a reduction in the wastage rate through failure. Its chief proposals were that:

1 Students should begin at a technical college as soon as they left school, and preliminary courses in evening institutes should be discontinued.

2 The selection of students for courses should be undertaken with more care. The colleges should experiment with full-time induction courses and with tutorial methods.

3 Courses would include National Certificate and Diploma Courses for students aiming to become high-grade technicians at least; technician courses specifically organized for particular industries; craft courses and courses for operatives.

4 O.N.C. courses would last for two years and not three. Standards of entry were to be raised.

5 There would be new courses for four or five years specially for technicians.

6 New general courses would be introduced, which would lead to either technician courses or O.N.C. and O.N.D. courses.

7 Craft courses would be modified in various ways.

8 There should be a vigorous development of operatives' courses.

9 More time ought to be provided under day release schemes, and no student should have to rely entirely on evening study.

10 Sandwich courses (in particular for technicians) and block release courses should be increasingly developed (16).

Thus, the White Paper sought to develop and implement some of the suggestions of the Crowther Report, particularly with reference to a greater variety of 'alternative routes', and a new form of full-time 'practical' education for those who were unsuited to the full-time academic route, or who would suffer from a wasteful part-time course.

E THE ROBBINS REPORT AND AFTER

In February 1961 the Committee on Higher Education was appointed by the Prime Minister under the chairmanship of Lord Robbins; it reported in October 1963. In addition to the report proper there were five appendices in six volumes, and the total cost of producing it was £128,770—just about £8,000 more than that of Plowden. Its terms of reference were very comprehensive, requesting the committee:

'to review the pattern of full-time higher education in Great Britain and in the light of national needs and resources to advise Her Majesty's Government on what principles its long-term development should be based. In particular, to advise, in the light of these principles, whether there should be any changes in that pattern, whether any new types of institution are desirable and whether any modifications should be made in the present arrangements for planning and co-ordinating the development of the various types of institution' (17).

Chapter X was given over to a consideration of 'Institutions for Technological Education and the System of Further Education', and we are here concerned with three main areas of recommendations made in that chapter:

(a) Institutions of Technology at University Level:

1 The volume of postgraduate study and postgraduate courses in both technology and science ought to be considerably increased.

2 There should be a major effort to encourage an increase in technological and scientific research.

3 In order that departments might use their resources to the best advantage larger institutions and faculties should be built.

4 A certain number of university institutions concerned in high level teaching and research, chiefly technology and science, should be

selected for accelerated development. Financial support should be available for them similar to that provided for the Imperial College.

5 These institutions should each contain about 3,500–4,500 students, half of whom should be engaged on postgraduate work. Staffing ratios should be good, and adequate provision should be made for equipment and technical assistance.

6 It was recommended that the Imperial College, and the Colleges of Science and Technology at Manchester and Glasgow should provide the nuclei of three such institutions.

7 A fourth completely new institution should be immediately planned and a fifth should be developed from one of the existing C.A.T.s.

8 These two new special institutions should have an independent constitution.

(b) Colleges of Advanced Technology:

1 These colleges should in general be designated as technological universities, with the power to award first and higher degrees.

2 The Grants Commission should be responsible for their finance.

3 Attached to each college there should be an academic advisory committee in order to supervise courses and examinations until the college was ready for complete independence.

4 Their chief emphasis should be upon the teaching of technology and science and in research in those fields, but the development of other subjects should be encouraged.

5 Each college should ultimately contain between 3,000 and 5,000 students.

(c) The Council for National Academic Awards.

The National Council for Technological Awards (N.C.T.A.) was established by the Ministry of Education in 1955. It was responsible for the award of the Dip. Tech., which was recognized as being of honours degree standard. The Robbins Report suggested that this council should be replaced by the Council for National Academic Awards (C.N.A.A.), which should cover the whole of Great Britain and might be established under Royal Charter. Its function would be to award honours and pass degrees to students in regional and area colleges. More will be said about the development of the C.N.A.A. later; it is sufficient here to say that it was established by Royal Charter in September 1964 (18).

In 1966, the Department of Education and Science presented to Parliament a White Paper (Cmnd. 3006) entitled *A Plan for Polytechnics and*

Other Colleges. This was an attempt to discuss and make proposals about higher education in the further education system. The colleges of advanced technology had now been transferred to the university sector of education, and the N.A.C.E.I.C. had emphasized the pressing need for further concentration of courses in order to achieve the most effective utilization of resources. The White Paper noted the rapidly increasing demand for higher education within the further education system, and the fact that the Government believed the demand could best be met by establishing a limited number of new, strong centres with adequate staffing, buildings and equipment 'needed both to achieve and maintain high standards and to provide the right setting for an active community of staff and students' (19). The Government considered the best results could be achieved by creating a number of polytechnics which would be comprehensive academic communities catering for students at all levels of higher education. In the appendix to the White Paper twenty-eight such institutions were proposed, although the final number was not precisely fixed in advance. Before a polytechnic was finally designated account would be taken of the possibility of associating a number of colleges by merger, or in some other way, in order to form the most effective unit possible. One of the proposals was to reduce substantially the number of colleges engaged in full-time higher education, but colleges which were not designated as polytechnics would continue to offer full-time courses of higher education provided they could satisfy the criteria for approval of courses in force from time to time. Unless there were exceptional circumstances colleges not already engaged in higher education would not be expected to embark on it.

In January 1965 the Universities Central Council on Admissions reported that in pure science the universities would have admitted 1,080 more students if suitable candidates had presented themselves, and they could have also admitted 420 more students in technology. The Council for Scientific Policy was requested on February 25, 1965, 'to examine the flow of candidates in science and technology into higher education', and in consequence a working group was set up under the chairmanship of Dr F. S. Dainton, Vice-Chancellor of Nottingham University. In February 1966 the Group produced an interim report, and two years later, in February 1968, a full report. This made a number of recommendations after stating that science and mathematics were, relatively, losing ground in the sixth form. The proportion of school leavers specializing in them had declined in relation to other subjects of study since 1960. It was clear that there had been an increasing preference for the social sciences, and the report deprecated this relative decline in technology and science which it regarded as 'potentially harmful both to individuals and to society' (20).

We cannot deal with the recommendations of the Dainton Report in any detail here, but briefly they included the following. It considered that in the sixth forms there should be a broad span of studies, and any irre-versible decisions for or against science, technology or engineering should be postponed as long as possible. All pupils should, normally, study mathematics until they left school, and mathematics teaching should show some relationship to other studies, such as economics and the experimental and engineering sciences. The report felt that there was an urgent need to infuse into the teaching of science and its curriculum a breadth, humanity and up-to-dateness. It was the responsibility of schools and L.E.A.s to ensure that within five years of the report (by 1973), the majority of secondary pupils should come into early contact with sound science teaching. There was a great need, especially in science and technology, for the participation of teachers in in-service courses; and the development of teachers should ensure that younger and uncommitted pupils received high quality teaching in science. Positive incentives should be offered to an increasing number of graduates of high ability in order to recruit them into science teaching. The responsibility should be firmly placed upon L.E.A.s to recognize the additional costs of curriculum reform, and to be prepared to finance promising new proposals. The universities were recommended to look again at their entry requirements and encourage a broad span of studies in the sixth form and to increase the actual flow of candidates into science, technology and engineering. They should also experiment with new courses in these fields in order to attract into these disciplines able students who were uncommitted. Employers, in their turn, should recog-nize their own responsibility to ensure that careers in the areas already mentioned were made both possible and attractive to students. Finally,

'there should be continuing review of trends in subject specialization and their implications for manpower; research into career choice should con-tinue; statistics on the flow of pupils from education through to employ-ment should be further developed' (21).

F THE COUNCIL FOR NATIONAL ACADEMIC AWARDS
The Council for National Academic Awards received its Royal Charter in September 1964, and is a self-governing body. It has the power to award degrees, which are comparable with those awarded by universities, to students who complete approved courses in further education established in colleges and other institutions which do not have power to grant their own degrees. By 1969 there were about fifty institutions providing courses for C.N.A.A. degrees, including polytechnics, colleges of technology, colleges of commerce, and at least one college of education. In September 1968 students taking C.N.A.A. courses numbered nearly 16,000—full-time, part-time and sandwich. The C.N.A.A. degrees included B.Sc., B.A., M.Sc., M.A., M.Phil., and Ph.D.; B.Ed. was added to this list shortly

afterwards. Although the official prospectus lists over 190 courses being pursued by this large number of students, each college may, in fact, be following its own particular version of a course, provided its planning has been approved by the Council and it is examined by the Council's appointed examiners. There can be no doubt that the Council represents one of the strongest and most progressive academic forces in our society for the development of higher education, not simply in the fields of science, engineering and technology, but also in business studies, architecture, economics, languages, law, librarianship, public administration, social science and even education itself. The Robbins plan of October 1963, in less than five years from its inception in September 1964, mushroomed into an organization of colleges and students greater than any single university with the exception of London University. Within a short time its number of students will unquestionably be doubled. The members of the council and its many committees, as well as its examiners, include some of the most outstanding names in higher education.

G TECHNICAL AND LIBERAL EDUCATION

So much has been written of the dangers of a purely 'technical' education that it may be necessary here to say something briefly on the other side. Technical schools, colleges and institutes, from the secondary technical school to the college of advanced technology or technological university, are all aware of the necessity of a broad, liberal education. In 1938 the Spens Report had stated that

'we are satisfied that it is the aim and purpose of the junior technical schools to liberalise every subject in their curriculum' (22).

If the schools were aware of such a purpose at that time they have been made even more conscious of the need for this 'liberalising' influence during the post-war years. The Crowther Report of 1959 emphasized the need for a discriminating use of 'minority time' in the sixth-form curriculum for this purpose, and liberal studies have become the latest offspring of the colleges of technology.

In May 1957 the Ministry of Education issued its *Circular 323* on *Liberal Education in Technical Colleges*. It stressed the importance of the liberal element in technical education in order to develop in the student not only a broad outlook but also 'a sense of spiritual and human values'. The circular made the point that it was not just a question of *what* was being taught but also *how* it was being taught; and it suggested that less formal methods such as group discussions, seminars and project assignments should be used, and whenever possible the tutorial system should be introduced. In 1962 the Ministry published a pamphlet, entitled *General Studies in Technical Colleges*, which had in mind courses in technical education lengthened to the 330 hours per year recommended by the Crowther Report. In these extended courses there should be an increase in the time given to English and general subjects, including physical education. The students undertaking such courses would in the main be young men between fifteen and eighteen years of age, and when not attending college they would be at work in industry. The first need was to develop their communication skills, to assist them to make themselves understood in speech and writing, and to understand other people. To this end, the teaching of general studies and English should be regarded as a single operation, and each college should make the attempt to estimate its students' progress towards greater fluency and accuracy in both speech and writing, increased clarity of thought and discrimination, and more awareness of the potential sources of information and a critical attitude towards them.

The Jackson Report of 1957 on *The Supply and Training of Teachers for Technical Colleges* had emphasized the need to introduce a more liberal outlook into technical education. The student must be enabled to see his own science or technology 'in the wider context of industrial activity and the economic life of the country and of the world'. He must also be concerned with moral problems, cultural issues, and the question of taste. To accomplish this it was important for teachers to possess wide interests themselves, and to have sufficient *savoir-faire* to mediate to their students a liberal education (23).

The whole problem of the relationship between technical and liberal studies is well expressed by A. N. Whitehead in his *The Aims of Education and Other Essays*, in which he says that

'The antithesis between a technical and a liberal education is fallacious. There can be no adequate technical education which is not liberal, and no liberal education which is not technical; that is, no education which does not impart both technique and intellectual vision' (24).

REFERENCES

1 Maclure, J. S., *Educational Documents—England and Wales: 1816–1967* (Methuen, 1968, 2nd ed.), p. 108.
2 Ibid., p. 110.
3 Ibid., p. 122.
4 Ibid., p. 123.
5 Ibid., p. 126.
6 Ibid., p. 142.
7 Ibid., p. 142.
8 *Vide* Abbott, B. A., *Education for Industry and Commerce in England* (O.U.P., 1933). Abbott maintains that there was a comparative neglect of technical education for about twenty years, from 1904 to 1924.

9 Consultative Committee, *Secondary Education* (Spens Report) (H.M.S.O., 1938, reprinted 1959), p. 371.
10 Ibid., pp. 372–3.
11 Ibid., Appendix IV, pp. 429–38.
12 *Vide* White Paper on Education (Cmnd. 6458) (H.M.S.O., 1943).
13 Maclure, J. S., op. cit., p. 229.
14 Op. cit., p. 2, para. 4.
15 Ministry of Education, *15 to 18* (H.M.S.O., 1959, reprinted 1962), pp. 365–370.
16 Ministry of Education, *Better Opportunities in Technical Education* (H.M.S.O., 1961), pp. 3–4.
17 Committee on Higher Education: *Higher Education* (Robbins Report) (H.M.S.O., 1963), p. 1.
18 Ibid., p. 280–3.
19 Op. cit., p. 3.
20 Council for Scientific Policy, *Enquiry into the Flow of Candidates in Science and Technology into Higher Education* (H.M.S.O., 1968), p. 1.
21 Ibid., '*Summary of Recommendations*', opposite p. 1.
22 Op. cit., p. 270.
23 Ministry of Education, *The Supply and Training of Teachers for Technical Colleges* (Jackson Report) (H.M.S.O., 1957), pp. 35–6.
24 Whitehead, A. N., *The Aims of Education and Other Essays* (Williams and Norgate, 1929), p. 74.

BIBLIOGRAPHY

Abbott, B. A., *Education for Industry and Commerce in England* (O.U.P., 1933).
Argles, M., *South Kensington to Robbins* (*1851–1963*) (Longmans, 1964).
Cotgrove, S. F., *Technical Education and Social Change* (Allen and Unwin, 1958).
Dobinson, C. H., *Technical Education for Adolescents* (Harrap, 1951).
Hutchings, D. W. and Hayworth, P., *Technology and the Sixth Form Boy* (Oxford University Department of Education, 1963).
Millis, C. T., *Technical Education, Its Development and Aims* (Arnold, 1925).
Price, B., *Technical Colleges and Colleges of Further Education* (Batsford, 1959)
Reese Edwards, K. H. R., *The Secondary Technical School* (University of London Press, 1960).
Richardson, W. A., *The Technical College* (O.U.P., 1939).
Silberston, D., *Youth in a Technical Age* (Parrish, 1959).
Venables, P. F. R., *Technical Education* (Bell, 1955).
Venables, P. F. R., *British Technical Education* (Longmans, 1960).
Venables, P. F. R., *The Smaller Firms and Technical Education* (Parrish, 1961).
Wood, E. M., *The Polytechnic and Quintin Hogg* (Nisbet, 1932).
Young, J. T., *Technicians Today and Tomorrow* (Pitman, 1966).

REPORTS AND WHITE PAPERS

Ministry of Education, *The Education of the Adolescent* (Hadow Report) (H.M.S.O., 1926).
Ministry of Education, *Secondary Education* (Spens Report) (H.M.S.O., 1938).
Ministry of Education, *Curriculum and Examinations in Secondary Schools* (Norwood Report) (H.M.S.O., 1943).

Ministry of Education, *Higher Technological Education* (Percy Report) (H.M.S.O., 1945).

Ministry of Education, *Further Education* (Pamphlet 8) (H.M.S.O., 1947).

Ministry of Education, *The New Secondary Education* (Pamphlet 9) (H.M.S.O., 1947).

White Paper: *Higher Technological Education* (Cmnd. 8357) (H.M.S.O., 1951).

Ministry of Education, *Circular 255/52* (H.M.S.O., 1952).

White Paper: *Technical Education* (Cmnd. 9703) (H.M.S.O., 1956).

Ministry of Education, *Organization of Technical Colleges* (Circular 305/56), (H.M.S.O., 1956).

Ministry of Education, *Liberal Education in Technical Colleges* (Circular 323/57) (H.M.S.O., 1957).

Ministry of Education, *15 to 18* (Crowther Report) (H.M.S.O., 1959).

White Paper: *Better Opportunities in Technical Education* (Cmnd. 1254) (H.M.S.O., 1961).

White Paper: *Industrial Training* (H.M.S.O., 1962).

Ministry of Education, *General Studies in Technical Colleges* (H.M.S.O., 1962).

Ministry of Education, *Higher Education* (Robbins Report) (H.M.S.O., 1963).

White Paper: *A Plan for Polytechnics and Other Colleges* (Cmnd. 3006) (H.M.S.O., 1966).

Schools Council, *A School Approach to Technology* (Curriculum Bulletin 2) (H.M.S.O., 1967).

Council for Scientific Policy, *Enquiry into the Flow of Candidates in Science and Technology into Higher Education* (Cmnd. 3541) (H.M.S.O., 1968).

Chapter 7

The Universities

A BEFORE 1800

Without entering into any partisan controversy concerning the precise dates of the foundation of the ancient universities of Oxford and Cambridge, we may note that it now seems generally agreed that Oxford was established in the late twelfth century, somewhere about 1185, and Cambridge about forty-five years later. Elizabethan prose provides some interesting and revealing pictures of life at these centres of learning. Paul Hentzner, in his *Travels in England*, published in 1598, found the life of students at Oxford almost monastic. In 1628, however, John Earle, in *Microcosmographie*, somewhat caustically referred to the 'young gentleman of the university' as

'One that comes there to wear a gown, and to say hereafter he has been at the university. His father sent him thither, because he heard there were the best fencing and dancing schools; from these he has his education, from his tutor the over-sight. The first element of his knowledge is to be shewn the colleges, and initiated in a tavern by the way, which hereafter he will learn of himself . . . he is now gone to the Inns of Court, where he studies to forget what he learned before—his acquaintance and the fashion' (1).

In his *Liberal Education*, published in 1789, Vicesimus Knox had some very harsh words to say about the universities in his time, and he insisted upon some reform. According to Knox, rather than seats of learning Oxford and Cambridge had become seats of ignorance and corruption; everything was performed in a perfunctory and superficial way. The universities were still open only to members of the Established Church, the Church of England; and the acceptance of the Thirty-Nine Articles was almost a guarantee of graduation. Oxford and Cambridge were virtually clubs for the idle rich.

In 1800 the Public Examination Statute of Oxford University insisted upon a written examination, as at Cambrige, in addition to the *viva voce* which has always been retained. Honour Schools in classics and mathematics were established in 1807 at Oxford, and at Cambridge considerably more interest was beginning to be shown in science. Dissenters of all kinds, whether Roman Catholic or Protestant Nonconformists, were still rigidly excluded from a university education, and in consequence they had established their own academies. Outstanding Dissenters of the eighteenth century, such as Joseph Priestley, F.R.S., and Philip Doddridge, demonstrated that the highest levels of cultural development could be reached by those to whom the more normal university channels were closed. Indeed, the academies provided an education much broader in its content, more liberal in its approach, and more practical in its application, than that which could be obtained at the universities. It is true, of course, that the Scottish universities of St Andrews (1410), Glasgow (1451), Aberdeen (1494) and Edinburgh (1583), had always been open to Dissenters, and many an Englishman migrated to Scotland in order to receive a higher education.

B NINETEENTH-CENTURY REFORMS

Reforms came slowly at Oxford and Cambridge—too slowly for many Dissenters who pressed for the establishment of an institution of higher learning at which there would exist no barriers of belief. In 1828 a college was opened in Gower Street, London, referred to by Thomas Arnold, then headmaster at Rugby, as 'that godless institution'. The college was to be the first element in London University, which was undenominational and lacking in any credal tests. In 1831 King's College was added to the Gower Street 'blasphemy' in order to provide teaching in religion and morals, as well as the classics, mathematics, science, modern literature, philosophy, history and commerce. In Gower Street there was an emphasis upon law, economics, history and modern studies generally, and in 1834 a Hospital School for the study of medicine was erected next door. The Gower Street College was officially christened University College in 1836, and London University was given a charter to grant degrees in arts, laws and medicine; in this way it became a large, public examining body to which students from colleges in London might go, after a suitable course in a particular 'faculty', to be examined and to receive graduation. London is the one university which, in addition to internal degrees, still makes provision for the external candidate who has pursued a recognized and acceptable course of study. Fees at these colleges of London University were extremely low compared with those of the older universities.

Reforms in education have come about through the work, effort and thought of individual reformers as well as through the investigations and considered recommendations of committees. Two such thinkers, John Henry Newman (1801–90) and Mark Pattison (1813–84), took up somewhat different positions in their views of the university although they were clearly both concerned with the status of higher education. Newman, who became a Catholic in 1814, was appointed the first Rector of Dublin University which was founded in 1854. He argued that it was essential to the development of true learning to have a residential community, such as a college, in which a tutorial system operated. For him research belonged to a different, supervisory body. Pattison claimed that the teaching of university tutors could be meaningful only if they themselves were actively involved in the advancement of knowledge or research. The tutor's function was to initiate his students into particular, viable methods, not to lay down sterile principles. He was an investigator who took his assistants, namely his students, along with him upon his path of investigation. The 'idea of a university' today combines both levels; the student is there to receive information, to acquire knowledge, and also to develop understanding, wisdom, and initiative. Not all are suited to further higher education, or research, although an increasing number of students are becoming involved in the furtherance of their academic work after they have taken their first degree.

We have said that the reforms at Oxford and Cambridge were slow, but they were certainly going on, and in 1849 there was a request for the setting-up of a Royal Commission. This request, or petition, was signed by renowned Fellows of the Royal Society who were also members of the older universities. When it was set up the authorities at Oxford proved very uncooperative; there was, however, a different atmosphere at Cambridge. In the main the commissioners supported the lecture system of the university as opposed to the tutorial system of the college, and this was generally in line with the views expressed by Mark Pattison. The university was, as its name implied, a place where universal research was going on, and where students received a liberal form of education.

The commissioners looked for a more democratic form of government at both universities, and suggested that the time had come for Senate discussions to take place in English instead of Latin. The reports, published during 1852–3, dealt with a variety of topics including discipline, aims, and finances. The Report of the Royal Commission on Oxford maintained that

'The grosser exhibitions of vice, such as drunkenness and riot, have in Oxford, as in the higher classes generally, become rare. . . . Of existing evils the most obvious are sensual vice, gambling in its various forms and extravagant expenditure. . . . Driving, riding and hunting are . . . causes of great expense. Of these amusements the most expensive is hunting. It seldom costs less than four guineas a day' (2).

And it was considered that any parent who managed to get his son through his university course on not more than £600 had reason to congratulate himself—particularly if he had no debts to discharge at the end of the course. The report recommended that the poorer students, who could not afford the college fees demanded for residence, should be permitted to live in private lodgings on very moderate terms. It considered, somewhat forcefully, that it should be the aim of the university to offer the best education to all those qualified to receive it, and to place it within their reach.

Whilst it was not within the terms of reference of the commissioners to consider the question of religious tests applied to candidates for membership of the University of Oxford, in general discussion with various members of the university it was elicited that there existed a strong opinion against such tests. In their report the commissioners went so far as to refer to 'this evil', and they expressed their strong conviction that enforced subscription to the Thirty-Nine Articles of the Church of England led to a considerable amount of sophistry. The university was a lay organization, and here it was demanding that laymen should subscribe to articles of belief—as a condition of membership—which the Church itself did not require before they could participate 'in its most sacred Ordinance' (3).

The report went on to deplore the decay of professional preparation at the university. Oxford had altogether ceased to be a school of medicine, whilst its large number of graduated theologians were, *qua* theologians, unlearned and inexpert. The same applied also to the study of law as a profession: few were being trained at Oxford as barristers. The commissioners obviously felt that this represented a great loss to the professions in that, whilst the professional demand might still be met, those liberal elements of mind which were somehow elicited by study at the older universities were no longer permeating the new representatives of the professions. They said, somewhat sadly, that whilst young men came into residence at a much more advanced age than formerly the university was, for most of them, 'a mere grammar school from first to last' (4).

As a result of the reports of the commissioners on the universities, the Oxford University Act of 1854 and the Cambridge University Act of 1856 were passed. These Acts gave considerably more power to representatives of the universities other than the Hebdomadal Board and the Council of the Senate, and more freedom generally to the universities to develop in any way they wished without interference from the State. Discussions in Council could take place in English instead of Latin, many more students would be able to enter the universities despite their lack of means, and there would be more opportunities for research and lecturing, and less emphasis upon the tutorial system.

In 1832 a new university had been mooted at Durham, to be established in the Norman castle and organized mainly along the lines of Oxford and Cambridge. Students were to be in residence and work was to be run on tutorial lines. It received its charter in 1836, but initially, as at the older universities, students had to subscribe to the Thirty-Nine Articles. It was not until 1871 that the religious tests were finally abolished at Oxford,

Cambridge and Durham; Dissenters could now take full advantage of the system of higher education. During the seventies and eighties there was expansion in a number of directions; the impact of science upon industrial society was leading inevitably to a serious look at educational organization and curricula. The setting up of the Royal Commission on Scientific Instruction and the Advancement of Science showed clearly, from the terms of reference, that there was concern to make scientific instruction, at the higher education level, as effective as possible. In 1872–5 the commissioners, under the chairmanship of the Duke of Devonshire, published their report. It emphasized in particular the need for more science teachers, and therefore the need to train such teachers both at university and training college level.

Whilst Oxford and Cambridge Universities were expanding their college system, a similar process was going on in London. In 1849, the first of the colleges for women, Bedford College, was established. The University of London Act of 1898 saw a reconstitution of the university, as a result of which it examined external students, but was not directly involved in their tuition. The university, through the deliberations of the various Faculty Boards and Senate, established the syllabuses that had to be followed, but students could pursue their studies privately, or in an institution which specifically prepared them for London degree examinations, or in a constituent college of the university.

C TWENTIETH-CENTURY DEVELOPMENTS
In his speech to introduce the Education Act of 1902, A. J. Balfour, the Prime Minister, stated that the educationalist

'has seen in the last 10 or 15 years a development of university life by private liberality which has no parallel except in America, which has covered, and still is covering our great industrial centres with universities and university colleges where the very highest type of university instruction is given by men well qualified for their duty' (5).

It was certainly a period of university expansion. The eighties had seen the development of a federation of provincial colleges, which originated with Owens College, Manchester. This college was given a constitution by Act of Parliament in 1871 and prepared its students for degrees of London University; Liverpool University College joined Owens College, Manchester in 1884 to form the federal university of Victoria. Students were no longer prepared externally for London University degrees, but Victoria University had a charter to award its own degrees. The federation was further augmented in 1887 by the advent of Leeds.

At Birmingham a similar process of development had been taking place;

Mason College was founded in 1880 and became Birmingham University in 1900, awarding its own degrees. In 1903 the Victoria federation ceased to exist, and the Universities of Manchester, Liverpool and Leeds were born. Sheffield University followed in 1905, and Bristol University in 1909. These universities are usually termed 'older civic universities', founded to meet the needs of various localities; but, like all true universities, they have developed as national institutions of higher learning open to students from all over the United Kingdom—in fact, from all over the world.

The University of Wales had developed in a way similar to that of the older civic universities, particularly the federated University of Manchester. In 1872 a university college was founded at Aberystwyth; this was followed by a college at Cardiff in 1883, and one at Bangor in 1884. At first, these university colleges prepared their students for London University external degrees; in 1893, however, a charter was granted to the University of Wales to award degrees to students who were prepared at its three constituent colleges. In 1920 the federation was further developed by the addition of the University College of Swansea and a School of Medicine.

In 1926 the University of London Act was passed. This provided a new constitution for the increasing number of teaching bodies which had developed since the end of the nineteenth century. In 1895 the London School of Economics had been founded, and the Imperial College of Science joined the University in 1907. The University of London today has more students than any other British university, and whilst each college has its own governing body, the University senate is finally responsible for the appointment of all senior members of staff, and for the organization of curricula and degree examination conditions.

The pattern followed by the 'younger civic universities' has, until recently, been a preliminary period spent as a university college preparing students externally for London University degrees. After this 'trial period' the college has been granted a charter to award its own degrees. The following universities were developed in this way: Reading (1926), Nottingham (1948), Southampton (1952), Hull (1954), Exeter (1955), Leicester (1957). In 1949 the University College of North Staffordshire broke with this traditional form of development by being granted a charter to award its own degrees immediately. It had, however, a period of supervision and sponsorship by three other universities until, in 1962, it became the University of Keele; it has always been largely residential. During the sixties there was a vast development of the university sector of education; proposed new universities were to receive their charters at their foundation without going through the embryonic stage of university colleges. The University Grants Committee considered the establishment of about a dozen new universities, which would initially be organized and administered by members of existing universities.

In 1961 the University of Sussex, at Brighton, received its charter, and its first fifty-two students. Other universities quickly followed, beginning with the University of Essex which was founded in 1962 with a development plan which made provision, eventually, for up to 20,000 students. Its first Vice-Chancellor, Dr A. E. Sloman, believed that 'bigness' was important, and that a university was not just a place of teaching and research.

'It is, or should be, a self-governing academic community. Universities are people, not places, people with different interests living and working together' (6).

Dr Sloman, however, was fully aware that 'bigness' had to be reconciled with intimacy, and that in consequence a great deal of planning had to go into the integration of the social and working life of this new university. The whole story of how tradition and innovation were brought together in the pursuit of learning at Essex University has been told by Dr Sloman in *A University in the Making*.

In 1963 the University of Newcastle-upon-Tyne was formed from King's College, which had been an offshoot of Durham University. Newcastle had a target of 6,000 students by 1970. During the same year the Royal College of Science and Technology at Glasgow became Strathclyde University; and the Universities of York and East Anglia, at Norwich, received their charters. Kent University, at Canterbury, and Warwick University, at Coventry, followed in 1965 and Lancaster University in 1966; Bath University was chartered in 1967 and Brunel, at Uxbridge, in 1968. The total number of students continues to rise—in October 1967 there were 199,372, whilst in October 1968 there were nearly 212,000 (7).

One of the interesting factors in the development of the newer universities has been their determination to experiment in new and mixed courses, with a maximum of academic freedom. A number of these universities have opposed very vigorously any over-specialization in a first degree. When the University College of North Staffordshire was first established it decided to experiment with a four-year course involving a balanced curriculum for a Bachelor of Arts degree. The first-year curriculum was compulsory for all students, and it dealt with the development of human civilization, current problems, and the methods and influence of the experimental sciences. Only after this preliminary and general course was the student permitted to proceed to greater specialization; but even now this was extended for a further three years, and the specialization was not a narrow one, although permitting certain options. A student had, in fact, to select four subjects, two of which he studied for three years and two for one year. The principal subjects chosen had to include one from the sciences and one from the humanities and social sciences. Other modern universities have followed similar patterns for the first year, at least, but not many have been prepared to make the degree course a four-year one.

D TECHNOLOGICAL AND OTHER DEVELOPMENTS AT
UNIVERSITY LEVEL

The Percy Report on higher technological education, published in 1945, complained of the lack of trained technologists and of the weakness in their training. It recommended that a number of technical colleges should be designated as colleges of technology, and that they should develop full-time courses for degrees, such as Bachelor of Technology, or diplomas, such as a Diploma in Technology. In the event little came of the recommendations until, in 1956, the colleges of advanced technology (C.A.T.s) were established. In 1946 a report on scientific manpower was published by a committee appointed by the Lord President of the Council, working under the chairmanship of Sir Alan Barlow. The Barlow Report recommended a wholesale expansion of the universities within the sphere of the training of scientists and technologists, in order to double their output. It argued that

'At present rather less than 2 per cent of the population reach the universities. About 5 per cent of the whole population show, on test, an intelligence as great as the upper half of the students who amount to 1 per cent of the population. We conclude, therefore, that only about one in five of the boys and girls, who have intelligence equal to that of the best half of the university students actually reach the universities' (8).

The committee stated that it would deprecate any attempt to increase the output of scientists and technologists at the expense of the number of students reading the humanities, and it considered that there was a sound case for the establishment of another university which might leave to posterity 'a monument of its culture'. Between the years 1938 and 1958 the student numbers at the universities doubled, and there was a steady increase in the number of universities.

In 1956 the White Paper on *Technical Education* put forward a proposal for a programme to expand technical education particularly within the universities and through the development of colleges of advanced technology. The White Paper was dissatisfied with the progress being made in this country as compared with the scientific and technical manpower of the U.S.A., Russia and Western Europe. And in the production of an ever-increasing number of technologists it wished to see a greater degree of independence afforded the C.A.T.s. The Robbins Report recommended that the latter should be placed in the hands of a Grants Commission. Soon after the publication of this report in 1963 the Government accepted the proposal that C.A.T.s should become universities, or affiliated to universities, and that other technological universities should be developed. The process of conversion has been proceeding steadily, and when, in 1967, the Royal College of Technology, Salford, and the Welsh College of Advanced Technology, Cardiff, received their charters as the University of Salford and the University of Wales Institute of Science and Technology, all the C.A.T.s had achieved the status of university institutions which the Robbins Report recommended.

In general, the Robbins Report considered that there were two weaknesses in university training; one was the small proportion of students who took first degrees of a broader nature, and the other was the inadequate provision for postgraduate study and research. It considered that there should be more courses involving the study of more than one main subject; and that arrangements should be made wherever possible to permit a student to postpone his selection of a special subject until the end of his first year at the university, or even to change his course of study then. In the development of postgraduate study an element of systematic teaching should normally be included; and the proportion of graduates proceeding to postgraduate study should be increased from 20 to 30 per cent by 1980.

One of the fascinating features of academic freedom and university autonomy is the development of a vast variety of courses throughout British universities and the incredible variation of nomenclature and content. The Robbins Report pleaded for some sort of rationalization in the process of establishment of both courses and degrees:

'Both in the creation of new undergraduate courses and in the provision of more varied facilities for postgraduate students, we recommend that universities should consult together. It is desirable that the universities should complement each other in the provision of new courses and that there should be some attempt to secure a measure of uniformity in the nomenclature of degrees. It is particularly important that in the matter of diplomas and higher degrees there should be a general equivalence in standard and some uniformity in the nomenclature of awards' (9).

Some would consider this sort of rationalization long overdue since there are anomalies, both in the content and title of the degree courses, which many employers find misleading. The practice varies from university to university. Some universities have a different degree title for each faculty; others have the same. Some universities call their initial degree 'bachelor';

at others it is 'master'. At one university a master's degree may be obtained by examination; at another by dissertation and examination; at another by thesis; and at yet another by 'keeping terms'. In Scotland, since 1858, the first degree has been the M.A., and other awards such as Ed.B. and B.LL., were granted for postgraduate study. At Oxford and Cambridge the B.A. is awarded in all faculties, whether science, arts or theology; B.Sc. and B.Litt. at Oxford are postgraduate awards, as also is the B.D. The M.A. at Oxford and Cambridge is not a higher degree awarded for further study, or for a thesis, but it is automatically granted to those who elect to pay a fee so many terms after their graduation. The degree of Ph.D., or D.Phil., may be awarded for almost any class of research in any faculty, provided the standard of research is of sufficiently high quality; but it is certainly not restricted, as many imagine, to a study in 'philosophy'.

These many variations are, perhaps, only of relative importance provided one knows all the levels and standards involved, but apart from full-time academics few people, in fact, have the time or inclination to make a study of these graduation oddities. It does become important, however, in the realm of the professions to have certain standards for evaluating a man's worth in terms of those professions. Whilst one may accept that one School of Law may be better than another, the legal profession still demands certain standards of attainment as well as certain elements of content in the qualifying courses. The same applies also to the medical profession. When, however, the Robbins Report recommended that a B.Ed. degree should be instituted for college of education students, in view of its avowed desire for 'a measure of uniformity', it could hardly have anticipated the amazing variety of degrees that would eventually be christened 'Bachelor of Education'. Quite apart from the variety of content in the degree at different universities there are at least nine different levels of award, from an unclassified pass to a fully classified honours degree. It is not surprising that students themselves are dissatisfied with this situation, or that headmasters are already at a loss to evaluate the real worth of a B.Ed. The Robbins Report assumed that by the middle of the 1970s provision would be made for 25 per cent of the entrants to colleges of education to take a four-year course. In the academic year 1968–9 there were approximately 6 per cent over the country as a whole who were proceeding to a fourth year. To reach the target of 25 per cent by 1975 will require, from present experience, far more teaching resources than are now available at college of education level.

E THE OPEN UNIVERSITY

In February 1966 a White Paper was published, entitled 'A University of the Air', outlining the possibilities of an Open University. In September 1967 a Planning Committee, under the chairmanship of Sir Peter Venables, was appointed by the Secretary of State for Education and Science with the following brief:

'To work out a comprehensive plan for an Open University, as outlined in the White Paper of February 1966, "A University of the Air", and to prepare a draft Charter and Statutes' (10).

In its report the committee clearly set forth the objects of the Open University. It maintained that the greatest educational opportunity was being denied to the greatest number of citizens: higher education was no longer the adventitious social right of a few, it was a basic individual right of all. As a result of a survey of the interest of the adult population in the Open University, the committee considered that there were good grounds for expecting a substantial number of candidates. In addition it was noted that out of some 100,000 applicants for university entrance in 1966–7 barely half were granted places. About 20,000 of the remainder were unsuccessful in achieving the minimum standards required for university entrance. This left some 30,000 who were qualified to proceed to a university course, and who were, in fact, interested in taking a degree but who had failed to do so through the usual university channels. Some would, of course, proceed to colleges of technology, polytechnics, and other institutions of higher education, but many of them would be disappointed.

The work of the Open University would be focussed mainly upon adults; where it was possible for younger students to attend sandwich courses, part-time day release, or block release courses they would not be considered for enrolment in the Open University. It would also serve a useful function in providing refresher and updating courses through broadcasting, residential short courses and correspondence courses; it was important that employees in particular professions and occupations should keep abreast of the most recent developments in technology, science and industry. The committee underlined in particular the fact that there were many young married women who had been denied the educational opportunities currently available to men. The Open University would 'have an unrivalled opportunity to rectify the long-continuing imbalance' (11).

In its consideration of the techniques to be used by the Open University, the committee accepted as beyond controversy the fact that the imaginative use of the broadcasting media was an efficient means of instruction, which could draw on a nation-wide pool of specialists and expert teachers. But students needed to undertake some regular written work, and the only method which could be made available everywhere and to a very large number was that of correspondence tuition. The report noted that this had, in fact, been the main agent of university expansion in Russia, and that nearly half of all Russian students in higher education were pursuing correspondence courses. The Robbins Report had supported the use of correspondence courses, with television as an ancillary (12); it had also suggested that British universities should experiment with such courses. The Venables Committee saw the Open University as a way of integrating a number of teaching systems including sound radio and television, correspondence courses, specially programmed textbooks, group discussions, and part-time face-to-face teaching.

This concept of the Open University has clearly seized upon certain features of modern society, and the vital element of motivation in adult study. Society is an ever-increasingly 'viewing' society; people have formed the habit of watching the television and it is the means of entertainment and information most convenient to the majority of people. The presentation of academic topics by experts can make a maximum impact through this medium. The 'fall-out' rate has always been high in organized courses of adult education, where after a day's heavy work a man may have to travel some distance to attend a course of study, and then travel back home again thoroughly tired, and certainly unprepared for further concentrated study. The correspondence course combined with organized television would help to reduce the fatigue element and the customary 'fall-out' rate, which is as high as 50 per cent in some diploma courses. Already in this country the National Extension College has worked in conjunction with the British Broadcasting Corporation and Independent Television in providing 'O' and 'A' level courses in English and physics.

The Open University is, by its charter, an independent, autonomous institution in much the same way as all other universities and the Council for National Academic Awards. Despite the general scepticism expressed concerning both the necessity for such a university and its techniques and modes of operation, the Venables Committee felt that there was very little basis for the fears and doubt expressed. But in order that its degrees might be comparable with those of other universities, the Open University must ensure that the quality of its staff is high. In January 1969 Professor Walter Perry, at that time Vice-Principal of the University of Edinburgh, was appointed the first Vice-Chancellor of the Open University. In order to cope with its 'integrated systems approach' the new university appointed a Director of Studies for Home Tuition and Correspondence Services, and a Director of Studies for Local Centres and Tutorial Services, their overall aim being

'to provide the necessary expertise in the educational technologies associated with specialised course design, with correspondence tuition, with radio and television broadcasting, with the special problems of adult education, and with the problems of programmed learning and of the assessment of student performance' (13).

It was decided to provide both ordinary degrees and honours degrees, which would be obtained by the accumulation of 'credits' in individual courses, each lasting for one academic year. Six credits would be required for an ordinary degree and eight for an honours degree; and the normal minimum period for obtaining a degree would be four years. The university would award a certificate to indicate the acquisition of a credit, and would issue this to any student who was successful in both continuous and final assessments. There were certain foundation courses which each student would have to pursue before proceeding to further study; each foundation course would count as one credit and all students would have to be credited with two foundation courses. Foundation courses would be offered in

1 Understanding Science
2 Mathematics
3 Understanding Society
4 Literature and Culture.

These foundation courses correspond to main degree 'lines'—science, technology, social science and arts. After the initial study of the foundation courses, each 'line' would be broken down into a number of components for further study in detail and depth. Mathematics, for example, might be developed into pure mathematics, statistics, computer science, and so forth. After the two foundation courses, selected from the four provided, a student might concentrate the rest of his study upon the components of one of the lines, for example, mathematics. Although, initially, full-time staff would be small in number, it was obvious that a large number of part-time tutors would be required to deal with students' written work and to guide and assist them in their studies. Some of these tutors might be recruited from housewives who were prevented from full-time work because of the demands of young families. The majority, however, would be recruited from the staffs of colleges of education, technical colleges, polytechnics and existing universities.

REFERENCES

1 Wilson, J. Dover, *Life in Shakespeare's England* (C.U.P., 1925), pp. 65–6.
2 Maclure, J. S., *Educational Documents—England and Wales: 1816–1967* (Methuen,1968), pp. 65–6.
3 Ibid., p. 67.
4 Ibid., p. 68.
5 Ibid., pp. 152–3.
6 Sloman, A. E., *A University in the Making* (B.B.C., 1964), p. 11.
7 D.E.S., *Education and Science in 1968* (H.M.S.O., 1969), p. 87.
8 Maclure, J. S., op. cit., pp. 231–2.
9 Committee on Higher Education, *Higher Education* (Robbins Report) (H.M.S.O., 1963), p. 106, para. 307.

10 Open University Planning Committee, *The Open University* (H.M.S.O., 1969), p. 1.
11 Ibid., p. 5.
12 Op. cit., p. 262, para. 821.
13 *The Open University*, p. 14.

BIBLIOGRAPHY

Adamson, J. W., *English Education, 1789–1902* (C.U.P., 1931).

Armytage, W. H. G., *Civic Universities* (Benn, 1953).

Curtis, S. J. *et al.*, *An Introductory History of English Education Since 1800* (Chapters XV and XVI) (University Tutorial Press, 1964).

Davies, W. C. *et al.*, *The University of Wales* (Hutchinson, 1905).

Dent, H. C., *Universities in Transition*, Cohen and West, 1961.

Evans, B. E., *The University of Wales: A Historical Sketch* (Cardiff, 1953).

Flexner, A., *Universities, American, English, German* (O.U.P., 1930).

Gardner, A., *A Short History of Newnham College, Cambridge* (Bowes and Bowes, 1921).

Hamilton, M. A., *Newnham* (Faber, 1936).

Humberstone, T. L., *University Reform in London* (Allen and Unwin, 1926).

Lowe, A., *The University in Transformation* (Sheldon Press, 1940).

Mallet, C., *A History of the University of Oxford*, 3 vols. (Methuen, 1924–7).

Moberly, W., *The Crisis in the University* (Student Christian Movement Press, 1949).

Newman, J. H., *On the Scope and Nature of University Education* (Everyman Library, Dent).

Roberts, S. C., *British Universities* (Collins, 1947).

Roberts, S. C., *Introduction to Cambridge* (C.U.P., 1945).

Sloman, A. E., *A University in the Making* (*Essex*) (B.B.C., 1964).

Smithells, A., *From A Modern University* (O.U.P., 1921).

Truscot, B., *Redbrick University* (Faber, 1943).

Tylecote, M., *The Education of Women at Manchester University, 1883–1933* (Manchester University Press, 1941).

Whyting, C. E., *The University of Durham* (Sheldon Press, 1932).

Wilson, G. S., *The University of London and Its Colleges* (University Tutorial Press, 1923).

Winstanley, D. A., *Early Victorian Cambridge* (C.U.P., 1940).

Winstanley, D. A., *Later Victorian Cambridge* (C.U.P., 1947).

REPORTS, ETC.

Board of Education, *Teachers and Youth Leaders* (McNair Report) (H.M.S.O., 1944).

Ministry of Education, *15 to 18* (Crowther Report) (H.M.S.O., 1959).

Committee on Higher Education, *Higher Education* (Robbins Report) (H.M.S.O., 1963).

A.T.C.D.E., *Handbook of Colleges and Departments of Education* (Lund Humphries, 1969).

U.G.C., *University Teaching Methods* (Hale Report) (H.M.S.O., 1964).

U.G.C., *University Development: 1957–1962* (Murray Report) (H.M.S.O., 1964).

D.E.S., *Education and Science in 1968* (H.M.S.O., 1969).

Open University Planning Committee, *The Open University* (H.M.S.O., 1969).

Chapter 8

Teacher Training

A RECRUITMENT OF TEACHERS BEFORE 1900

The National Society and the British and Foreign School Society found it necessary to train teachers for their own schools; their courses were inevitably unsatisfactory through pressure of time and lack of adequate facilities. The Glasgow Normal Seminary was founded by David Stow in 1827, and this was a landmark in the development of teacher training. Its success resulted in attempts and proposals during the next decade to establish similar 'normal schools' elsewhere, such as at University College, London. In 1834 the Parliamentary Committee on the State of Education discussed in its report the question of teacher training and the social status of teachers. In reply to a questionnaire it was stated by one witness that one of the principal objects of the National Society was 'to promote the training of masters and mistresses in its own central schools . . . throughout the country' (1). Since all of those employed as teachers must have had some employment before the age of twenty-one, most of them, with very few exceptions, had been in some type of work other than school-teaching. This maturity was regarded as more valuable to the schools than greater academic proficiency acquired by younger boys given a superior education as schoolmasters. Sheer knowledge or academic ability was not regarded by the witness as sufficient; the teacher needed a flawless character, morally and religiously, and if a man were sufficiently skilled in reading, writing and arithmetic he might learn 'the difficult art of teaching' in three to five months!

The evidence provided at the same committee by another witness, the Secretary of the Sunday School Union, has a strangely modern ring about it. It was his belief that one requisite improvement in the teacher situation was adequate encouragement and remuneration; for the fact was that

'if a man is very clever as a teacher, he is generally picked up for some other employment, and it is not worth his while to continue in that pursuit; and for a man to be a clever teacher, he must have qualifications that would entitle him to double the remuneration he would get in average day schools' (2).

The witness went on to underline the fact that there was no adequate system of supplying trained and competent teachers, and insufficient funds to reward them at any level higher than the recompense given to 'porters or ploughmen'. Another witness, the Rev. Samuel Wood, considered that the establishment of normal schools by the Government would be the most beneficial way for it to take active steps to promote education. Wood based his arguments on the success of the Borough Road College at Southwark, which had been founded by Joseph Lancaster about 1798. Yet another witness, a member of the committee of the National Society, considered it not worthwhile to furnish schoolmasters with qualifications higher than those already enjoyed, without materially raising their salaries, since they would very soon be lost to the profession.

In 1839 a plan for a State or national normal school came under consideration by the committee of the Privy Council on education. There was a great deal of opposition to this scheme from Churchmen and Dissenters alike, and it was soon dropped. In 1840 Dr Phillips-Kay (afterwards Sir James Kay-Shuttleworth), Secretary of the committee, established a training school for teachers at Battersea which quickly grew and received a grant from the committee. Training colleges, as well as schools, were permitted by the committee to be established by voluntary societies out of the grant provided by the Government, which in 1842 was £40,000. As a result training colleges were founded by the National Society, the British and Foreign School Society, the Wesleyan Conference and the Roman Catholic Poor School Committee, and other such societies; the college at Battersea was itself transferred to the National Society in 1843, and within a few years the Church of England had organized over twenty training colleges. At first they were modelled largely upon the experience of the Swiss in their normal schools, and as well as the study of the more elementary work, practical subjects such as drawing, geography, science, mensuration and accounts were engaged in. There was also now an organized attempt to look upon education as a 'subject' to be studied in its own right, in both theoretical and practical terms.

In 1846 a scheme was launched by the committee of the Privy Council to develop a five-year apprenticeship scheme for pupil teachers. It had by now been generally accepted that the monitorial system as such was a failure, and in any event unsound educationally. The method of the apprenticeship was to attach the pupil teacher to a master or mistress competent to see him through the course of instruction laid down. As a reward for instructing these apprentices for at least one-and-a-half hours during five days in the week, before or after school hours, the master received a fee scaled according to the number of trainees attached to him. Pupil teachers had to be at least thirteen years old before they could be so apprenticed, and they had to be physically fit. In the light of more recent demands it is interesting to note the minimum requirements of the candidate. He had to be competent in reading, 'with fluency, ease and expression'; able to write neatly and correctly; knowledgeable about the table of weights and measures and the 'first four rules of arithmetic, simple and compound'; possessed of an elementary knowledge of geography; and facile in the distinguishing of parts of speech in a simple sentence. In addition, all candidates had to teach a junior class 'to the satisfaction of the inspector', and girls must show competence in knitting and sewing. If the candidate were connected with a Church of England school he was required to repeat the Catechism, show some understanding of it, and have acquaintance with scripture history. The parish priest would assist in this part of the examination. In schools other than Anglican the managers were responsible for certifying the candidate's state of religious knowledge (3). After each year the candidate was subject to examinations, and at the end of the fifth year a certain selected number of pupil teachers entered an open competition, by means of a public examination, for a course at a 'normal school' or training college. Successful candidates were awarded exhibitions of £20 or £25 and became 'Queen's Scholars'.

The training college course was, by 1856, fixed as one of two years' duration, and any student who left after the first year was regarded as an 'uncertificated teacher'. It was at this time that the 'pledge' was introduced whereby a candidate who entered a training college declared that it was his avowed intention to become a teacher in a school 'recognized' by the Education Department. This 'pledge' never had, throughout its long history, any binding legal force: it was a matter of honour and moral pressure.

The Newcastle Report of 1861, which investigated popular education in England pretty thoroughly, had something to say about teachers and their shortcomings. The commissioners clearly had in mind what children came to the elementary school to learn, namely, 'to read, write, and cypher' (4). They were equally clear that many children did not even learn to read, and if they did they very soon lost the skill when they left school. Religious instruction, which was a *sine qua non*, was, according to the report, 'unintelligent, and to a great extent confined to exercises of merely verbal memory'. The commissioners had, apparently, received reports that trained teachers were 'conceited and dissatisfied'. It may well be that there is a high correlation between knowledge and conceit, but the report at least did not accept the charge in relation to teachers as a class. They did, however, admit the second charge 'to a certain degree'; and noted that teachers' emoluments rose too soon to the highest level, although they would not agree that they were too low.

The task of the training colleges and of the pupil teacher system was no easy one. The colleges were increasingly drawing their students from pupil teachers who left school at the age of thirteen in order to begin their five-year apprenticeship. Each student had to spend at least 150 hours in practical teaching, and in addition he had to reach a certain accepted standard in his academic work. All this left him with very little time for professional training. It was the Cross Commission of 1888, investigating the working of the Elementary Education Acts, which pinpointed in both its majority and minority reports, some of the more important problems of teacher training. It had been obvious that the revised code of 1862, with the institution of Robert Lowe's system of payment by results, had had deleterious effects upon the pupil teacher system as well as upon training colleges. The narrow application of study to those subjects which alone would be taught in the schools, and the somewhat nervous desire to satisfy the inspectorate with the 'right answers' to inevitable questions, led to a pressurized system of rote-learning of required material. The defects of the teacher training system were, in fact, a reflection of the defects of the educational system at large, and a certain reluctance to enter the profession resulted, as well as a growing apathy amongst those ahead in the profession towards true and liberal learning.

The 1870 Education Act and the formation of the school boards did something to alleviate the situation. Apprenticeship was to begin at the age of fourteen, instead of thirteen, which gave a little more maturity, as well as a little more knowledge, to the trainee. And after 1875 there was a strong interest in the formation of pupil teacher centres which would afford several advantages to the 'apprentices'. Much of the instruction they received in the elementary schools was piecemeal, discontinuous, and often misinformed. In the centres they would have the possibility of a certain communal life, the development of a professional outlook, better and more continuous instruction of a less disparate nature than that provided in the schools, and some teaching of educational theory as well as practice. The centres became a fact in 1881.

The evidence which the Cross Commission received concerning the pupil teacher system was obviously not unmixed. There were those who considered that the whole system was injurious to the work of teaching, that it was cheap and 'the very worst possible system of supply' (5). There were others, however, who spoke highly of the system, not merely because it afforded the best means of keeping up the supply (although this was clearly a great consideration), but also because it was felt that there were certain practical advantages in the pupil teacher system, particularly in the development of the right sort of staff relationships at an impressible and malleable age. This may, of course, have meant quite simply that younger teacher candidates were easier to handle and more amenable to the authoritarian régime of the school. At any rate, the commission felt that, where moral considerations were involved, there was no other 'equally trustworthy source from which an adequate supply of teachers is likely to be forthcoming' (6). The majority report concluded that the apprenticeship of pupil teachers ought to be continued but with educational improvements.

The Cross Commission also had a look at the training colleges, and it is evident that considerable pressure was being brought to bear from a number of areas to extend the training to a third year or even more. The commissioners showed some sympathy for this point of view, arguing that students in training needed not so much more knowledge as a greater penetration of their minds by that knowledge. Students needed time to absorb what they were being taught and to think more deeply about it whilst they were still in training. On the whole, the commissioners felt that, however desirable a three-year course might be for some students, there were others unable or unwilling to extend their time of training to three years, and, further, their own hesitation in recommending the extension of the course at the time was on the basis of feasibility. There would be insufficient staff and funds to implement such a development. The interest and keenness of the majority of the members of the commission, however, were still expressed in the belief that certain selected students might yet with advantage be brought together for a third year's course of instruction at certain convenient centres. Whilst the report considered, on the whole, that the residential system of colleges was best, it nevertheless recommended the establishment of a number of day training colleges. There was a serious shortage of accommodation for students in the forty-three existing colleges; of these only eight were undenominational, and most of the remainder were Anglican. The minority report of the Cross Commission felt particularly strong about the 'liberal recognition of the rights of conscience' of the student body. Whilst the majority report had rejected the right of students to contract out of religious attendance, the minority report felt that the arguments put forward for this rejection lacked real foundation. The signatories of the minority report also felt that there should be greater extension of facilities for day students, and the eventual dispensing with the employment of untrained teachers. They also rejected the arguments put forward to claim that youthful pupil teachers were the most trustworthy source of supply: indeed, the suggestion by the majority that they wanted more 'women of superior social position and general culture' obviously militated against such arguments.

The Education Department accepted, in 1890, the principle of day training colleges attached to universities and university colleges; moreover, day students were permitted to attend residential colleges, although the number was at first strictly limited. A third year of training was also authorized in certain instances, and before very long some students pursuing a three-year course were allowed to read for university degrees. The Education Department was still responsible for the professional examination in the principles and practice of teaching. The attack on the pupil teacher system did not abate, and a special departmental committee, which sat from 1896 to 1898, finally damned it as wasteful in terms of finance and economy, and generally unsatisfactory educationally. Where pupil teacher centres existed they should be liberalized. Many were still working with very limited academic programmes and extremely narrow syllabuses. The committee wanted their work to be extended in the direction of secondary education and not simply for them to exist as a piece of machinery for reproducing the elementary school curricula. In addition they felt that more teachers should be recruited from the secondary schools, and that the age for the commencement of apprenticeship should be raised to fifteen and eventually to sixteen. By the turn of the century the period of apprenticeship had been set as three years; many of the pupil teacher centres had been greatly improved and were nearer to secondary schools in their academic aspirations. And finally university graduates were given the opportunity of becoming qualified teachers after a year of teacher training. This could be pursued during their degree course, concurrently with their academic work, or it could be completed during a year's course after their graduation.

B FROM THE EDUCATION ACT OF 1902 TO 1944

In his introductory speech to the Education Bill of 1902, Mr A. J. Balfour deplored the existing situation concerning the education of teachers. He maintained that 36 per cent of the pupil teachers 'have never got through the examination for the certificate', whilst 55 per cent of the existing teachers had never been to any sort of training college (7). Balfour felt that our society was not achieving the best results when one considered the amount (£18 million) spent each year on elementary education. The passing of the 1902 Education Act changed the system of pupil teacher training. The minimum age for pupil teachers was raised to sixteen in urban districts and fifteen in rural, and the normal period of apprenticeship was reduced to two years. Half their time would be spent in observing teaching in a school, and the other half in the pupil teacher centre receiving instruction. The centre itself might be attached to a higher elementary school or a secondary school, and its aim was to provide a liberal education for the trainee, and not a cramming course in order to obtain a certificate. Schools employing pupil teachers were to be certified as suitable and adequate for their training, and no school would be permitted to have more than four at once.

The system was criticized as a disruption of the education of pupil teachers, and so the Board of Education put forward an alternative in 1907. This proposed that any secondary school pupils who had received instruction in the school for two or more years could, if they wished to become teachers, claim bursaries for a year and then pass on to a training college or serve another year as a student teacher. In 1910 it was decided to raise the minimum number of years in the secondary school to three. Many local education authorities adopted this alternative scheme.

When, in 1904, separate training college regulations were issued many L.E.A.s were encouraged to develop their own colleges, and building grants were awarded for this. Some of these colleges were wholly residential; others accepted a proportion of day students. Before the outbreak of World War Two about thirty colleges had been established by L.E.A.s, and their most proficient students were being encouraged to stay on for a third year. There was a concerted attempt to improve the general standards of training and to broaden the students' curriculum. At the universities, after 1921, it became the normal practice for students who wished to become teachers to spend three years on their degree work, and then a fourth year on professional training. These graduates, if they were successful, were awarded a university diploma, or certificate, in education. Gradually the number of trained teachers in secondary schools increased; and many of them began to enter elementary and higher-grade elementary schools.

In 1925 a departmental committee was set up under the chairmanship of Vincent Burnham to review the arrangements for the training of teachers for public elementary schools. It recommended that university-trained teachers should continue to spend four years over the process, whilst the teacher training college course should last for only two. The report, however, was strongly in favour of greater co-operation between the universities and the training colleges; it considered that one way to achieve this was to establish a special examination for the whole body of the training college students under the auspices of the universities instead of under the control of the Board of Education. The Board should accept a pass at these examinations as qualifying for the Teacher's Certificate. In fact, schemes of this kind were already in operation at Goldsmiths' College, London, and they were being mooted for all the other training colleges in the London area. The departmental committee felt not only that contact with the universities would help to improve the academic standards of the colleges, but also that it would provide a means of affording more autonomy to the latter. The central authority of the Board of Education was imposing too rigid a control upon the curricula and examinations of colleges which were widely scattered over the country; closer links with individual universities would provide a greater freedom and variety for particular colleges and groups of colleges. The committee was convinced that

'the universities, as a whole, are anxious to accept a larger responsibility for the training of teachers in its various aspects, in no sense as a means to power but as part of the normal evolution of their functions' (8).

As a result of this view, the Burnham Committee recommended that joint examining boards should be set up for groups of colleges in association with the universities. Students would be examined by panels of examiners from members of the colleges (internal examiners), and members of the universities (external examiners). This recommendation was accepted by the Board of Education, and in 1930 nine regional joint boards were organized with a central advisory board whose purpose it was to supervise the standards that the regional boards adopted. This was a big step towards the present situation with regard to the organization of teacher training, but the universities as such were not yet directly responsible for the training of teachers, although they were very much involved in their examination and final qualification.

There was, however, a great deal of dissatisfaction expressed by the teaching profession about the resulting situation of the training colleges. Their links with the central authority, the Board of Education, had been loosened; their connections with the universities were, apart from the moderation of their students' work, extremely tenuous. The colleges felt strongly that they were not so much 'autonomous' as out in the cold. In 1938 the Joint Standing Committee of the Training College Association and Council of Principals issued a report entitled *The Training of Teachers*, followed in 1939 by a report published by the National Union of Teachers entitled *The Training of Teachers and Grants for Intending Teachers*. These reports expressed some of the disquiet felt by the profession generally, and stressed a number of principles considered essential for the proper development of teacher training. It was felt that more than two years were needed to improve the quality of the teachers, on whom the whole success of the schools depended. There was some criticism of the formal lectures and their pre-digested material, and a suggestion that the individual student's powers of constructive thinking and his creative ability were the important elements for development. A course which lasted for three years would provide the student with more time for reflection and leisured thought. The reports also looked for a greater equivalence between the qualifications obtained by those teachers who had been to university and those who had been trained in a training college. To achieve this it was argued that every training college should become an integral part of the university in whose area it was situated. All teaching qualifications should be university awards.

Before we consider the proposals of the McNair Report, which went most of the way towards meeting these demands, at least in principle, there is one interesting development of teacher training which was both in the nature of an experiment as well as an urgent utilitarian measure in time of national need. As a result of the Second World War there threatened to be a very serious shortage of teachers, and in consequence, in 1943, the Board of Education issued a scheme for the provision of emergency teachers' training colleges. The object was to provide the additional number of teachers which would be required in the immediate post-war years and the chief sources of recruitment were obviously the Forces and other areas of· National Service. There was, of course, a natural as wel l as undisguised fear on the part of the teaching profession that the recruiting campaign would lead to the introduction of inferior material, which some expressed very forcibly as 'dilutees'. The course itself would be a shortened one, and *ipso facto* inferior, and the standards of teaching would be generally lowered. The full story of this 'experiment' may be read in Pamphlet 17, *Challenge and Response*, published by the Ministry of Education.

Altogether about 126,000 candidates made application, 95,000 of whom were interviewed; 54,000 were accepted for training; 36,660 eventually entered college, and 35,728 finally completed their training successfully. Of these 23,808 were men and 11,920 were women. A pilot course was tried out at Goldsmiths' College in September 1944, involving twenty-eight students, and from the experience gained it was decided that an intensive course of thirteen months, involving forty-eight working weeks, could give a satisfactory basic training, which should then be followed up by two years of part-time study during the teacher's first appointment. By the end of 1947 a total of fifty-five such colleges, with 13,500 places, had been opened; and when the scheme ended in October 1951, thirty-two of these colleges were finally closed, whilst the remainder either became permanent colleges or their buildings were taken over by already existing colleges.

The Ministry pamphlet underlined certain important points in relation to the much maligned 'dilutees'. These students displayed a great keenness, singleness of purpose and capacity for sustained effort; they possessed a larger and deeper experience of life than the normal run of students, and their greater maturity of personality and attitude provided them with a certain motivation which many younger students lacked. There was amongst them a wide range of talents and accomplishments which strongly affected the quality of union activities and creative productions. Most of them possessed a sense of purpose after, in many instances, a period of dispirited desperation; this in itself provided them with a certain vitality and genuine interest in those with whom they worked. There can be no doubt—although these are not the terms used by the pamphlet—that many of these students saw themselves as architects of social reconstruction after an involvement in social devolution. And in this respect they saw the *social* importance of the schools as well as their more narrowly academic purpose. Because of their experience both in the Services and in all walks of life, most had some powers of organization and considerable initiative. There was certainly no lack of leaders in these emergency colleges. Finally, it is frequently suggested that students entering college should be as free as possible from domestic ties and problems, so that they can concentrate upon the difficult job of training for a profession: on balance the Ministry felt that as far as the emergency students were concerned domestic responsibilities had proved a steadying influence upon their college work. Special situations clearly demand special remedies: this was a success story which many have preferred to sweep under the carpet.

C THE MCNAIR REPORT 1944

In 1942 the President of the Board of Education appointed a committee under the chairmanship of Arnold McNair, who was Vice-Chancellor of the University of Liverpool. Their terms of reference were:

'To investigate the present sources of supply and the methods of recruitment and training of teachers and youth leaders and to report what principles should guide the Board in these matters in the future' (9).

There were ten members, including Sir Fred Clarke, who was the Director of the London University Institute of Education, and Sir Frederick Mander, who was General Secretary of the National Union of Teachers. On the issue of area training authorities concerned with the organization of training, the committee was evenly divided and alternative schemes were provided.

The report regretted very much the difference in practice in the appointment of 'elementary' school teachers and 'secondary' school teachers; and the Board of Education was blamed for two such different systems for two branches of the educational service. Moreover, the difficulties would become even more acute as new reforms were implemented, since the failure to make the distinction between 'primary' and 'secondary' education in 1902 had 'resulted in the creation of disparate yet overlapping systems of elementary and secondary schools' (10). In the past the code for elementary schools had set out prescribed qualifications for its teachers: these were (a) certificated, (b) uncertificated, (c) supplementary, (d) teachers of special subjects; on the other hand, the regulations for secondary schools merely required that members of the teaching staff of the school should be suitable in number and qualifications. The report went on to analyze the supply of intending teachers, and suggested ways in which the field of recruitment might be widened. It recommended that H.M. Inspectors should be instructed by the Board of Education to satisfy themselves that the claims, the conditions and the prospects of the teaching profession were adequately presented to the older children in secondary schools.

The report recommended very strongly that married women should be permitted to continue to teach, and that provision should be made for refresher courses for those women who were returning to school after a prolonged period of absence. Considerable concern was shown over the salaries received by teachers, and comparability tables were presented which featured certificated teachers, clerical officers and junior executive officers. It was clear that the teacher was getting a raw deal. The committee felt that salary scales should satisfy four main tests:

(a) a test of personal need: salaries should be related to the cultural levels of the people concerned, i.e. they should make possible the sort of life which teachers of the quality required ought to be enabled to live;

(b) a market test: in order to ensure the supply of teachers of the right quality, their salaries should be comparable with those of other professions and occupations;

(c) a professional test: salary scales should not give rise to injustices or anomalies within the teaching profession;

(d) an educational test: they should not have consequences which might damage the efficiency of the education provided in any particular type of school or area (11).

They recommended that the Board should recognize 'qualified teachers', that is, teachers who normally had completed in a satisfactory way the minimum course of training necessary to provide them with the basic professional qualification. This would mean a three-year course for those students who entered college at about eighteen years of age, or a shorter course for older students whose experience or qualifications justified this. Others, such as graduates who had served in industry, might, subject to the Board's discretion, be recognized as 'qualified' without further training.

In considering the organization of the training of teachers, the committee's chief concern was to end the isolation of the training colleges. The report considered that there was an urgent need to integrate the whole service of teacher training by effecting a much closer connection between the existing training colleges and the universities. This could be brought about by establishing a Central Training Council, and a number of area training organizations. On the methods to be employed the committee was evenly divided, and the following two schemes emerged:

Scheme A: University Schools of Education: Each university was to establish a School of Education consisting in 'an organic federation of approved training institutions working in co-operation with other approved educational institutions'; and these university Schools of Education should be responsible for both the training and the examination of all students who were seeking the status of 'qualified teacher' from the Board of Education.

Scheme B: The Joint Board Scheme: This was a continuation of the existing joint boards in closer relation with the universities represented on them. The University Training Department and the training colleges would preserve their identity and be in direct relation with the Board of Education and the Central Training Council.

In both schemes the Area Training Organization (A.T.O.) was given the responsibility for the approval of curricula and syllabuses for all types of students under training. The A.T.O. would make the final assessment of the students' work by some agreed procedure, and would then recommend to the Board of Education that certain students should be accepted for recognition as qualified teachers. The Board of Education would retain the right to inspect every aspect of the work of the A.T.O.; the system of the pledge was to be abandoned; and only one grade of teacher was to be recognized—'qualified'. In passing, it is interesting to note that it was sixteen years before the recommendation to extend the normal course to three years was adopted.

D THE EDUCATION ACT OF 1944 AND AFTER

The 1944 Act had a number of sections which dealt with the question of teacher training. Section 62 dealt with the duties of the local education authorities in this matter. It stated that the Minister would make such arrangements as he considered expedient for ensuring that sufficient facilities should be available for the training of teachers for service in schools, colleges and other establishments maintained by the local education authorities. For this purpose the Minister might give any L.E.A. such directions as he thought necessary, requiring the authority to establish, maintain and assist the provision of any other facilities specified in the directions. Another Section, 81 (c), dealt with the financial provisions for students undergoing courses in teachers' training colleges, and at the same time it gave power to L.E.A.s to grant scholarships, exhibitions and other allowances to pupils over compulsory school age, including those undergoing training as teachers. Section 89 compelled the Minister to ensure that a committee, such as the Burnham Committee, existed to draw up salary scales for teachers and to submit them to him for approval. Teachers were reclassified by the Act as 'qualified' and 'temporary'; unqualified teachers were to be eliminated from both primary and secondary schools, and all qualified teachers had to be trained.

In 1949 a National Advisory Council on the Training and Supply of Teachers was set up to provide the Minister with factual knowledge, analyzed in an expert manner, and with advice. It was the Council's function to keep the national policy on training and conditions under review. It was also to consider such problems as the qualifications of teachers, their recruitment and distribution, and the way in which the needs of schools and colleges could best be met. In the same year the Standing Conference of Representatives of the Area Training Organizations was established in order to consider matters on which it was thought a common policy was desirable. These included assessment and examination methods, the facilities available for teaching practice, and the curricula involved in the award of certificates and diplomas.

The Ministry published, in 1950, *Circular 213* which stated that five passes at the G.C.E. 'O' Level examination would be the minimum academic qualifications normally required of candidates for admission to teachers' training colleges. The A.T.O.s, however, were given certain powers to admit students who appeared to be suitable in all other respects but who, for one reason or another, had not obtained the prescribed qualifications. The Ministry's publication in 1954, entitled *Education in 1953*, provided an excellent summary of teacher training at that time, the functions of the existing A.T.O.s, the nature of the training colleges, the grants available to students, and the various types of courses and curricula. It also elicited a very vital principle in the training of the teacher:

'The teacher can no longer hope or expect to prepare himself by learning specifically at college all he will need to know for the educating of the children he will teach. The emphasis is therefore on the teacher as an educated person with interests, ideals, and ideas, who has had the chance of reaching in at least one field of study the highest standard of which he is capable and of acquiring in others some experience of the ways in which children learn and grow' (12).

One important section of the Crowther Report of 1959, *15 to 18*, was Part Seven on 'Institutions and Teachers'. It pleaded for an increased supply of teachers because of the additional duties to be placed upon the schools by the raising of the school-leaving age, and because of the need to improve the quality of the work already in progress in the schools. It was felt that a longer average school life would inevitably produce more candidates for teacher training. The Central Advisory Council concluded that there was need for different kinds of teachers, and that good teachers required a range of qualities that were not easily acquired. Staffing ratios were still far from what the council regarded as desirable, and there were too many overlarge classes. There were two sources of supply—the universities and the teachers' training colleges—and the problems of the two sources were largely distinct, despite the fact that there was considerable overlapping between them, both in regard to the candidates they recruited and the variety of posts taken up in the schools.

One of the chief difficulties was the number of places available in training colleges; and the report argued that there was little doubt that the number of qualified entrants could be increased. It recommended that the National Advisory Council on the Training and Supply of Teachers should be requested to advise on the additional number of teachers necessary to raise the school-leaving age. The report accepted that further measures would be required to supply the necessary number of college-trained teachers, and special attention would need to be paid to see that the arrangements for training were flexible enough to meet the needs of more mature men and women attracted to teaching. The chief difficulty in increasing the supply of graduates was the inadequate numbers who showed any desire to enter teaching. If there were to be a vigorous campaign to explain its attractions to a university graduate, it would require also a revision of material rewards to make them comparable with those of other professions open to graduates. The council felt that married women had a specific contribution to make to the profession, and if large numbers of them were to be attracted special attention was needed to the terms and conditions of employment. In general, it argued that teachers were *not* a homogeneous body, and there was therefore a great need for more variety of conditions of employment (13).

E THE THREE-YEAR TRAINING COURSE

A three-year course was first recommended in 1919 by the Committee of Principals in Training Colleges; it was also recommended in the McNair Report of 1944. In 1956 the Fifth Report of the National Advisory Council on the Training and Supply of Teachers accepted the criticism of the McNair Report of the two-year course, and considered that the three reasons provided by that report still held good. They were:

1 The schools require better educated men and women, and this better education cannot be ensured unless students are released from the strain and sense of urgency which at present conditions many of them.
2 Students in general have not, by the time they are twenty, reached a maturity equal to the responsibility of educating children and young people.
3 The committee intended that a longer amount of time should be spent in contact with and teaching in the schools (14).

The Fifth Report of the N.A.C. underlines the educational advantages of a three-year course; it considered that such a course would 'go some way also to reflect the modern concept of a unified profession teaching in all types of schools' (15). It went on to suggest that the Education Act of 1944 had brought together the teachers trained in training colleges and those from the universities in a common task of making secondary education available for all. A formal relationship had now been established between the colleges and the universities by the Area Training Organizations; it now remained to make the courses available to both types of student of more nearly equal length and scope (16). The report considered that more time was required not only for the student's personal education but also for the inculcation of the principles of education. The advice given to the Minister was that the new course should be introduced in 1959 or 1960.

The Ministry felt that the colleges should be prepared for the extension of the course to three years as soon as possible, and a group of H.M. Inspectors, who had experience in the work of training colleges, produced a pamphlet entitled *The Training of Teachers* (17). They warned against doing in the three years what was already being done in two, and emphasized that continued study, reflection and experience were essential ingredients in the maturing process of the teacher. Students, for the most part, entered college as adolescents with adolescent attitudes and sense of responsibility; during the course of training they had to be assisted to become adults. This was a progressive affair involving the acceptance of new responsibilities, the ability to organize themselves and their own work, and the competence to study independently, and conscientiously, for considerable periods of time. They should also be able to discuss all sorts of problems, intellectual, moral, social and so forth, 'with their tutors on as level terms as may be' (18).

The pamphlet warned against using the extra year as an opportunity for piling Pelion upon Ossa; instead of adding courses on more and more topics to the college curriculum, the extra time should be used for tutorials and seminars. The greater maturity of the students in their final year would have a considerable effect upon the life of the college, and would result in a more mature product entering the schools. It was pointed out that few students were mentally able to benefit from a deeper study of everything that came under the umbrella of education, but there were those who could certainly benefit from a specialized study of one aspect of the subject. And in its concluding section the pamphlet emphasized once more that the increased time should be made available for the student's own thinking, reading, discussion and writing—and not for lectures. It felt that the weakest candidates, who were currently a matter of considerable concern to the colleges, and for whom remedial or 'life-saving' courses had to be devised, should no longer be admitted to college (19).

F THE FUTURE PATTERN OF TEACHER TRAINING

The three-year course began in 1960, and in 1962 the N.A.C. produced its Eighth Report, entitled *The Future Pattern of the Education and Training of Teachers*. It looked ahead to at least the 1980s and produced three fundamental long-term objectives:

'(a) the need for a substantial enlarged teaching force and consequently for an enlarged educational base from which to draw additional teachers;

(b) the need for a flexible teaching force adaptable to the inevitable changes in demand and educational developments;

(c) the need for a teaching force of high quality, universally and fully trained for its professional task' (20).

After considering these three long-term objectives the report went on to discuss the types of courses, academic and professional, that such a pattern demanded; and the sort of institutional framework and government within which they could be provided. It accepted that if the teaching force were to be adequately enlarged, there had to be much more recruiting from among those who were being educated in art colleges, colleges of commerce, technical colleges, and colleges of advanced technology. The objective of flexibility and mobility among the teaching force could be achieved by the production of, broadly speaking, two types of teacher—the specialist in his own field, and the general practitioner who had been educated through the study of more than one subject. Flexibility could also be achieved through the provision of academic courses at two distinct levels and by a professional training based not on the school organizational divisions which separated children into infant, junior, secondary and so forth, but rather on 'the continuous development of children through the whole age-range' (21).

With regard to the third long-term objective the council set its sights high. It considered that before very long the majority of students on three-year college courses would possess, on entry to college, academic qualifications comparable with the minimum which university students currently possessed. It was already a fact that one-third of such college students possessed two or more passes at the G.C.E. 'A' Level, whilst another one-third had one such pass. Career prospects in teaching, for young men at least, almost demanded the possession of a degree; and the conclusion of the council, which included some quite outstanding names of people involved in higher education, was a very weighty one indeed. Despite the shortage of teachers existing at the time of the report (1962), the council felt that the ultimate objective at which teacher training should aim was a four-year course of education and training, whether taken concurrently or consecutively. The personal education of *all* teachers ought to culminate in the award of a degree, 'or of an equivalent qualification', and this academic qualification should be distinct from the professional qualification (22).

The year 1963 was a big year in the general consideration of the training of teachers; it was the year of the publication of the Robbins Report, entitled *Higher Education,* of the Newsom Report on *Half Our Future,* of the Year Book of Education entitled *The Education and Training of Teachers,* and of Professor R. K. Kelsall's report on an independent Nuffield survey, entitled *Women and Teaching.* From this spate of reports and literature at this time it was clear that those involved in teacher training of any sort were concerned with quantity, quality and status. The Newsom Report emphasized that the Central Advisory Committee considered that the day of the untrained graduate in the schools was over. It recommended that a training requirement for graduates should be introduced at the earliest practicable moment, and that a date should be announced in advance. The raising of the school-leaving age would make new demands upon teachers, and their training should, therefore, be adapted to meet these requirements. The committee felt that training college students should be equipped to teach a main subject and at least one other to pupils of secondary school age. All potential teachers should be made aware in their training of the social and environmental problems involved in the education of secondary pupils; this meant that their training should include some knowledge of sociology and environmental studies. The report recommended research and experiment, and thought that the recruitment should be strongly encouraged of candidates from other fields to teaching (23).

The Committee on Higher Education was set up in February 1961, and its terms of reference involved a review of the pattern of full-time higher education in Great Britain, and the giving of advice on the principles of its long-term development. The report, which appeared in 1963 as the Robbins Report, had some radical changes in mind. The committee noted that many colleges were still very small, some with less than 250 students, and it recommended that in the future the average size of training colleges should be increased so that, eventually, colleges with less than 750 students should be the exception rather than the rule. Whilst the three-year course which led to a professional qualification should still be available, it was argued that there should be provided, for suitable students, a four-year course leading to a professional qualification and also a degree. It was felt that by the middle of the 1970s provision should be made for 25 per cent of the entrants to training colleges to take the degree course. At the conclusion of the four-year course a B.Ed. of the university of which the college was a constituent member, should be awarded to successful candidates.

The emphasis upon the all-round education of the educator was endorsed by the recommendation that training colleges should be renamed colleges of education; and the status of these colleges would be improved, it was argued, by a closer association with the universities. The committee felt that this could be achieved by adopting something a little more like the Scheme A of the McNair Report rather than the Joint Board Scheme

(Scheme B), which was eventually accepted. This would mean that the colleges in each university's Institute of Education and Department of Education should be formed into a School of Education. Under the auspices of this school suitable college students might be awarded degrees. Transfer to a university from a college of education might be appropriate for some students. Each School of Education would be responsible to the university for the degrees awarded to students in the colleges of education, and it should have its own academic board and board of studies. The committee held that by 1980/1 there should be about 145,000 places for intending teachers in colleges of education (24); in 1968 there were some 107,000 compared with about 97,000 in 1967.

G SOME SPECIAL PROBLEMS

The Third Report of the National Advisory Council, entitled *Graduate Teachers of Maths and Science*, was published in 1953. It pointed out that whilst the small increase in the early 1950s in the number of men and women graduates who were teaching maths and science in maintained schools, had remained steady, the supply was already inadequate in quantity and quality to meet the current demands of schools. Extraordinary methods would be required if the much greater needs of the period 1955–60 were to be met. The current supply was about 570 per year whilst the average annual requirement during that period was estimated at 1,020. This shortage of graduate teachers in maths and science was a national problem; industry, the universities and the schools were all competing for the services of graduates in these fields—and it looked as if industry was winning. But the needs of the schools were fundamental, since any truncation in quantity or quality here would, in the long term, harm industry, science and technology. Whilst the council had certain 'first-aid' recommendations to make of a temporary and patchwork nature, it felt that the main factor in the situation was the *financial* prospects of teachers. This was the one field where the law of supply and demand operated freely in an open market, and it was clear that the teachers' salary scales were not adequate for the struggle. There is still a shortage of fully-qualified teachers of maths and science; finance is one of the reasons, but the greater interest expressed in the arts and the social sciences, and the general disillusionment at the destructive usages of science, are strong contributory factors.

The training of technical teachers was one of the matters considered by the McNair Committee in 1944 when the members pointed out that the technical teacher was frequently teaching students who were earning their living, many of whom were attending classes voluntarily and had some specific personal motivation. It became doubly important that teachers concerned with such students should understand the psychology of the semi-independent, younger adolescents, and of the adult students, and should also know something of their working conditions and social background (25). The Jackson Report was provided by a special committee appointed by the Minister of Education in September 1956; and it was published in May 1957 as *The Supply and Training of Teachers for Technical Colleges*. Its terms of reference were to consider the supply and training of both full-time and part-time teachers for technical colleges, and to make recommendations. The report considered that there were three factors for success in recruitment: firstly, additional sources must be found; secondly, there must be a growth of partnership between colleges and associated fields; and thirdly, teaching must be made more attractive.

The Jackson Report contended that whilst the bulk of the teachers required by the technical colleges must be recruited from industry, university teaching and the schools, more use might be made of late entrants from the Services as well as the Scientific Civil Service. There were also possibilities for the greater employment of married women and of men who had retired, after wide and prolonged experience in the field of industry and elsewhere. The report recommended the appointment to colleges of special lecturers from higher levels of technology, industry and industrial science. It also recommended a number of ways in which the profession of teaching could be made more attractive to candidates from industry—not least of these being, as usual, an improvement in salary scales.

The report also advocated an increased and improved provision for professional training, with more generous financial incentives for those wishing to undertake it. It emphasized the need for students to undertake some work, during a minority of time, in liberal studies; and if this were not possible it was essential to present technical subjects in a liberalized way. It recommended the further development of the one year pre-service courses available (in 1957) at the technical training colleges of Bolton, Huddersfield and Garnett (London); and a fourth college to be established in the Midlands (later at Wolverhampton). Area Training Organizations should be asked to consider the awarding of a technical teacher's certificate to teachers who had satisfactorily completed one year of training. The existing technical training colleges needed new up-to-date buildings, with residential accommodation; each college should have a strong governing body representative of industry, technical colleges, L.E.A.s and universities; and the staff should be sufficient in both number and quality to implement the various courses required. Finally the report emphasized

'the function of a liberal education in enabling a student to see his own particular technology in the wider context of industrial activity and the economic life of the country and of the world; and in bringing him face to face with moral problems, such as those of purpose, and cultural issues, such as those of taste. We accept the importance of these aspects of technical education and we realize that only teachers who are alive to their value, possess wide interests, and have some knowledge of how to draw them into the teaching of a craft or a technology, can successfully give a liberal education to their students' (26).

Briefly, we should mention one final problem in relation to teacher training, namely that of the training of teachers who work in a variety of special schools. In 1954 the National Advisory Council published its Fourth Report, entitled *The Training and Supply of Teachers of Handicapped Children*. When the council, under the chairmanship of Professor R. A. C. Oliver, investigated this problem, no special qualifications were demanded of teachers of the handicapped, except for those concerned with the blind, the deaf, and the partially deaf children. They enquired whether there were any changes that ought to be made in the special qualifications of such teachers, and whether the teachers of any other categories of handicapped children should require special qualifications. The council recommended that teachers of handicapped children in special schools should successfully complete an approved course of training as a teacher, have at least two years' experience in ordinary schools, have sufficient preliminary experience of handicapped children, preferably in a special school, up to a maximum of about one year, and undergo special training and obtain a special qualification as a teacher of handicapped children. It also recommended that a portion of teachers in schools for normal children should have similar experience and training, and that teachers in special schools should be seconded from time to time for short periods to ordinary schools.

H THE PLOWDEN REPORT 1967

The Central Advisory Council published its report, *Children and Their Primary Schools*, in 1967; and in Chapter 25 it discussed in particular 'The Training of Primary School Teachers'. In its introduction to Part Six on 'The Adults in the Schools' the council made the point that, despite all the efforts of the colleges of education, the primary schools were '20,000 teachers short of the number needed on present staffing standards' (27). Out of the 67,000 students taking courses in general colleges of education in January 1967, in England and Wales, only one-third of them, nearly all women, were preparing to work with very young children by taking nursery-infant, infant, or infant-junior courses. About 19,000 students were taking junior-secondary courses, and half of those were men. The average quality of men applicants was lower than that of women, and there was a particularly marked shortage of able men wishing to enter primary courses. The report felt that the newly established B.Ed. degree ought to be a major, if not *the* major, source of supply of graduates for primary schools.

The report criticized the qualifications and experience of some members of college of education staffs; there were too few lecturers with up-to-date knowledge and experience of primary school work, whilst the colleges themselves were too remote from the problems of the schools. It went on to make certain quite specific recommendations, beginning with a suggestion that there should be a full enquiry into the system of training teachers, an enquiry which is long overdue: in an age of violent and sudden change, when many worship change for change's sake, it might prove salutary to enquire not only what we are doing but also why we think we are doing it. The report noted the fact that a choice of career was forced on many students at the age of eighteen, or even earlier, before some of them knew their own minds; and having made their choice they were, as potential teachers, segregated from those preparing for other types of work. The number of courses in which candidates for teaching could be trained side by side with entrants to other social services should be increased; in this way closer collaboration would be encouraged in the field. The council regretted the fact that a quarter of the men and two-fifths of the women who entered college had not reached 'O' Level in G.C.E. mathematics. All primary school teachers needed to be numerate as well as literate, and efforts should be made to improve qualifications in these subjects. There were more men needed in the primary schools, and the attention of the secondary schools should be drawn to this fact.

The recommendations included an extension of the network of day colleges and outposts in which mature students, with adapted hours and modified timetables, had proved their value; an increase in the number of graduates in primary schools, and more facilities for their training; professional training for any graduates who proposed to teach in primary schools; and the encouragement of closer contact and partnership between the colleges and the schools. Arrangements for teaching practice should take note of the needs of the schools, and, whilst final responsibility for the supervision of students should rest with the colleges, the schools could play a bigger part. To aid this general co-operation between schools and colleges there should be more joint appointments to college and school staffs. There were also a number of other recommendations relating to probationary periods, travelling expenses for teachers attending short courses and the availability of the B.Ed. degree course for serving teachers (28).

The report emphasized that the modern demands being made upon teachers were 'frighteningly high'. The teacher was required to have far more knowledge than previously when he used to give set lessons, and could use the same material repeatedly. Today the teacher had to exercise a considerable amount of judgment, to 'think on his feet', and to keep in mind long and short term objectives. The important thing was not to teach a set lesson or to mediate a particular body of knowledge; it was to select an environment for the purpose of encouraging interest, observation, and curiosity. Within this environment, or field of enquiry, and given a willingness on the part of the teacher 'to lead from behind', and to collaborate with the children rather than to stand aloof and direct like a general, the pupils would begin to make exciting discoveries within the framework of their own, living world. But such a programme or curriculum, demanding as it did a considerable flexibility of mind and a capacity in a whole realm of inter-disciplinary enquiry, required a different sort of teacher, and so a different sort of training.

REFERENCES

1 Maclure, J. S., *Educational Documents—England and Wales: 1816–1967* (Methuen, 1968, 2nd ed.), p. 29.
2 Ibid., p. 31.
3 Ibid., pp. 53–4.
4 Ibid., p. 78. Other quotations in this paragraph are also from this page, which is an extract from Chapter 2, pp. 168–9 of the report.
5 Ibid., p. 131.
6 Ibid., p. 132.
7 Ibid., p. 151.
8 Ibid., p. 178.
9 Board of Education, *Teachers and Youth Leaders* (McNair Report) (H.M.S.O., 1944, reprinted 1961), p. 5.
10 Ibid, p. 9.
11 *Vide* ibid., p. 32.
12 Ministry of Education, *Education in 1953* (Cmnd. 9155) (H.M.S.O., 1954), p. 84; pages 31–9 summarized the position of teacher training in 1953.
13 Op. cit., pp. 427–46.
14 Op. cit., p. 65.
15 N.A.C., *Three-Year Training for Teachers* (5th Report) (H.M.S.O., 1956), p. 3.
16 Ibid., p. 4.
17 Ministry of Education, *The Training of Teachers: Suggestions for a Three-Year Training College Course* (H.M.S.O., 1957, reprinted 1962).
18 Ibid., p. 2.
19 Ibid., p. 4.
20 N.A.C., *The Future of the Education and Training of Teachers* (Eighth Report) (H.M.S.O., 1962), p. 1.
21 Ibid., p. 12.
22 Ibid., p. 15.
23 Op. cit., pp. 98–108.
24 Committee on Higher Education, *Higher Education* (Robbins Report) (H.M.S.O., 1963), pp. 107–25.
25 Op. cit., pp. 119–20.
26 Op. cit., p. 36.

27 C.A.C., *Children and Their Primary Schools* (Plowden Report) (H.M.S.O., 1967), p. 312.
28 Ibid., pp. 309–67.

BIBLIOGRAPHY

A.T.C.D.E., *Handbook of Colleges and Departments of Education* (Lund Humphries, 1969).
Bereday, C. Z. F. *et al.*, *The Education and Training of Teachers* (Year Book of Education 1963) (Evans, 1963).
Byrne, H. J., *Primary Teacher Training* (O.U.P., 1960).
Dent, H. C., *To Be A Teacher* (University of London Press, 1947).
Gurney, P., *Education and Training of Teachers* (Longmans, 1963).
Jeffreys, M. V. C., *Revolution in Teacher Training* (Pitman, 1961).
Judges, A. V. (ed.), *The Function of Teaching* (Faber, 1959).
Rich, R. W., *The Teacher in a Planned Society* (University of London Press, 1950).
Rich, R. W., *The Training of Teachers in England and Wales during the Nineteenth Century* (C.U.P., 1933).
Richardson, C. A., *et al.*, *The Education of Teachers in England, France, and the U.S.A.* (Paris, UNESCO, 1953).
Sadler, J. E. and Gillett, A. N., *Training for Teaching* (Allen and Unwin, 1962).
Selincourt, A. de, *The Schoolmaster* (Lehmann, 1951).
Stow, D., *The Training System* (Glasgow, 1840).
Tropp, A., *The School Teachers* (Heinemann, 1957).

REPORTS, ETC.

Board of Education, *Teachers and Youth Leaders* (McNair Report) (H.M.S.O., 1944).
Central Advisory Council, *15 to 18* (Crowther Report) (H.M.S.O., 1959).
Central Advisory Council, *Half Our Future* (Newsom Report) (H.M.S.O., 1963).
Central Advisory Council, *Children and Their Primary Schools* (Plowden Report) (H.M.S.O., 1967).
Committee on Higher Education, *Higher Education* (Robbins Report) (H.M.S.O., 1963).
Ministry of Education, *Circular 213* (H.M.S.O., 1950).
Ministry of Education, *Challenge and Response* (Pamphlet 17) (H.M.S.O., 1950).
Ministry of Education, *Training of Teachers: Suggestions for a Three-Year Training College Course* (Pamphlet 34) (H.M.S.O., 1957).
Ministry of Education, *The Supply and Training of Teachers for Technical Colleges* (Jackson Report) (H.M.S.O., 1957).
Ministry of Education, *The Supply of Teachers in the 1960s* (H.M.S.O., 1958).
Ministry of Education, *Teachers for Further Education* (H.M.S.O., 1961).
National Advisory Council, *Graduate Teachers of Maths and Science* (3rd Report) (H.M.S.O., 1953).
National Advisory Council, *Training and Supply of Teachers of Handicapped Children* (4th Report) (H.M.S.O., 1954).
National Advisory Council, *Three-Year Training for Teachers* (5th Report) (H.M.S.O., 1956).

National Advisory Council, *Scope and Content of the Three-Year Course* (6th Report) (H.M.S.O., 1957).

National Advisory Council, *The Demand and Supply of Teachers, 1960–80* (7th Report) (H.M.S.O., 1962).

National Advisory Council, *The Future Pattern of the Education and Training of Teachers* (8th Report) (H.M.S.O., 1962).

National Advisory Council, *The Demand and Supply of Teachers, 1963–1986* (9th Report) (H.M.S.O., 1965).

Nuffield Survey, *Women and Teaching* (Kelsall Report, 1963).

Chapter 9
Further and Adult Education

A CONTINUATIVE AND ADULT EDUCATION: SOME ORIGINS

Before 1800 there was very little in the way of adult or continuative education, apart from one or two isolated examples of philanthropic teachers with a deep sense of religious or social mission, who took in hand small groups of youths and adults in order to provide them with a minimum of literacy. The development of the revolution in industry and science led many adults to realize their sheer inadequacy in a world of business, in which they often possessed some skill in management and administration but were baulked by an inadequacy in knowledge and learning. Gradually there arose both religious and philanthropic groups anxious and willing to deal as best they might with the situation. Between 1800 and 1850 there was a considerable expansion of such voluntary movements, which sought to help their students at least to read and write, as well as to do some simple arithmetic.

The number of such adult schools and scholars gradually declined after 1850 for several reasons, some of which have been expressed by a contemporary historian, J. W. Hudson, in his *History of Adult Education*. Voluntary associations were finding it increasingly difficult to employ good teachers; and there were, according to Hudson, objections to teaching the poor to read and write. These were being voiced by the upper and middle classes who desired to retain their superiority, at least in the realm of literacy, in a society which was already changing with some rapidity in its economy and social relations. As more and more children were receiving a minimal elementary education, there was less need to develop adult schools simply for the purpose of encouraging people to read and write.

Another development in adult education was also currently taking place which had strong links with industry, commerce and engineering, and which began to capture more strongly the imagination of adults than did the Bible-reading and often socially unsophisticated voluntary groups. The Mechanics' Institutes provided an identity based on work and social betterment within the context of a career; whereas many of the adult schools which had arisen were teaching largely *in vacuo*, albeit with a sense of personal and frequently spiritual mission. Many industrial cities were becoming conscious of the need to supply a form of education for adults which gave them not merely a superficial literacy, but also an introduction to the wealth of new ideas and invention currently developing; whilst a certain unity of purpose was provided by the very nature of the institutions. Dr Birkbeck was responsible, in 1823, for the founding of the Mechanics' Institute in London, and the movement spread until, in 1850, there were over 600 literary and mechanics' institutes in England, with a membership which was calculated as being somewhere between 100,000 and half-a-million. Many of these institutes went on to develop a variety of courses involving scientific knowledge and embryonic technology. They were the forerunners of the 'techs' which afforded so many partially-educated youths in later years some further education, as well as advancement and encouragement in life. The London Mechanics' Institute eventually (in 1907) became Birkbeck College, and in 1920 was recognized as a constituent college of London University for both part-time and evening students. Gradually, and probably because the academic levels were becoming more demanding, the nature of these institutes began to change; and the students, who originally were mechanics, tended increasingly to come from the ranks of the middle classes.

Another type of college was also developing at this time, variously termed people's colleges or working men's colleges. The first of the people's colleges was opened in Sheffield in 1842 by a minister of religion; and it was so successful that it was later re-established as Firth College and ultimately received a Royal Charter as the University of Sheffield. The working men's colleges, as such, have now disappeared, but originally they were founded to provide further education for manual workers over the age of sixteen and able to read, write and do simple arithmetic. Most of these colleges were liberal in outlook and lacked the religious *penchant* of most of the adult schools of the first half of the nineteenth century.

In this general development towards the further acculturation of our adult society, it was only natural that the universities should take a part, and this has taken the form of university extension movements. The first university extension lectures and courses took place in the 1870s, inspired by a Scotsman named James Stuart, who prevailed on a number of university authorities to organize them. They began at various centres in Cambridge, Leicester, Nottingham and Derby, and by 1880 a number of university extension societies had been formed, including one at London and another at Oxford. Money was eventually forthcoming from the Board of Education to help provide fees for lectures and tuition by university dons and other teachers. Some of the centres of the university extension movement became established as university colleges and finally chartered as universities.

During the last three decades of the nineteenth century a large number of adult schools and colleges were established by the Society of Friends, or

Quakers, and other philanthropic groups. The year 1875 saw the creation and development of a number of local unions of such schools and in 1889 a National Council of Adult School Associations was formed to give some cohesion to adult education. This was renamed the National Adult School Union in 1914. Several educational settlements, residential and non-residential, began to appear at the turn of the century; and they have continued to arise in the present century. The first was opened in 1884, and was christened Toynbee Hall; it was established in memory of the work done in the East End of London by Arnold Toynbee. Ruskin College was founded at Oxford in 1899; its aim was to train working-class students to become leaders within their own social class. Out of the dissatisfaction of its students there developed, in 1909, the Labour College which became the National Council of Labour Colleges. Ruskin College itself was reorganized, and it was afterwards governed by trades' unions and working-class societies. Other settlements were established at Woodbrooke (1903), Swarthmore, Leeds (1909), St Mary's, York (1909), the Homestead, Wakefield (1913), Hillcroft College, Surbiton (1920), Catholic Workers' College, Oxford (1921), and Coleg Harlech, Wales (1927). L.E.A.s have in recent years taken a keen interest in these forms of adult education, partly because the student body is already there and no further motivation is required to get attendance, and partly because the creation of new centres with fresh buildings and tutorial staff is always a costly business. It is a much more viable and economic proposition in education to develop something already there, and working healthily, rather than create something nebulously new.

In 1903 the Association to Promote the Higher Education of Working Men was formed, and various branches of the association were developed throughout the country. Its somewhat ungainly name was changed to the Workers' Educational Association in 1905. It was, in fact, a sort of amalgam of trade union tenacity and intent to get on equal terms educationally with the best brains in society, the co-operative movement's desire to improve socially but also cohesively, and the university extension movement's mission to provide culture for the educationally deprived. S. J. Curtis has referred to it as 'certainly the most important agency for adult education in the last half-century' (1). Tutorial classes for the W.E.A. have been supported by nearly all the universities in our society, including Oxford and Cambridge. One of the great forces behind the movement was R. H. Tawney, who was later to become a member of the Consultative Committee of the Board of Education. Since 1924 the central authority for education has been prepared to make grants for adult education of a voluntary nature, with the proviso that the approach to educational studies is non-political and unsectarian. Today, the D.E.S. may be persuaded to make not only direct grants to national associations for adult education, but also special grants for particular purposes, as for example in 1967:

'The Department also made a special grant of £1,000 to the National Institute of Adult Education towards the costs incurred in eradicating dry rot at the Institute's premises' (2).

Although the large percentage of the W.E.A. members have usually been manual workers, a fair cross-section of the community is represented by the students attending the courses of the association. The W.E.A. has always insisted upon as wide and liberal an educational programme as possible, but it has left any instruction in the realm of technology to technical colleges and the various types of colleges of technology. Courses vary in nature and in length; they may be residential or non-residential; they may last for a term or for three years; they may be full-time or part-time. Whilst the D.E.S., L.E.A.s, and the extra-mural departments of the various universities are all interested in adult education and support it, the W.E.A. remains a voluntary organization. Its grant from the D.E.S. in 1967 was £3,230, and in 1968 it had risen to £3,550.

B THE MYTH OF COUNTY COLLEGES: DAY RELEASE

When he introduced the Education Bill on August 10, 1917, the President of the Board of Education, Mr H. A. L. Fisher, made as one of his six specific proposals the statement that

'we desire to establish part-time day continuation schools which every young person in the country shall be compelled to attend unless he or she is undergoing some suitable form of alternative instruction' (3).

He detailed this proposal by stating that 'young persons' not undergoing full-time instruction should be freed from their work for the equivalent of three half-days a week during forty weeks. Two half-days were to be spent in school, while one half-day would be a holiday for them. When the Act was passed in 1918 provision was made for 'young persons' between the ages of fourteen and sixteen to attend day continuation schools for 320 hours in the year. This might be reduced to 280 hours during the preliminary period of seven years if the L.E.A. wished. After that preliminary period, however, the L.E.A. would have to enforce the time of 320 hours, and 'young persons' would now be boys and girls between the ages of fourteen and eighteen years. In the event the only authority which established such a college was Rugby; and Rugby has operated a statutory scheme of day release ever since, whilst other authorities have worked such release only on a voluntary basis.

In 1944 the Butler Education Act, Section 43 (1), stated:

'not later than three years after the date of the commencement of this Act, it shall be the duty of every local education authority to establish and maintain county colleges, that is to say, centres approved by the Minister for providing for young persons who are not in full-time attendance at any school or other educational institution such further education including physical practical and vocational training, as will enable them to develop their various aptitudes and capacities and will prepare them for the responsibilities of citizenship' (4).

There are nine sub-sections relating to county colleges and to the various conditions concerning the duties of L.E.A.s and compulsory attendance up to the age of eighteen. Under the County Colleges Order, 1947, it became the duty of every L.E.A. to establish and maintain county colleges —some day; but no date was specified. The Crowther Report, in 1959, stated that the Minister should reaffirm his intention to implement at the earliest possible date the provision of compulsory part-time education for all young people of sixteen and seventeen who were not in full-time education; and it stated that it was the widespread lack of belief in this intention which had almost stopped the growth of all part-time release other than that which was clearly essential for technical reasons. The Central Advisory Council was particularly concerned over the loss of contact with the least skilled and the least able members of the community as soon as they left school, and with their resultant loss of morale. The council finally recommended a phased introduction of county colleges by three stages; the progressive sequence of development would reach its final stage of compulsory part-time day education some time in the 1970s (5).

Even in 1960, the Central Office of Information could publish its third edition of the pamphlet, *Education in Britain*, with the sanguine statement that

'It is intended that county colleges shall take their place within the environment of local colleges of further education and that these local colleges may also provide full-time vocational courses for young people under eighteen, and part-time day and evening courses and activities of all kinds, both vocational and general' (6).

In November 1962, however, the Minister of Education appointed a committee to investigate the whole question of release from employment of young persons under the age of eighteen to attend both technical and other courses of further education. The Chairman nominated by the

Minister was Mr C. Henniker-Heaton, who was chairman of the Industrial Education and Training Committee of the British Employers Confederation. The committee presented its report, entitled *Day Release*, in 1964. It began by accepting that the concept of county colleges as a sector separate from the rest of further education had now been modified. 'The balance of educational opinion' at the time probably took the view that the local colleges of further education—whatever they were called—provided a natural focus for the development of county college work (7).

Before the Second World War there were about 40,000 young people who were being granted day release by their employers, presumably almost entirely on a voluntary basis. By 1960 the number had grown to something over 200,000, including 42,000 girls. Whilst the absolute numbers of both girls and boys receiving release increased in 1961–2 and 1962–3, the actual percentages decreased. The numbers rose from 200,000 to 209,000 boys, and from 50,600 to 52,000 girls; but the percentages fell from 18·64 to 18·3 (boys), and from 4·93 to 4·77 (girls). Whilst, however, there was a percentage fall in the fifteen to seventeen age group receiving day release, there was a sharp percentage increase in the eighteen to twenty age group. The Henniker-Heaton Report recommended that for the year 1969–70 a target should be set for obtaining day release from employment, for the purpose of further education, of at least an additional 250,000 boys and girls, thus doubling the numbers existing in 1962–3. The essential provision of additional accommodation for these students should be authorized by the Ministry of Education, and made by the local education authorities. As the need developed so additional teachers should be recruited. At first, the report argued, there should be a concentration of effort upon young people who were currently being trained in occupations which required skills and knowledge with which courses of further education were associated. Day release of such young people would generally be accepted as worthwhile by both employers and employees. The report also emphasized the importance of day release for general education: the needs of *all* young people must be met. There were many boys and girls who received little or no education or training through their employment, and they did not require specially vocational education; it was hoped, therefore, that there would be a systematic development and evaluation of such non-vocational courses (8).

It is salutary to reflect, after reading the recommendations of the Henniker-Heaton Report of 1964, that it was in 1943 that the White Paper on *Educational Reconstruction* had clearly emphasized that when the period of full-time compulsory education had come to an end the young person would 'continue under educational influences up to eighteen years of age', either as a full-time pupil at a secondary school, or by 'part-time day attendance at a young people's college' (9); whilst the Crowther Report, sixteen years later in 1959, could say that

'There is no escaping from the fact that the ladder of further education is at present too steep for most of those who are attempting to climb it. . . . If the ladder cannot be made less steep, the only alternative is to provide more help for the climbers' (10).

And for this the Crowther Report had one prescription—namely, more time. It is a familiar cry in education, at all levels. It may seem odd that something which should be supremely enjoyable should be conducted with such unseemly haste, with incredible stress, and with an almost soul-destroying sense of urgency. Further education is not alone in this. It was once thought by many students that the removal of the awful burden of the final day of judgment epitomized in 'the exam' would release them for the pleasurable pastime of becoming educated. The alternative of 'continuous assessment' has provided them instead with a whole series of dead-lines to be kept, and the day of judgment turns out to be *every* day instead of 'the exam' at the end. Part of the prescription may certainly be more time; but unfortunately there are always the voracious pedants and academics who see more time simply as an opportunity for more content in the syllabuses. Students need more time: but they also need more time just to sit and think.

C OTHER DEVELOPMENTS IN FURTHER EDUCATION

In 1928 the first village college was built at Sawston in Cambridgeshire mainly through the energy and imagination of Mr Henry Morris, the Education Secretary of the Cambridgeshire County Council. It was essentially the realization of a vision of a planned community. The village college aimed at bringing the whole life of the village, or of a group of villages, into one focal point. Here the children would attend day school; the adults would listen to evening lectures; youths would participate in dramatic productions, sports and dances; young women would learn the arts of cookery and housewifery; the old would rest in the reading rooms with books borrowed from the lending library; and all would pursue their interests, hobbies and a variety of leisure activities together. The village college at Sawston was an undoubted success—it brought old and young together in a communal life of learning and purposeful activity. Three more colleges were opened in Cambridgeshire before the Second World War curtailed this development as it did so many other valuable experiments, but by 1960 there were nine such colleges altogether in Cambridgeshire, Leicestershire and the Soke of Peterborough.

The Physical Training and Recreation Act of 1937 empowered the

Board of Education to make capital grants and local authorities to provide community centres and maintain them. These had developed after the First World War as another serious attempt to establish community, particularly in newly-built housing estates. So that these community centres might be developed more efficiently, the New Estates Community Committee had been formed. In 1945 the recently established Ministry of Education stated in *Community Centres* that it had taken over the general responsibility, with the L.E.A.s, for their development. All villages with a population of over 400 should have a village hall and some sort of community organization and development. In 1968 the number of grants provided under the 1937 Physical Training and Recreation Act increased from £452,650 (the 1967 figure) to £569,078. These capital grants were spent on village halls and community centres, which provide not merely possibilities of recreation but also further education.

Other developments in adult and further education included the establishment of Women's Institutes and Townswomen's Guilds, the Y.M.C.A. and the Y.W.C.A., church associations and many other voluntary bodies. The Women's Institutes originated in this country during the First World War, as a transplant from Canada; and their activities over the years have included educational and cultural programmes. There is a National Federation of Women's Institutes which established its own college in 1948 at Abingdon in Berkshire. The Y.M.C.A. had its beginnings in a small Bible class for young men at Ludgate Hill in 1844. From this humble origin many groups developed wherever there were youths living in lodgings; and the purpose of the association was to provide them with social and educational facilities, as well as hostel accommodation. The Y.W.C.A. provides similar amenities for women. Church associations include the Mothers' Union, the Catholic Social Guild, the Church of England Men's Society, and Free Church Men's Fellowships, all of which are interested in providing opportunities for cultural activities. During the Second World War, the Council for the Encouragement of the Music and Arts (C.E.M.A.) was instituted, and as the Arts Council it received a Royal Charter in 1946, deriving its income from the Treasury. The aim of the Arts Council is to bring the fine arts to the people through the Government subsidy, and to educate our society at large in an appreciation and understanding of the arts.

D CORRESPONDENCE EDUCATION

One of the most controversial elements in further education has been that of tuition by correspondence. Writing in *New Society*, on September 22, 1966, Anne Corbett said that

'Theirs is a slow and private progress towards respectability, but the correspondence colleges have nearly made it. The Secretary of State recently gave conditional approval to an accreditation scheme drawn up by the Association of British Correspondence Colleges, representing sixteen schools, and the Cleaver-Hume Company, with five schools—they are the two major groups of commercial colleges and claim 80 per cent of the market. It's a scheme the colleges themselves would organize and finance' (11).

Correspondence colleges began during the last decades of the nineteenth century, not long after the passing of the 1870 Elementary Education Act. The first outstanding foundation was the University Correspondence College which Dr William Briggs created in 1887, and which was ultimately incorporated in the National Extension College, Cambridge, in 1964. Wolsey Hall, Oxford, was founded by Joseph William Knipe in 1894 as the almost inevitable outcome of his own personal experience. As a trainee teacher at Cirencester Grammar School, Knipe prepared himself in a systematic way for the Certificated Teachers' Examination. He afterwards thought that his orderly notes might be of some use to other students, so he advertised in the *Schoolmaster*, and as a result was able to enrol a number of students. Having seen them all through their examination he proceeded to enrol another thirty students; and gradually there developed an organization which prepares students all over the world for degrees, diplomas, and certificates, or in single subjects for personal improvement and pleasure. In 1907 the college which Knipe founded moved to Oxford, to a house in St Aldates called Wolsey Hall, which became the name of the Diploma Correspondence College; in 1930 it moved again to Banbury Road, its present address.

Today there are probably something like eighty or ninety correspondence colleges of one sort or another, claiming nearly half a million students. International Correspondence Schools, for example, provides courses which range from sailing and flower arrangement to electronics and computer programming.

During the Second World War several correspondence colleges, including Wolsey Hall and the Metropolitan College at St Albans, were appointed to provide correspondence tuition to members of the Forces by arrangement with the Institute of Army Education. This service still continues and many thousands of servicemen have benefited by being able to take not only G.C.E. subjects at 'O' and 'A' levels, but also external degrees of London University by correspondence.

The advent of the G.C.E. in 1951 very greatly increased the demand for correspondence education, because of the freedom, granted for the first time, to take subjects singly or in any combination. This is an age and society of examinations and demonstrable paper qualifications, and these private schools and colleges which provide tuition by correspondence enable many children and adults to study at home, and at their own pace, subjects which they might not otherwise be able to tackle.

In more recent years some considerable concern has been shown regarding the educational standards of institutions outside the State system. The result was the foundation in 1955 of the Association of British Correspondence Colleges (A.B.C.C.), which was later incorporated in 1962 as a non-profit-making body. The membership of the A.B.C.C. today numbers about twenty colleges, some large, some small, but providing between them tuition in almost every conceivable subject. The object of the association is to maintain a code of conduct for the day-to-day operation of the member colleges, whilst membership is restricted to correspondence colleges which have, for a minimum of five years, provided a reliable tutorial service. The aims as detailed by the association are:

'(a) To maintain and enhance the prestige of British institutions that provide postal tuition for university, professional, and other examinations, or in vocational, technical and cultural subjects.

(b) To be a centre of information and advice on matters pertaining to postal tuition.

(c) To co-operate with the Department of Education and Science, local education authorities, universities, professional societies, institutions and other bodies and persons interested in further education.

(d) To safeguard the interests of postal students.

(e) To engage in such other activities as may further the best interests of postal tuition' (12).

In 1966 the Gurr Report made a number of recommendations for an Accreditation Council to be set up which would have the chairman and half the members appointed by the Secretary of State for Education and Science, and the remaining members nominated in the first instance by the sponsoring correspondence colleges but ultimately elected by accredited colleges (13). In August 1968, the Secretary of State announced that he was ready to nominate the chairman and five other independent members of the proposed Accreditation Council, as an independent body incorporated under the Companies Acts as a non-profit making company, and limited by guarantee. Its main function is to accredit colleges which conform to the standards it sets, to raise generally the standards of postal tuition, and to protect the interests of the colleges and students alike. The company was incorporated in September 1968.

In discussing the new Open University we have mentioned the fact that it will inevitably use the method of correspondence tuition as well as specially programmed textbooks and TV lectures. The National Extension

College, Cambridge (N.E.C.), has already linked a number of its courses with television study programmes, and will certainly be co-operating very closely with the work of the Open University. In his introduction to the *Guide to Courses* (1968–69) of the N.E.C., the Director, Brian Jackson, has said that

'An establishment was needed, run by qualified educationalists who were prepared to examine the problems of distance teaching and establish real educational standards, with no commercial motivation' (14).

It would be quite wrong to assume that a commercial motivation necessarily results in bad educational standards; and even university dons are not altogether disinterested in their promotion of learning. But it is also true, to use the phrase of Anne Corbett, that there has been a 'shady trader image' attached to the correspondence college, and it is therefore time that there was a more exacting educational control over what is rapidly becoming one of the most important sectors of further and higher education (15). Even a casual glance at the literature and prospectuses of the N.E.C. will reveal a list of names of some of the most outstanding figures in the field of education and academic learning. One can be certain that these names were not given lightly in such a field as home study. Thus with the support of the Association of British Correspondence Colleges Ltd, the Cleaver-Hume Group, the Accreditation Council, the National Association of Local Government Officers' (N.A.L.G.O.) Correspondence Institute, and the National Extension College, we can hopefully look forward to a vastly improved standard of correspondence and home courses.

The TV-correspondence courses appeal to a large number of students whose needs are not fully met in any other way, or whose peculiar situation may prevent those needs being fulfilled in any other way. Some students find it quite impossible to attend regular tutorials or classes outside their own home; some are interested in learning, but wish to proceed at their own steady (or even very fast) pace; some have never had the opportunity to succeed in any other way and may find the group learning situation embarrassing or unsatisfactory; some are not interested in the more cultural or educational content of a course—they merely want to pass an examination, and have a very strong 'commercial motivation'; and some students want a specially-devised course for a particular interest or situation, whilst some correspondence colleges are willing to prepare such an individual and personal course.

Unlike university, college or school courses, a correspondence course can be started by a student at any time. Much motivation for further education is lost by long waiting periods—because there are too many applicants, or because it doesn't happen to be September. Terms and academic years are irrelevant—the only fixture for most students is the date of the examination. There is also something reasonably objective about a course of tuition designed through a correspondence college: the courses, though written by individual tutors, are open to correction and revision by others, and can be updated at any time. And the tuition provided is individual: tutors do much more than mark papers, they frequently carry on a lengthy correspondence with students. Face-to-face relationships are, admittedly, much more difficult, particularly when students may come from any one of eighty countries. But wherever the zoning of students is possible personal contact with tutors has become increasingly a reality.

But correspondence study does make certain peculiar and heavy demands upon the student. The interesting 'red herring' of the tutorial group, which has so often proved to be the most educationally beneficial element in a particular class discussion, is not possible in home study: nor is it, of course, necessarily desirable where the supremely important thing is to gain a qualification rather than to be 'educated'. This is more a reflection of the sort of society in which we live than an intrinsic weakness of the home study system.

In large countries, such as Australia, U.S.S.R., and America, where the population is often scattered and staff difficult to obtain, systems of extension-correspondence and supervised home study are being fully used. Fully supervised correspondence study is also used in Sweden on a fairly wide scale, in which local education authorities collaborate with local 'course leaders'. The Swedes claim that the method has been highly successful.

Success, however, cannot be guaranteed with correspondence teaching any more than with university teaching, or any form of further or higher education. Reading and writing are personal skills demanding concentration, assimilation, and also ease and rapidity if a wide field of study is to be covered. Many students undoubtedly begin courses which are beyond their competence because of their basic lack of these skills. They frequently blame the correspondence schools for not 'getting them through'; more realistically they ought, perhaps, to blame them for ever allowing them to start. But without much more initial personal contact it is virtually impossible to say whether any particular applicant is likely to succeed, provided he has the foundation qualifications for any specified course, unless he is clearly illiterate as judged from his application form. But, as we have already emphasized, there are drop-outs in all areas of further education and at all levels.

Finally, correspondence courses have a very large part to play in retraining. After a number of years in any profession we all get rusty and need some form of updating and sometimes complete retraining. Six years of active service during war can play havoc with mental development; but so can sixteen years of constantly teaching the same basic material, to the exclusion of newer and more fascinating developments in other areas of thought. The motivation with teachers to be 'knowledgeable' is strong; and, where sabbatical leave or secondment may be impossible, one very real solution is to pursue a correspondence course simply to update, or to obtain further and more specialist qualifications.

REFERENCES

1 Curtis, S. J. and Boultwood, M. E. A., *An Introductory History of English Education Since 1800* (University Tutorial Press, 1964, 3rd ed), p. 325.
2 D.E.S., *Education and Science in 1967* (H.M.S.O.), p. 72, para. 112.
3 Maclure, J. S., *Educational Documents—England and Wales: 1816–1967* (Methuen, 1968, 2nd ed.), p. 174.
4 *Education Act, 1944* (7 and 8 Geo. 6, Ch. 31), pp. 34–5, Section 43 (1).
5 *Vide 15 to 18* (Crowther Report) (H.M.S.O., 1959), pp. 195–6.
6 C.O.I., *Education in Britain* (H.M.S.O., 1960, 3rd ed.), p. 45.
7 D.E.S., *Day Release* (H.M.S.O., 1964), p. 11.
8 Ibid., pages 9 and 10 provide a summary of the committee's recommendations.
9 Maclure, J. S., op. cit., p. 207.
10 Op. cit., p. 367.
11 *Vide New Society*, September 22, 1966, p. 451, col. 1.
12 *Handbook of the Association of British Correspondence Colleges*, 1968, p. 5.
13 *Report of the Committee on Accreditation of Correspondence Colleges* (Gurr Report, 1966). Obtainable from the Association of British Correspondence Colleges Ltd, 4–7 Chiswell St, London, E.C.1., and the Cleaver-Hume Group, Aldermaston Court, Aldermaston, Berks.
14 National Extension College, Cambridge, *Guide to Courses 1968–69*, N.E.C., Shaftesbury Rd, Cambridge. *Vide* p. 5.
15 *Vide 11 supra*, p. 451, col. 1.

BIBLIOGRAPHY

Currie Martin, G., *The Adult School Movement* (National Adult School University, 1924).
Davies, L. J., *The Working Men's College* (Macmillan, 1904).
Delisle Burns, C., *A Short History of Birkbeck College* (University of London Press, 1924).
Dent, H. C., *Part-time Education in Great Britain* (Turnstile Press, 1949).
Harrison, J. F. C., *Learning and Living: 1790–1960—English Adult Education* (Routledge, 1961).
Hawkins, T. H. *et al.*, *Adult Education: The Record of the British Army* (Macmillan, 1947).
Hudson, J. W., *History of Adult Education* (Longmans, 1851).
Kitchen, P. I., *From Learning to Earning* (Faber, 1944).
Livingstone, R., *The Future in Education* (C.U.P., 1942).
Mansbridge, A., *An Adventure in Working-Class Education* (Longmans, 1920).
Mansbridge, A., *University Tutorial Classes* (Longmans, 1913).

Parry, R. St. J. (ed.), *Cambridge Essays on Adult Education* (C.U.P., 1920).

Peers, R., *Adult Education in Practice* (Macmillan, 1934).

Pole, T., *A History of the Origin and Progress of Adult Schools* (Bristol, 1814).

Price, T. W., *The Story of the W.E.A., 1903–24* (Labour Publishing Co., 1924).

Raybould, S. G., *W.E.A., The Next Phase* (Workers' Educational Association, 1949).

Raybould, S. G., *The English Universities and Adult Education* (Workers' Educational Association, 1951).

Raybould, S. G., *Trends in English Adult Education* (Heinemann, 1959).

Sadler, M. E., *Continuation Schools in England and Elsewhere* (Manchester University Press, 1907).

Scott, R., *The Story of the Women's Institutes* (Village Press, Idbury, Oxon., 1925).

Stocks, M., *The W.E.A.—The First Fifty Years (1903–1953)* (Allen and Unwin, 1953).

Wedemeyer, C. A. and Childs, G. B., *New Perspectives in University Correspondence Study* (Chicago: Centre for the Study of Liberal Education for Adults, 1961).

White, A. C. T., *The Story of Army Education, 1643–1963* (Harrap, 1963).

Wilson, N. Scarlyn, *Education in the Forces—The Civilian Contribution, 1938–1946* (Evans, 1948).

Yeaxlee, B. A., *Spiritual Values in Adult Education*, 2 vols. (O.U.P., 1925).

REPORTS, ETC.

Ministry of Reconstruction, *Final Report of the Adult Education Committee* (H.M.S.O., 1919).

The Development of Adult Education in Rural Areas (H.M.S.O., 1922).

Adult Education in Yorkshire (H.M.S.O., 1927).

Pioneer Work and other Developments in Adult Education (H.M.S.O., 1927).

Ministry of Education, *Community Centres* (H.M.S.O., 1945).

Ministry of Education, *Youth's Opportunity* (Pamphlet 3) (H.M.S.O., 1946).

Ministry of Education, *Further Education* (Pamphlet 8) (H.M.S.O., 1947).

Ministry of Education, *Evening Institutes* (Pamphlet 28) (H.M.S.O., 1956).

Ministry of Education, *15 to 18* (Crowther Report) (H.M.S.O., 1959).

Committee on Higher Education, *Higher Education* (Robbins Report) (H.M.S.O., 1963).

D.E.S., *Day Release* (H.M.S.O., 1964).

Chapter 10

The Youth Services

Before the First World War the existing youth services were entirely
voluntary bodies and self-supporting. The war years inevitably saw an
increase in juvenile crime and a Government that was alarmed at the
possible consequences. It is always wise to use and extend available
resources rather than create entirely new ones, provided they are successfully fulfilling their purpose; and this is precisely what the Government did
here. It set up, in 1916, the Juvenile Organizations Committee as a standing
committee for the purpose of organizing the extension of the existing
voluntary bodies that helped to provide recreation and various forms of
community for young people. The 1918 Fisher Education Act empowered
L.E.A.s to assist in these developments by providing, or assisting the
maintenance of, centres for physical training, equipment, playing-fields,
school swimming baths, and other facilities for social and physical training.

It was not long before the Juvenile Organizations Committee was
transferred to the Board of Education, which from 1920 became responsible for the encouragement and expansion of youthful recreations.
This expansion went on up to the early thirties when economic pressures
and depression put a stop to further development, and by 1939 most of the
local juvenile organizations had ceased to exist. The Board's *Circular
1486/39* was published in 1939 informing all the L.E.A.s that the Board
would be directly responsible for the youth welfare services, and at the
same time would work in close association with both the L.E.A.s and the
still existing voluntary organizations. The term 'juvenile' had developed
certain pejorative connotations, linked as it was with such words as
'delinquency' and 'behaviour', used in a deprecatory sense. So the Board
replaced it by 'youth', and the 'Juvenile Organizations Committee' now
became 'Youth Organizations Committee'. The work of those committees
had been taken over, since their inception, by the National Fitness Council,
which was a body mainly concerned with allocating grants in order to
improve the amenities available for physical training and recreation. When
it was dissolved in September 1939 the Board established a National Youth
Committee.

The process of name-changing is more than an arbitrary one; in this
context 'fitness', at first blush, relates simply to physical development and

health, whereas 'youth' refers to the sum total of youthful activities—educational, social, physical and recreational. The L.E.A.s were urged to become fully involved in the project by setting up local youth committees, through which an organized policy might be developed in their areas. These committees had advisory powers only, however; and it was their function to advise the L.E.A.s on three issues:

(a) The provision of staff, clerical assistance and office accommodation;
(b) The provision of grants for the upkeep and renewal of buildings, and the purchase and maintenance of equipment;
(c) The provision of instructors for recreational activities, physical activities and crafts.

All three categories would rank for grants from the Board of Education of up to fifty per cent.

This, briefly, is how the present-day youth service originated and developed. L.E.A.s responded to the obvious need and demand for youth centres and organizations, and great enthusiasm was shown in the setting up of youth committees, which were essentially a part of the administrative service of the local authorities. In March 1940 the Board published *Circular 1503/40*, by which it reiterated its willingness to provide grants of up to 50 per cent of the costs incurred by the youth services. *Circular 1516/40*, which followed in June, recognized the youth service as a part of further education itself. Whilst it was not compulsory, its function was being clarified. Existing voluntary bodies could not make provision for all youths in all areas, and they needed support both in the realm of finance and through the supplementation of their efforts and resources by the creation of state organizations. In December 1941, *Circular 1577/41* was published in order to encourage youths liable for registration by the Ministry of Labour and for National Service to become members of youth organizations.

B THE YOUTH ADVISORY COUNCIL: THE 1944 EDUCATION ACT
The National Youth Committee was dissolved by the Board of Education in 1942, after it had been working for nearly three years. In its place a body was created to include representatives of people working in all areas of the youth service; this was the Youth Advisory Council which was formed of members of youth committees, administrators and younger people involved in some of the voluntary organizations as well as pre-National Service organizations. The main functions of this council were to consider fully any problems submitted to them by the Board of Education, and then to advise on particular courses of action. It was also to act as a channel so that the Board could be kept informed about the youth service and its

problems, and to train individuals to provide new ideas for the development and general improvement of the service, and to place its suggestions before the Board.

The Butler Education Act of 1944, by the all-embracing terminology of Section 7, made it quite clear that there was a duty for all L.E.A.s to develop, as a part of the third stage, the service of youth:

'The statutory system of public education shall be organised in three progressive stages to be known as primary education, secondary education, and further education; and it shall be the duty of the local education authority for every area, so far as their powers extend, to contribute towards the spiritual, moral, and physical development of the community by securing that efficient education throughout those stages shall be available to meet the needs of the population of their area' (1).

In the sections of the Act relating specifically to further education (sections 41 to 47), the duty was firmly laid upon every L.E.A. to secure adequate facilities for further education, including leisure-time occupation, organized cultural training and recreative activities for any one 'able and willing to profit by the facilities provided for that purpose' (2). Section 53 went on to list the sort of facilities which L.E.A.s, with the approval of the Minister, might establish, maintain and manage, such as camps, holiday classes, playing-fields, play centres, playgrounds, gymnasia and swimming baths. Thus the Act gave statutory recognition to the youth service under the aegis of further education schemes initiated and evolved by L.E.A.s.

In 1945 the Youth Advisory Council issued a report *The Purpose and Content of the Youth Service*. This was a general review from 1943 to 1945, when, as a result of its recognition as a part of the educational services of the L.E.A.s, it made rapid progress. The report claimed that the aim and purpose of the youth service was both preventive and palliative; it helped young people to learn the elements of community living, and to apply that knowledge to both active service and communal effort. The organizations provided had a specific appeal, as for example, the scouts, the guides, church fellowships, and so forth. These services were largely of a voluntary nature though they received support and finances through the local authorities. But the service also provided organizations with a more general appeal, without attachment to any particular religious or social group, and thereby catered for people who were not sure of what they wanted.

Until April 1, 1959, L.E.A.s received grants for the youth service from the Ministry in exactly the same way as for any other part of the educational system. Since then the responsibility for particular areas of expenditure has been largely handed over to the L.E.A.s by the system of block grants now paid to them by the Ministry. The latter still pays direct grants to recognized national voluntary youth organizations for assistance with headquarters administration. Thus, in 1968, the grants of the Department of Education and Science to national voluntary youth organizations towards their headquarters and training expenses increased to £346,725 from £330,050 the previous year. In all, forty-eight organizations received these grants. The Department also made a special grant to the University of Leeds for a research project involving an examination of the youth service provision made by L.E.A.s and voluntary organizations in York-shire. Another grant was made to the National Association of Youth Clubs for the appointment of a national field officer to work with immigrants. The Duke of Edinburgh's Award scheme received £13,750, and the Scout Association the sum of £15,800. Grants were also made under the Social and Physical Training Grant Regulations of 1939, totalling £1,067,897, in order to assist 390 local capital projects. It will be seen that today the Department takes a very live and practical interest in the youth service.

Local education authorities all have youth committees which have been formally constituted. These are representative of the authority, of minor local authorities within the area, of the voluntary youth organizations, youth leaders, teachers, religious organizations, youth employment ser-vices, and of the local, industrial and civic life. Today most authorities employ a youth officer, who may in large areas have assistant officers; whilst the youth committee itself is one of the main sub-committees of the education committee.

What, with all its expenditure, regarded by some as far too small and insignificant to achieve any solid or lasting success, has the youth service attained? Professor W. O. Lester Smith, writing in 1957, said:

'Unfortunately during the post-war years the youth service lost much of the force and drive that characterized it during its initial period. For this the public conscience must take some of the blame' (3).

Professor Lester Smith went on to develop this theme in his book where he suggests, in a chapter on 'Education and Industry', that the emphasis in our Welfare State has been on material necessities rather than upon the cultural and social needs of individuals, 'on the standard of living rather than on the quality of life' (4).

C THE MCNAIR REPORT 1944

The McNair Report was not concerned with the supply, recruitment and training of teachers only, since the Board of Education brief included also youth leaders. In its analysis of the staffing situation in 1944 the report argued that there was a need for full-time workers, such as organizers, wardens, heads of large centres and institutions who would, almost invariably, be paid workers. There was also a need for part-time workers, who could be paid or unpaid. Voluntary workers were regarded as vital because they brought to their work a variety of experience of contemporary life which most full-time workers could not bring in the same measure. There was about voluntary work a certain degree of altruistic interest, and an example of unrewarded service which, according to the report, young people were quick to appreciate; and which, additionally, provided a safeguard against over-professionalization (5).

When it came to discuss the qualifications which a youth leader had to possess, the report discovered there were none recognized as such; and there existed only a few courses which offered, by their scope and length, any systematic training. These varied in length from a few months to two and a half years and were provided by only a small number of the voluntary organizations. There was one course which included a social science diploma of a university. As a result of all these courses together, no more than 150 trained youth leaders had been produced each year. There were, however, other workers possessing diverse qualifications; some were graduates, some had been trained as teachers and others as social workers. Since 1939 the Board of Education had taken two steps in the sphere of training: they had conducted a number of short courses, many of which had been residential and were not training courses so much as conferences; and they had announced their willingness, by *Circular 1598/42* of 1942, to grant financial assistance, on a student capitation basis, to institutions and organizations which were willing to conduct emergency courses to be regarded as experimental only. There were several universities, a teachers' training college, and some voluntary organizations which had taken advantage of these arrangements; and approval had been granted for certain courses ranging from three months to one year, and some part-time courses (6).

The McNair Report had a number of recommendations to make, including a qualified assessment of the emergency courses recognized under *Circular 1598*. It argued that the course of training for those without any special qualifications, who were trying to prepare themselves for full-time posts as youth leaders, should extend over a period of three years of full-time study and practice. Moreover, courses of not less than one year's duration should be available for any whose previous experience and qualifications made the full three-year course unnecessary. Apart from exceptional cases, the minimum age for recognition of full-time leaders should be twenty-three. It was also recommended that the salaries of youth leaders should be comparable with those of teachers, that service as a youth leader should be pensionable, and that transfer between the two services should be facilitated (7).

D THE CROWTHER AND ALBEMARLE REPORTS

In Part Four, entitled 'A Majority without Education', the Crowther Report of 1959 briefly analyzed the way in which the youth service provided for the needs of children who left school as soon as they were legally entitled to do so; and it argued that 'the majority . . . are without that help in growing up which is acknowledged to be necessary' (8). As a result of a close examination of the Social Survey undertaken during spring-summer 1957, and the National Service Survey made in 1956–7, involving altogether nearly 11,000 youths, the Central Advisory Council for Education came to a number of conclusions.

It was clear that the great majority of pupils during their school life belonged to some youth organization which had their welfare as its objective, and which might therefore be said to be educational in purpose. When boys and girls left school, however, there was a radical change. As far as boys were concerned, the National Service Survey revealed that about one-fifth of the Army recruits had belonged to some youth organization for three years continuously after leaving school. Even when membership for a shorter period was considered, the proportion rose only to little more than one-third. It was clear that the sons of semi-skilled and unskilled workers participated less in youth organizations than did the sons of skilled workers and the professional classes. A comparison showed that 17 per cent of the former group, as compared with 22 per cent of the latter, had three years' continuous active membership. Girls had less connection with youth organizations after they left school than had boys; the ratio of girls' club membership to boys' was 1:5.

After school-leaving age there was a noticeable decline in the interest in uniformed organizations, such as the scouts, guides and various kinds of cadets. General youth clubs now began to play a larger part, and, especially from the age of eighteen onwards, political and cultural organizations had a stronger appeal. Girls who had been pupils in non-selective schools were particularly attracted to dance clubs, which accounted for 23 per cent of all the clubs to which such girls belonged. In general, boys and girls from non-selective schools were less likely to belong to any sort of club, after they had left school, than those from selective schools. In addition, those who pursued no courses in further education were less likely to be members of clubs than those who did. It was clear that time itself was not a controlling factor, since those who perhaps had least time to spare became involved in youth club activities: it was mainly a question of social, intellectual, and cultural background and training. In general, it was true to say that boys were more interested in playing games regularly after leaving school than in continuing to be members of youth organizations.

The general picture presented by the Crowther Report was that the youth service, as a whole, failed to attract the youths who probably needed it most—those in the bottom quarter or third of the population from the point of view of intelligence, ability and attainment. The less able and less steady elements in our society were somehow slipping through the net of both further education and the youth service.

'Thus an enquiry in one inner London borough showed that, while 55 per cent of the 16 year-old boys and 30 per cent of the 16 year-old girls belonged to some youth organization, the percentage of members among those who had been in the lowest stream in ability in modern schools dropped to 41 per cent and 22 per cent respectively' (9).

It was not the function of the Crowther Report to make specific recommendations on the youth service, since problems in that area and the question of priorities had already been remitted to the Albemarle Committee, but it was the opinion of the Crowther Committee that in no other field of education could the expenditure of public funds 'accomplish so much so readily' (10).

In November 1958 the Minister of Education appointed a committee under the chairmanship of the Countess of Albemarle, and in 1960 it presented its report, *The Youth Service in England and Wales*. Its terms of reference were to review the contribution which the youth service of England and Wales could make in assisting young people to play their part in the life of the community, in the light of changing social and industrial conditions and of current trends in other branches of the education service; and to advise according to which priorities best value could be obtained for money spent. In its introduction, the Albemarle Report indicated that the youth service was in a state of acute depression, and that those working in this service felt themselves neglected and held in small regard, in educational circles and by the public generally.

The report recommended that the youth service should be available for all young people aged fourteen to twenty inclusive. The Minister of Education was advised to initiate a Ten-Year Development Programme, divided into two equal stages; he was also recommended to appoint an advisory committee, of not more than twelve persons, to be called the Youth Service Council, whose function it would be to work closely with the Ministry and H.M.I.s.

The Albemarle Report also recommended that L.E.A.s should ensure that in each area a sub-committee of the education committee itself was charged with responsibility for the youth service. The report considered it was essential to develop the voluntary principle at every level of activity, and that there should be a national campaign for more voluntary helpers, including people with skills to serve self-programming groups. Young people should be given opportunities for participation as partners in the youth service. The Minister was asked to consider the provisions of larger grants to national and voluntary youth organizations, and to ensure that the expenditure of L.E.A.s would be sufficient to sustain the momentum of development. The Minister should also put in operation the long-term training arrangements for full-time leaders, and there should be ease of transfer from youth leadership to other professions. The report finally held that all its recommendations depended for success on the assumption that the Government intended to make the youth service adequate for the needs of young people today. It needed to go forward on all fronts, and if this were to be possible the Minister must declare his policy to advance it; only in this way could it produce a generous return for the money spent.

Since the publication of the Albemarle Report other reports relating to the youth service have appeared. In 1962 there was a report on *The Training of Part-Time Youth Leaders and Assistants*, and another on the same subject in 1966. Committees of the Youth Service Development Council also reported in 1965 on the service as a whole, and in 1967 on *Immigrants and the Youth Service*. The Newsom Report (1963) showed a keen interest in joint appointments of teacher/youth leaders and teacher/wardens, who would be attached to school staffs but would spend part of their time teaching in school, and part of their time working with young people in the evenings. It went on to say that

'These are developments which might foreshadow a more flexible teacher's day and a different range of responsibility for some members of the staff. Quite apart from any possible reorganization of the school day, we think it highly desirable that over the next few years thorough-going experiments in this type of joint appointment should be tried' (11).

The Second Report on the Training of Part-Time Youth Leaders and Assistants, published in 1966, recommended the provision of increased training facilities and a national recruiting campaign for more part-time youth workers. Reports received from L.E.A.s by the D.E.S. during 1967 indicated that there had, generally, been a good response to the recommendation for more training facilities; whilst the recruiting campaign had been launched. By the end of 1968 the number of full-time youth leaders in the country, and on the Department's Register, was 1,580; this was, in fact, twenty more than at the end of 1967. The actual number in training had dropped by three, from 247 in 1967; and whilst there were three more studying for the post-graduate diploma course at Manchester University, there were six less being trained in the five recognized colleges for full-time courses in youth leadership.

E YOUTH EMPLOYMENT SERVICE

Under the Labour Exchanges Act of 1909 a number of labour exchanges had been established, and included in some of these were special juvenile departments whose aim it was to assist boys and girls to choose the right career and work. In 1910 the Education (Choice of Employment) Act gave the power to L.E.A.s to provide this service to juveniles under seventeen years of age; and the Board of Education had the responsibility of supervising the administration of any schemes which might be initiated under the Act; it was also empowered to give grant aid where it considered it was necessary.

The Board of Trade was thus responsible for the work in exchanges, and the Board of Education was responsible where it was carried out by the L.E.A.s. Problems arose as a result of this dual interest in youth employment, and in consequence the two Boards made an agreement in 1911 to delimit their particular fields of interest. Those L.E.A.s which exercised the powers given them under the 1910 Act would restrict their activities to interviewing, advising, registering and selecting juvenile applicants; and the labour exchanges would do the rest: they would register vacancies as they arose, place juveniles with employers and have the oversight of their progress during their early employment. But the fields of interest were not so easily defined, and their precise areas of operation were difficult to keep distinct in practice. The position became even more complicated by the passing of the Unemployment Insurance Act of 1920, which made the Ministry of Labour (formerly the Board of Trade) responsible with reference to the unemployment of juveniles in all areas. The Board of Education, however, was responsible for the employment of juveniles in those areas where the L.E.A.s were exercising their powers.

In 1926 the Malcolm Committee, which had been appointed to investigate this uneasy sort of relationship, recommended the abolition of the dual central control by making the Minister of Labour solely responsible for the choice of employment services and the administration of unemployment insurance, whether the work was done by a local education authority or by the Ministry. This suggested change in central control was effected by the Ministry of Labour (Transfer of Powers) Order of July 25, 1927. This made the Ministry of Labour responsible for the central control of the whole system, including the payment of grants to local education authorities who were doing the work. The statutory power, given to L.E.A.s under the 1910 Act, was transferred to the Unemployment Insurance Act of 1935. The service had, since the Education Act of 1918, applied to juveniles under eighteen years. At the end of March 1945, 104 out of 315 local education authorities were operating the service.

In January 1945 the Minister of Labour and National Service appointed the Ince Committee to consider what measures were necessary to establish a comprehensive Juvenile Employment Service, and to make suggestions for a practical scheme. The committee's report was published in September 1945, and whilst the members unanimously recommended that the work should be done in all areas by one organization, they were unable to agree whether this organization should be the Ministry of Labour or the local education authority. The report proposed that a National Advisory Council on Juvenile Employment should replace the National Advisory Councils; it should be appointed by the Minister to consider all matters concerning the organization, procedure and development of the Juvenile Employment Service, and make recommendations to promote the efficiency of the service.

The Ince Committee recommended the provision of legislation to make it a statutory duty for all schools to register their leavers with the Juvenile Employment Service, which should be empowered to require the attendance of any school-leaver in order that he or she might be given vocational guidance by the department. If the provisions of the 1944 Education Act were to be fully effective for the benefit of young people, it was clear that an adequate Vocational Guidance Service was essential. The Ince Report recognized that, without the full co-operation of the schools and their staffs, no scheme would work satisfactorily. Vocational guidance was becoming of increasing importance in the schools, and the report noted four main stages in its plan. It considered that such guidance should start *in the schools*, and that the dissemination of information about careers in industry and the professions should be part of the normal teaching of a school. In particular, during the latter part of their time in school a more detailed consideration of their future work should be introduced into the curriculum for all girls and boys. Children should then be taken to see exhibitions and films as well as to visit factories, firms and industrial plants. Much of the Newsom Report supports this sort of activity for school-leavers during their final year. *School talks* should also be given, preferably by an officer of the Juvenile Employment Service, and within the school. The school-leaver's *interview* should be conducted by one expert officer, that is, the Juvenile Employment Officer, and he should be unaccompanied by anyone except the teacher and the parent. The interviewing officer should be supplied with sufficient information about a child, the chief source of such information being the child's school record card possessing details concerning physical qualities, intelligence, educational attainment, any special aptitudes, interests, qualities of disposition, club or society membership, home circumstances, and any special features of school attendance. Finally, there would inevitably be misfits in employment, and it was, therefore, important to have some machinery for *supervision* in order to rectify these.

In 1948 the Employment and Training Act provided the necessary statutory authority for putting into operation the Ince Report's recommendations. The L.E.A.s were given six months to decide whether they would be responsible for the Juvenile Employment Service in their areas. At the Annual General Meeting of the Association of Education Committees a resolution was passed encouraging all L.E.A.s to take on this responsibility, and the great majority of county and county borough education authorities agreed to do so. Any scheme submitted by a local education authority must provide for the constitution and appointment of a competent Youth Employment Officer (Y.E.O.). Provision also had to be made for the administration of unemployment benefit, which might be claimed by persons below the age of eighteen years under the National Insurance Act of 1946, and of assistance which might be claimed by the same group under the National Insurance Act of 1948. In addition, a scheme had to include the establishment of a Vocational Guidance Service.

In 1961 the Institute of Youth Employment Officers was formed to promote 'the advancement of the principles and practice of vocational guidance'. Although, quite naturally, it is concerned to promote the interests of members of the profession, it clearly has a major concern for the development of the fullest possible body of information and advice concerning careers and employment. It is also interested in further education, industrial training, and all the many problems involved in employment and unemployment. There is no doubt that the profession of the Y.E.O. demands individuals with adaptability, varied interests, enquiring and resilient minds, patience, and a strong sense of vocation. As a result of their efforts, and their collaboration with the schools on the one side and industry on the other, most children today can have a broad perspective of the jobs, professions and careers available, and detailed information about those forms of employment that interest them most. The supervisory powers of the Youth Employment Service also ensure that where misfits exist they are at least known, and some effort is made to rectify mistakes.

REFERENCES

1 *Education Act 1944* (7 and 8 Geo. 6, Ch. 31) (H.M.S.O., 1944), Part II, Section 7.
2 Ibid., Section 41 (b).
3 Lester Smith, W. O., *Education: An Introductory Survey* (Penguin Books, 1957), p. 85.
4 Ibid., p. 213.
5 Board of Education, *Teachers and Youth Leaders* (McNair Report) (H.M.S.O., 1944, reprinted 1961), p. 96, paras. 329 and 330.
6 Ibid., pp. 96–7, paras. 331–4.
7 Ibid., pp. 102–5, paras. 357–69.

8 Ministry of Education, *15 to 18* (Crowther Report) (H.M.S.O., 1959, reprinted 1962), p. 169. *Vide* paras. 262–4 for a summary of the C.A.C.'s main conclusions.
9 Ibid., p. 171.
10 Ibid., p. 172.
11 Ministry of Education, *Half Our Future* (Newsom Report) (H.M.S.O., 1963), p. 48, para. 144.

BIBLIOGRAPHY

Alexander, W. P., *Education in England* (Newnes, 1964, 2nd ed.).
Armfelt, R., *The Structure of English Education* (Cohen and West, 1961).
Board of Education, *Teachers and Youth Leaders* (McNair Report) (H.M.S.O., 1944).
Brew, J. Macalister, *Youth and Youth Groups* (Faber, 1945).
Button, L., *Youth Service* (National Association of Youth Service Officers).
Children Act of 1948 (H.M.S.O., 1948).
D.E.S., *Service by Youth* (H.M.S.O., 1965).
D.E.S., *The Training of Part-Time Youth Leaders and Assistants: A Second Report* (H.M.S.O., 1966).
D.E.S., *Immigrants and the Youth Service* (Hunt Report) (H.M.S.O., 1967).
Employment and Training Act of 1948 (H.M.S.O., 1948).
Heginbotham, H., *The Youth Employment Service* (Methuen).
Kuenstler, P. H. K., *Youth Work in England* (University of London Press).
Lowndes, G. A. N., *The English Educational System* (Hutchinson's University Library, 1960, revised ed.).
Ministry of Education, *Community Centres* (H.M.S.O., 1945).
Ministry of Education, *School and Life* (Report of C.A.C.) (H.M.S.O., 1947).
Ministry of Education, *Health Education* (Pamphlet 31) (H.M.S.O., 1957).
Ministry of Education, *15 to 18* (Crowther Report) (H.M.S.O., 1959).
Ministry of Education, *Circular 11/60: Youth Service* (Progress Report and Further Development) (H.M.S.O., 1960).
Ministry of Education, *Youth Service in England and Wales* (Albemarle Report) (H.M.S.O., 1960).
Ministry of Education, *The Training of Part-Time Youth Leaders and Assistants* (H.M.S.O., 1962).
Ministry of Education, *Half Our Future* (Newsom Report) (H.M.S.O., 1963).
Ministry of Labour and National Service, *Report of the Committee on the Juvenile Employment Service* (Ince Report) (H.M.S.O., 1945, reprinted 1964).
National Association of Youth Service Officers, *Leisure-Time Education of Young People* (National Association of Youth Service Officers).
Youth Advisory Council, *The Purpose and Content of the Youth Service* (H.M.S.O., 1945).

Part Three

Some
Educational Thinkers

Chapter 11

Johann Friedrich Herbart
(1776–1841)

A HIS LIFE AND WORK

In his discussion of the Apperception Theory of Herbart and his followers, Dr J. P. Wynne remarks that

'The Herbartians provided one of the first theories of education that enabled the merchant classes to justify philosophically and psychologically educational reforms in line with their economic and political aspirations' (1).

Any brief account of Herbart's work is bound to be an oversimplification; he was a pioneer psychologist as well as a philosopher and educator. But if Herbart was a philosopher he failed to achieve fame in this particular area of his interests; and he himself maintained that he was an experimenter whose chief work on education (*Science of Education*) owed as much to his carefully organized experiments and observations as it did to his theoretical ideas or philosophy. It was this pragmatic approach in the work of Herbart, and of his followers, that made it particularly useful and adaptable as an instrument and technique of indoctrination; but as Wynne is careful to point out, in the long run such a system is self-stultifying. The fixation of ideas and patterns, to which 'Herbartianism' lent itself, failed to deepen or extend human experience. Yet Herbart's approach and the crystallization of his 'Formal Steps' by his over-zealous followers were destined to affect teaching method, and the preparation of lesson notes, down to our own time.

Johann Friedrich Herbart was born at Oldenburg, in Germany, in 1776. His father was a lawyer whose wife was considerably cultured and able to assist her son in the study of both classics and mathematics. It was largely through his mother's persistent, and insistent, application that Herbart had already acquired some facility in logic and metaphysics before he proceeded to the local *gymnasium*, and then on to Jena University at the age of eighteen. He went there ostensibly to read law, but he found the attraction of the philosopher Fichte too great for him; and although, as S. J. Curtis suggests, 'he soon outgrew the latter's idealism' (2), there was a great deal of Fichte's thought that rubbed off on to him.

Johann Gottlieb Fichte (1762–1814) had advocated in his *Addresses to the German People* the practice of the ideas of Pestalozzi on the basis of idealistic Kantian philosophy. Fichte believed firmly that morality was the aim of education, and that this in turn involved the complete fixation of character so that each individual would do the 'right' as a matter of course. The motivating force for all conduct was to be found in a completely disinterested love of the right and not in any form of coercion or self-interest. Fichte also held that, if the personal activity of the individual pupil were aroused and excited, learning would be the inevitable consequence. Training in citizenship was the whole of education—its beginning, middle and end, and the corruption of the adult world must not be allowed to sully the young and innocent mind at any point. In order to attain to this ideal, almost Platonic, régime all the children were to be educated alike, irrespective of class or sex, and it was the duty of the State to provide such an education. It is also interesting to note the emphasis placed upon manual training by Fichte so that individuals might not only be self-sufficient, but might also help to make a positive and practical contribution to the society of which they were members. It will be seen subsequently how much Herbart owed, consciously or unconsciously, to the ideas of Fichte.

Herbart left Jena University at the age of twenty-one, without apparently completing a course in either law or metaphysics. The study of law he found particularly irksome and uninspiring, whilst Fichtean metaphysics proved to be somewhat disillusioning. In 1799 he went to Switzerland where the Governor of Interlaken employed him to instruct his three sons. During the two years which he spent as tutor to these boys he had to produce a detailed report of their conduct and progress every two months; indeed, this period of private tutorship represented for Herbart his apprenticeship in the profession of teaching.

Whilst he was in Switzerland Herbart visited Pestalozzi's school at Burgdorf, which was situated about thirty miles away from Interlaken. Herbart's study of Pestalozzi's work led him to believe that its principles could be applied to all levels of education, and he wrote several treatises to illustrate his theories. In 1802 he was awarded a doctorate at Göttingen University, where he became a lecturer in philosophy and allied subjects. His interests were, as ever, wide and not to be confined to some artificial specialism: pedagogics, aesthetics, ethics, logic—all absorbed him. In 1809 he succeeded to the Chair of Philosophy and Pedagogy, vacated by Immanuel Kant, at Königsberg.

Herbart was always prodigiously industrious, developing every aspect of his philosophy, evolving a psychology 'founded according to a new method on Experience, Metaphysics and Mathematics', and writing a great deal on pedagogy as well as supervising a practice teaching school in conjunction with the teacher training college which he had founded.

Despite all his accomplishments and successes, Herbart remained a disappointed man. He very much coveted Hegel's Chair at Berlin, but he failed to obtain it when Hegel died in 1831. In 1833 he returned to Göttingen where he continued to work until 1841, when he died of a stroke. It was during this final stage of his career that his most practical book, *Outlines of Educational Doctrine*, was written.

B HIS PHILOSOPHY AND PSYCHOLOGY

Herbart's philosophy is sometimes referred to as Realism, as distinct from the Idealism of such philosophers as Fichte and Kant. But, as W. Boyd points out, it is not Realism in any usual sense of the term, nor indeed is it a philosophy by any means antagonistic to Kantian modes of thought, since Herbart

'does not think that any of the things known to us are real or that their real nature can ever be known. He is a realist only in the strict philosophical sense of believing that "reality" lies hidden behind the appearance of things, and that by way of interpreting the facts of experience it is permissible to postulate the existence of simple entities or "reals", about which all that can be said is that they exist and that they are manifold' (3).

And Herbart applied this thesis as much to the experience that we have of our own mental states as to our experience of external objects.

Although he believed that psychology was a science based on experience, metaphysics and mathematics, and that the individual's field of consciousness could be observed empirically, Herbart held, nevertheless, that the simple nature of the soul was totally unknown and would remain so for ever. The soul, as we perceived it, was in fact the sum of the actual 'presentations' (*Vorstellungen*), or mental states, arrived at through our individual experience. Originally it was, as John Locke had argued, a *tabula rasa* in the most absolute sense; in it there were no primitive ideas or any predisposition to form them; time and experience alone could produce ideas.

Thus, for Herbart, the mind must evolve as a result of contact with the phenomena of space and time, with men and with things. Each experience is a presentation to the individual; a presentation which may become a permanent element of his awareness and comprehension of his environment. His mind is, or becomes, an interrelated collection of presentations, or *apperception mass*. It is the function of the mind, or soul, to receive, classify and relate experiences, or ideas based upon experience.

Presentations, then, are the basic elements of mental life, and their combinations, permutations and interactions are the cause of all forms of consciousness. The interactions of the 'empty arena' (4) of the pure soul with the external world produce derived presentations, which in turn comprise the greater part of the mind's contents. These, in their turn, can play their part as re-presentations, which form the material for the higher processes of thought. The masses of presentations in the mind (apperceptive masses) derive from experience and intercourse. It is from experience that the teacher seeks and helps to create knowledge, and from free intercourse sympathy. *Apperceptions* are, basically, the assimilation and identification of a new idea by the mass of ideas already in the mind. Herbart used the term 'idea' to include sense-impressions as well as intellectual and emotional impressions.

Contrary to the theory of Locke, ideas were for Herbart both active and operative forces. Some ideas, or presentations, are contrary, or opposite, and so diminish each other, because they are mutually exclusive. Some ideas are similar, or compatible, and so they retain their intensity and a fusion takes place. The new presentation has a greater strength than either idea regarded separately. Other ideas, again, may be disparate; that is, they do not conflict, nor do they fuse, but they remain members of a mass or complex. An object, for example, may be identified as an orange; it is, in fact, an apperceptive mass with presentations of colour, shape and smell which are neither in conflict nor in fusion. Thus Herbart developed, and gave a certain dynamism to, Associationist psychology, with laws of similarity, contrast, disparity, contiguity, and so on.

Many ideas *do* conflict and present areas of inhibition, which persist in activity below the *limen* or threshold of consciousness. Herbart considered that ideas in this area of unconsciousness were equally as important as other material in the formulation of consciousness.

'Ideas rise above the threshold only if they fit in with the temporary configuration. Once an idea rises above the threshold it is "apperceived"—it both becomes conscious and is assimilated into a complex of on-going experiences' (5).

In this respect Herbart provided the seeds of concepts of human consciousness which were later developed by Sigmund Freud and the psychoanalytical school. Herbart also believed firmly that the presentations of the mind were amenable to mathematical measurement and analysis. In this, however, Herbart was not conspicuously successful, and it was left to psychologists such as Gustav Fechner to develop the theme.

C THE AIM OF EDUCATION

One thing became quite clear in Herbart's thought: that the great aim of education was 'virtue'; in fact, this term 'virtue' expressed for him the whole purpose of education. It was the idea of inner freedom as a constant, perpetual state of mind. When an individual no longer finds a conflict in his actions between what 'is' and what he feels 'ought to be', he then possesses inner freedom. But in order to attain to this inner freedom man must possess knowledge; he must be many-sided in his approach to problems of action and their understanding. In fact, Herbart clearly understood that insight and conscience have to be educated and trained by experience.

The aim of education is thus seen by Herbart as the production of good men; a man's true worth is measurable in terms of will, and will in action, rather than in terms of intellect; and the educator's purpose is to make children good through the medium of learning. What exactly does Herbart mean by 'good'? For him goodness comprises five factors or moral ideas. There is the idea of *inner freedom* to which we have already referred, and in which the individual has the requisite dynamism to put into effect what he 'knows' to be right. For Herbart only the truly good man is perfectly free.

Secondly, there is the idea of *perfection*, or completion. This ethical idea involves complete knowledge, for Herbart seems to have been sufficiently Platonic to accept the notion that 'virtue is knowledge'. If it is true that only the completely good man is completely free, it is also true that the completely good man must know what is good, and such complete knowledge is the result of the interplay of experience and ideas, and of presentations woven into the totality of consciousness.

It is just at this point that Herbart emphasizes the importance and necessity of directing the process of apperception by a judicious selection, arrangement and presentation of sensations and impressions to be experienced by pupils. All undesirable presentations must be eliminated from the child's experience. Thus Herbart says:

'Those only wield the full power of education who know how to cultivate in the youthful soul a large circle of thought closely connected in all its parts, possessing the power of overcoming what is unfavourable in the environment and of dissolving and absorbing into itself all that is favourable' (6).

This, of course, raises all sorts of questions of censorship and indoctrination, but one is forcibly reminded of the Confucian programme of education in which there was a shift from a spontaneous to a deliberate, conscious and reinforced tradition. It was a programme in which moral ideas were drummed into people by every conceivable means until they became habits in daily life—through the media of schools, temples, homes and theatres to toys, proverbs, stories and history (7).

Thirdly, there is the idea of the *good will*, or benevolence, which is revealed in the attitudes assumed by individuals towards others. The operation of the will is the result of the struggle between opposing sets of ideas, and the strongest ideas will ultimately determine choices made and actions performed. But since the will is the outcome of the struggle between ideas, the will and disposition of the individual may be formed by educative instruction.

Fourthly, the idea of *rights* involves the whole question of private and public property, and of social institutions generally. Herbart considers that the child has to be educated in an understanding and appreciation of such institutions before he can fully involve himself in his social responsibilities. Fifthly, the idea of *equitable rewards*, both positive and negative, is Herbart's equivalent of the Eastern concept of *karma*. According to Herbart everyone should be justly, properly and adequately requited for the good and evil that he does: there is, in fact, a moral law of retribution at work in the world.

Herbart's concept of morality was both individual and social, and it depended upon a very wide knowledge of life. It was inculcated, gradually, through instruction until the whole man, possessing perfect will and inner freedom, was produced. Obviously this cannot be an immediate, classroom aim of education, and nowhere does Herbart suggest that it can; it is for him the ultimate end of education, the goal towards which all education is working. But,

'Perfection quantitatively considered is the first urgent task, wherever a human being shows himself pettier, smaller, weaker, more limited than he need be' (8).

In reality, educative knowledge for Herbart is not simply a store of facts, which one might possess or lack and yet be essentially the same person; educative knowledge is many-sided, involving a personal *interest* which does not merely absorb facts but gets absorbed in them in a vitally active sort of way.

D THE CONCEPT OF INTEREST

The concept of 'interest' in educational theory is a very popular one in our own times, but it is, of course, by no means new or revolutionary, although it is frequently misconceived. Herbart saw interest as a necessary condition for learning, but it was no superficial methodological idea about making things 'interesting' to the child. For Herbart it was something generated within the child himself—'interest means self-activity'. There is, in the presentation (*Vorstellung*), some special attraction for the mind; it compels attention. There is a natural attention, which is primitive and original; and there is the apperceptive or assimilating attention, which gradually displaces it. We progressively learn to select the objects of our attention, for the simple reason that we cannot attend to all the things that clamour for our interest. New experiences derive their character from previous experiences to which they are related; and the attention necessary for learning depends solely on the 'apperception', or mental appropriation, by which this process operates.

Herbart maintains throughout that interest must be many-sided, for it is only through the multiplicity of the facts of interest that perfection can be reached. Herbart was a strong believer in systematization in all his theorizing, and just as he had reduced his ethical aims to five so he classified the interests, or types of interest, under six headings, in two groups of three. The first three he termed *knowledge interests*, that is, interests which are empirical, speculative and aesthetic. The empirical interest comprises the pleasure derived by pupils from the objects of direct experience, such as the facts which inspire the botanist or the historian. The speculative interest involves the intellectual concern which the pupil has for the general laws or underlying causes of things, typical of the student of science, mathematics and logic. Here the individual is involved in some of the cosmic problems which mystify the most intelligent. The aesthetic interest derives from the contemplation of beautiful things or of an ideal through the medium of the senses. Here the pupil is involved in art, sculpture, poetry and literary productions generally.

The second collection of interests Herbart termed *ethical interests*, or interests which involved in some way or another the association with other people. These interests are the sympathetic, social and religious. The sympathetic interest is that which one has in one's fellows as individuals, in their many joys and sorrows. The social interest is that which is discoverable in national and civic life, and in one's general participation in group and community activity. And, finally, the religious interest is that involved in the contemplation of the Divine, or in a consideration of the meaning of the Infinite.

The 'cardinal sin of instruction' was to be boring or wearisome; but this was not for Herbart a general invitation to turn all instruction into some form of 'play' activity. It meant that the intensity of intellectual effort would be deepened, the range of interest would be widened, and there would be some unification of interest and knowledge on sound educational principles, bearing in mind always the general moral or ethical aims. The unification of interests could be achieved only through properly arranged methods of instruction.

E THE CURRICULUM

Herbart considered that the child's interests should be organized and integrated along specific curricular lines, if they were not to remain diffuse and very superficial. He saw our knowledge as being derived from two chief sources—from nature and from man himself. These two main threads —knowledge of nature and knowledge of humanity—would be spun to their uttermost limits in all the 'subject' areas of school learning.

Herbart saw the study of languages as important, with the proviso that they did not exist in their own right, as it were; they were instruments only. He says:

'But there are only two main threads which can and ought to be spun out in both directions—knowledge of nature and knowledge of humanity; languages are but the instruments' (9).

By this he did not mean, as some have suggested, that languages were unimportant; rather he meant that the time and effort expended on the grinding of classical grammar should be directed in a much more concentrated way upon the subject-matter of the literature involved. His pupils might not be able to parse the words in the *Odyssey*, but they would henceforth know its content and any lessons it had to teach. Not all children were suited to a detailed study of languages, and Herbart well understood the decreasing importance of Latin and Greek. To him ancient history was more important than the classical languages in which it was written.

The sheer boredom of language study and the prolixity of much historical study could be avoided, Herbart suggested, by the reading of simple biography and stories, such as those of Herodotus—in translation. He believed strongly in the use of all types of visual aid, such as maps and charts, portraits and pictures, in order to get historical ideas across. 'History should be the teacher of mankind', and should include not merely political history but also the history of inventions, of the arts and of the sciences. But politics were certainly not to be excluded, and should be taught with history, chronology and literature.

In general, Herbart considered the sciences and the humanities to be of equal importance in the development of that idea of perfection which formed one of his chief educational aims. In particular, he emphasized the value of elementary mathematics and science, especially on the practical side. It is of some interest to note that, well over 100 years ago, Herbart continually stressed the practicality of the subjects to be chosen for the curriculum. Counting, measuring, weighing, estimating and ideas of proportion and function were to him far more important than logical proofs or any underlying principles. For example, it was the use of logarithms in practice that mattered, not how they were arrived at theoretically. Elementary science should include some physics and astronomy, and practical activities should involve the construction and use of instruments and general manual training.

Herbart did not regard manual training simply as a preparation for any particular trade, although of course it could include such a preparation. It was to him a nexus between the understanding of natural phenomena and the direction of human purpose. The manipulation of material things in a course of manual training inevitably not only made the child a part of nature, but also provided him with some participation in its adaptation for human needs and survival.

Bound up with the curriculum there is inevitably the method and organization of material. Herbart suggested three principles for the organization of the curriculum—correlation, concentration and recapitulation, or the principle of culture epochs. The *correlation* of studies involved the combination of a variety of subjects and skills with some common purpose in mind. Thus, mathematics could be linked with physics and manual training. The principle of *concentration* was illustrated by geography, which Herbart regarded as an 'associating science'; it brought together history, politics, the arts and the sciences. Concentration was in reality a way of providing a core curriculum and a more systematic correlation of studies. The principle of *culture epochs* was the theory, based on evolution, that just as man evolved physically through certain biological stages so also he advanced culturally through specific phases and gradations. There was a progressive educational development of the human race through such stages, or epochs, as primitive, nomadic, agricultural, industrial and so forth. And just as mankind as a whole had evolved through these successive stages, so also each child developed mentally from a very primitive level, through 'culture epochs' similar to those of the race, to ultimate maturity. As A. E. Meyer remarks:

'It is only fair to add that . . . Herbart merely let fall a few vague and dulcet whispers about the possibility of such a parallelism. Nevertheless his successors, who entertained no such self-restraint, lost no time in pouncing on the suggestion and welding it into the canons of their psychology' (10).

The theory that the individual's development recapitulates that of the race, or that 'ontogeny recapitulates phylogeny', has received scant support in modern times, although more recently W. Kay has suggested that its value may lie in the fact that 'it can illuminate our understanding of individual moral development' (11).

F THE DOCTRINE OF FORMAL STEPS

Herbart argued that if the child were to learn in a consistent sort of way from the 'apperceptive masses' absorbed within his mind, then experiences within the learning situation should be presented in an orderly fashion, and in an associative manner, so that the mind became accustomed to certain patterns of apprehension. There was, he argued, an ideal way of instructing and of receiving instruction; and in this process there were *four* successive stages which were universal and which should be pursued in all instruction. These stages were clearness, association, system and method.

These stages of progression in teaching formed a very minor part in Herbart's doctrines, and as H. G. Good has shown (12) close parallels can be found in Cicero's *De Oratore* and in John Dewey's *How We Think*. They are, in themselves, almost self-explanatory, and whilst Herbart himself regarded teaching as an art, requiring considerable adaptation to the context and situation, his enthusiastic followers developed his stages into the 'Five Formal Steps', and thereafter proceeded to fossilize them into an almost unchangeable method for lesson preparation and teaching.

The first step in this scheme, *Preparation*, undertook to prepare the learner for receptivity. It began by revising, and bringing into the consciousness, previous knowledge which might be related to the new, or which might possibly throw some useful light upon it. The second step of *Presentation* was devoted to the setting forth and explanation of new material, whether of facts, principles, procedures or experiments. The third step of *Association* involved a comparison, or contrast, of the old and familiar material with the newly acquired presentations, which were fully analyzed until they were completely understood. Here, for Herbart, there was room for almost 'free association' in discussion and conversation, so that the mind could range freely over its experiences, and the new was not completely isolated, or seen out of relation with other material. The fourth step of *Generalization* was one devoted to the drawing of conclusions, or generalizations, after some recapitulation and systematization of the material under discussion. The fifth, and final, step, *Application*, represented the putting into practice of the new knowledge or skill on the assumption that true learning was the actual utilization of knowledge in an understanding way, and in a meaningful situation.

In planning lessons and experiments, as well as in the general process of empirical thought, these formal steps still have much to commend them. It is, to a large extent, the way we think; and, further, it suggests that our ideas and conclusions should be put rigorously to the test after some close analysis and examination. But to apply the method to every set of lesson notes and every piece of class activity would result in a stultification of the whole procedure.

G HERBARTIAN INFLUENCES

Herbart had many devotees both in Europe and later in America. Karl Volkmar Stoy (1815–85) lectured at Jena, and he there established a demonstration school similar to that founded by Herbart. Tuiskon Ziller

(1817–82) lectured at Leipzig from 1853, and as well as providing a seminary for the training of teachers and a teaching practice school, he wrote a number of works on education, including *An Introduction to General Pedagogy* (1856), *Foundations of Educative Instruction* (1864), and *The Basis of the Doctrine of Educative Instruction* (1865).

Ziller saw morality as the main concern of education, and accordingly he worked out a detailed correlation between general studies and moral training. He was responsible for founding a society called the Association for the Scientific Study of Education, which became a large, growing and powerful group, to a very great extent responsible, according to Professor A. E. Meyer, for the perversion of the original Herbartian doctrines (13).

Eventually, and inevitably, Herbartian teaching and influence made its way to America, where in 1882, the National Herbart Society was formed and supported by such figures as C. and F. McMurry and C. de Garmo. As the direct influence of Herbart became less and as the pioneering educative spirit evolved, the society changed its nature somewhat, and in 1902 it was renamed the National Society for the Scientific Study of Education.

Perhaps the most interesting feature of this whole process is the fact, not that a great thinker's ideas and ideals tend to be misinterpreted and become perverted, which of course they do, but rather that some original thinkers realize the impossibility of conserving and transplanting, without modification, ideas and methods that worked in one place, and at one time, into another place, and at another time. There was, undoubtedly, much of value in what Herbart taught and in his pedagogical ideas generally: but they were by no means immortal. Some of his ideas became ossified into a Herbartian doctrine and pattern, but many were modified and extended to meet a different age and varying conditions.

REFERENCES

1 Wynne, J. P., *Theories of Education* (Harper and Row, 1963), p. 80.
2 Curtis, S. J. and Boultwood, M. E. A., *A Short History of Educational Ideas* (University Tutorial Press, 1965, 4th ed.), p. 355.
3 Boyd, W., *The History of Western Education* (A. and C. Black, 1964, 7th ed.), p. 130.
4 *Vide* Curtis, S. J. and Boultwood, M. E. A., *An Introductory History of English Education Since 1800* (University Tutorial Press, 1964, 3rd ed.), p. 124, where the mind, or soul, of the new-born baby is delineated in Herbartian psychology as 'an empty arena' into which each experience enters as a presentation. According to W. Boyd (op. cit., p. 341) Herbart does, however, describe the soul as 'originally a *tabula rasa* in the most absolute sense, without any form of life or presentation'. (Quoted from *Psychologie als Wissenschaft*, para. 120.)

5 Thomson, R., *The Pelican History of Psychology* (Penguin Books, 1968), p. 32.
6 Herbart, J. F., *The Science of Education* (S. Sonnenschein, 1892), p. 92. Quoted by Curtis and Boultwood, op. cit., p. 359.
7 *Vide* Chiang Monlin, *Tides from the West* (Yale University Press, 1947).
8 Lange, A. F. (tr.), *Herbart's Outlines of Educational Doctrine* (Macmillan, 1901), p. 13.
9 Ibid., p. 71.
10 Meyer, A. E., *An Educational History of the Western World* (McGraw-Hill, 1965), p. 363.
11 Kay, W., *Moral Development* (Allen and Unwin, 1968), p. 91.
12 Good, H. G., *A History of Western Education* (Macmillan, 1966), p. 259.
13 Op. cit., p. 365.

BIBLIOGRAPHY

Adams, J., *The Herbartian Psychology Applied to Education* (Heath, 1897).
Boyd, W., *The History of Western Education* (A. and C. Black, 1964, 7th ed.), pp. 338–49.
Cole, P. R., *Herbart and Froebel: An Attempt at Synthesis* (Columbia University Press, 1907).
Curtis, S. J. & Boultwood, M. E. A., *A Short History of Educational Ideas* (University Tutorial Press, 1965, 4th ed.), Chapter XIV, pp. 355–68.
Davidson, J., *A New Interpretation of Herbart's Psychology and Educational Theory Through the Philosophy of Leibniz* (W. Blackwood and Sons, Ltd, 1906).
De Garmo, C., *Herbart and the Herbartians* (Scribner, 1895).
Eckoff, W. J., *Herbart's A.B.C. of Sense-Perception and Minor Pedagogical Works* (D. Appleton and Co., 1896).
Felkin, H. M. and E., *An Introduction to Herbart's Science and Practice of Education* (Heath, 1904).
Good, H. G., *A History of Western Education* (Macmillan, 1966, 7th printing).
Hayward, F. H., *The Critics of Herbartianism* (S. Sonnenschein, 1903).
Jones, R. H. and Turnbull, G. H. (tr.), *Addresses to the German Nation of J. G. Fichte* (Liverpool University Press, 1922).
Lange, A. F., *Herbart's Outlines of Educational Doctrine* (Macmillan, 1901).
MacVannel, J. A., *The Educational Theories of Herbart and Froebel* (Columbia University Press, 1905).
McMurry, C. A., *The Elements of General Method, based on the Principles of Herbart* (Macmillan, 1903).
Meyer, A. E., *An Educational History of the Western World* (McGraw-Hill, 1965), Chapter 23, pp. 358–66.
Mulliner, B. C., *The Application of Psychology to Education, by J. F. Herbart* (Scribner, 1898).
Rusk, R. R., *The Doctrines of the Great Educators* (Macmillan, 1965, 3rd ed.), Chapter X.
Smith, M. K. (tr.), *Herbart's Textbook in Psychology* (D. Appleton and Co., 1891).
Thomson, R., *The Pelican History of Psychology* (Penguin Books, 1968), pp. 30–33.

Turnbull, G. H., *The Educational Theory of J. G. Fichte* (Liverpool University Press and Hodder & Stoughton, 1926).

Ufer, C., *Introduction to the Pedagogy of Herbart* (Heath, 1901).

Wynne, J. P., *General Method: Foundations and Applications* (Century, 1929).

Wynne, J. P., *Theories of Education* (Harper and Row, 1963), pp. 64–81.

Chapter 12

Friedrich Froebel
(1782–1852)

A HIS LIFE AND WORK

Friedrich Froebel was born in a village in Thuringia, Germany, in 1782. When he was still a baby, his mother died, and he seems to have spent a somewhat lonely childhood, playing and walking in the countryside, until he reached the age of ten when he was sent to the village school where he was taught arithmetic and something about nature. His early home and school life appears to have made a deep impression upon Froebel, who loved everything related to the world of nature. He continued his country walks and observed everything in his environment—trees, plants, insects, pond-life and stones. This love of nature certainly affected his concept of education when he came to formulate it at a later date.

At the age of fifteen he was apprenticed by his father to a forester, so that he might study both forestry and surveying. Froebel seems to have had very little idea of what he really wanted to do in life, and yet there was an exceedingly lively interest developing in his mind in almost everything that entered his awareness. It was an interest which was not basically academic or organized in any particular way, but it arose out of his personal perception and awareness. This thirst for sheer information and knowledge about the things that attracted him most led him to the University of Jena, where he managed to attend a variety of courses in biology and mathematics. These absorbed him particularly at first because they arose quite naturally out of his childhood involvement in nature, in school arithmetic and in surveying.

Unfortunately for Froebel he had no steady income and no particular means of earning money at this time, so that before long he found himself in the university prison, condemned for nine weeks to be deprived of the mental sustenance that he so eagerly sought. After this unhappy experience he attended courses once more, spreading his net to include a wide variety of subjects from philosophy to zoology and architecture. In the realm of philosophy he was able to listen to such lecturers as Goethe, Fichte and Schiller, and the Idealist School generally appealed to him; in comparative zoology he was considerably influenced by A. J. Batsch.

Certainly Froebel's interests were catholic, and perhaps not quite as haphazard as might first appear. He had an intuitive, perceptive mind which seemed to see things whole almost from the beginning. He felt that there was a relatedness in things that extended beyond the boundaries and barriers of 'subjects', but which, nevertheless, had to be viewed and absorbed in a disciplined way. He was a sort of mystic who was prepared, nevertheless, to subject his insight to ordered and scientific method; he was aware of the *Gestalten*, the concepts of form and shape, but felt that comprehension could follow apprehension only if he looked into the very nature of things through man's systematic classification.

For a time he was content to teach drawing at a school in Frankfurt, if only to keep alive and out of debt; but whilst he was beginning to feel that teaching was in fact his *métier*, he also felt very acutely his ignorance and unreadiness for anything on a large scale. For three years, from 1807 to 1810, he took up the job of tutoring three boys at Yverdon in Switzerland. It was here that, as a student himself, he learned from his visits to Pestalozzi's school a great deal both of factual material and method. Froebel had a considerable amount of that humility which is characteristic of the really great—he was always aware of how much more there was to know and to learn, and he was willing to sit at anyone's feet in order to increase his knowledge.

Between 1810 and 1816 he assiduously continued his studies, particularly in science, maths and mineralogy. Nor was he content with a superficial look at science in some abstract philosophical manner; he delved practically into the mysteries of physics, chemistry and zoology, and specialized in mineralogy sufficiently well to be offered an academic post in the subject. He also studied philology for a spell at the Universities of Göttingen and Berlin, and acted at the museum of the latter city as an assistant curator, working with a research professor. After a brief, but active, period of service in the army he opened his first school in 1816, and then moved to Keilhau, Thuringia, the next year.

In 1826 Froebel published his first book, *The Education of Man*. Its content will be discussed when we consider Froebel's general educational principles; suffice it here to say that Froebel was an idealist and a dreamer. He dreamed up an institution which would serve all basic needs of education, from educating mothers to looking after their children in every type of school from nursery to technical. Moreover, such an institution would not depend upon the wealth of the parents or upon their social position; it would be open to the poor, orphans, socially outcast—in fact everybody without distinction of class or creed. Froebel did not fulfil his dream, but the ideal remained with him and with others.

He realized early the necessity of training teachers for his particular type of education and school, and in 1831 he went to Switzerland in order to become involved in this work. He became increasingly aware of the importance of studying children from their earliest years and of relating their education to their development, so in 1835 he went to Burgdorf and established a training college for teachers with a demonstration school attached. The next year he decided to travel in Germany to see infant schools at work; these proved to be, in the main, little more than day nurseries for the children of working mothers. Froebel decided it was time to experiment with early education, so he established, at Blankenburg in Thuringia, his first experimental school for psychological education. After providing it with various long and pompous appellations he finally hit upon the name *Kindergarten*—a garden for children, in which children were the tender plants to be reared and the teachers, or educators, were the gardeners. The emphasis in the kindergarten was essentially the provision of suitable situations, including materials and activities, in and through which the children might develop their observation and perception, and ultimately their understanding.

During the next decade Froebel was responsible for the founding of a large number of kindergartens and for training teachers for this specific kind of work. In the process it was discovered that certain forms of apparatus were of more use than others and these were established and further developed. Although a considerable amount of original and progressive work was done by Froebel and his followers in connection with the kindergarten, it was proscribed by the Minister of Education in 1851. The general view is that this proscription arose out of a confusion by officials between Friedrich Froebel and his nephew Karl who had decisively socialistic tendencies. But history is seldom so simple in its issues as this. It is much more likely that the combination of circumstances surrounding the whole of the project militated against Froebel and his work. It was a private enterprise; financially Froebel was always in trouble; and further he presented a view of the child and of education which was novel and not always popular. The emancipation of the child from teacher and parent domination has never been an easy one, nor always a popular or successful one, and the concept of the school as a place where children happily played, sang songs, did gardening and kept pets was not immediately seen by those in authority as educational. Certainly, it seems hardly likely that Friedrich should be confused with Karl for the next ten years, particularly as Friedrich died in 1852. The proscription was finally withdrawn in 1861, and kindergartens were re-established and were soon flourishing.

B HIS PHILOSOPHY

Froebel began, in his philosophical thinking about the world around him, with nature itself. In his early youth he had become a very close observer of natural life, and he found some identity with the whole of life around him. Apart from financial problems which made it difficult to pursue a normal academic career, there was also some fundamental element in the man himself, some mystical proclivity, which refused to allow him to divorce one part of life from another. His close observation of nature was synthetic rather than analytic. At heart he was an idealist, and although philosophically his thinking is linked with the work of Kant, Fichte, Schelling and Hegel, the link is a very tenuous one. It was largely a question of finding great names on which to foster his insight—a tendency which is universal.

For Froebel all material things in the world around were expressions of God's creative will, and there was a fundamental unity behind them all, a unity which found its origin in God himself. We are very prone to classify everything and everybody, to pigeon-hole their ideas and beliefs, and to give them pseudo-scientific terms, which are then accepted or rejected. Froebel's thought has frequently been referred to as 'pantheism' because he saw God as an active energy in matter and mind, continuously working and creating in the whole of nature. Pantheism, when 'sheer' or 'simply' is placed in front of it, becomes a pejorative word, and the pantheistic thinker is frequently rejected out of hand. It is interesting to note Professor A. E. Meyer's judgment on Froebel's philosophy:

'Much of Froebel's thinking sojourned in the lotus land of mysticism. In consequence, his writing, and even some of his Kindergarten practices, are frequently blanketed in a fog of half-tones, symbols, and allusions. Today, Froebel's mysticism carries no more weight than fortune-telling, and if the kindergarten continues to be well regarded, it is because in the main it is rooted in psychological and sociological verity' (1).

Froebel's philosophy was a personal one, however, derived from the philosophy, science, psychology and beliefs of his time. He was a theistic evolutionist in the sense that he saw life as an evolutionary process with God as the initiator and continuing agent in the process. But if one examines his writings, not for the 'half-tones, symbols and allusions' to which A. E. Meyer refers, but for the broad, general ideas of life, one finds almost a modern view of the cosmic process, as well as a seventeenth-century Leibnitzian Monadology. Teilhard de Chardin, for example, saw the organic whole as the Biosphere, with God, the Omega point, as the unifying factor. Leibnitz (1646–1716) saw all nature as constructed of myriads of unities or monads, minute 'wholes' with God as the Great Monad unifying the totality. Froebel saw God as the original Creator of the whole universe, whilst every single piece of matter, including man, was part of the Creator.

The evolutionary process of life was to a large extent in man's own hands. Julian Huxley has much more recently reiterated this theme, in what we no doubt regard as a more 'scientific' manner. But due regard must be given to the scientific ethos of Froebel's own day, and far from sojourning 'in the lotus land of mysticism' Froebel was, indeed, well ahead scientifically and educationally. He believed that man held his destiny in his own hands, and that his actual rate of development or evolution was, in addition, an *educational* matter, not a question of blind chance or accident. More will be said about this in the section on education, but it is sufficient to point out here that Froebel had a clearly conceived aim in education based on a philosophy of man's natural development within God's creation.

It was this belief in the potential of man for greater harmony, unity and development that led Froebel to question the existing methods for such personal integration and progress. It does not help very much to classify Froebel as an 'idealist' or a 'pantheist' or a 'transcendentalist'. His philosophy was certainly religious, and the stigmatization of everything religious as 'fortune-telling' is more of a comment on the classifier than upon religion or the religionist. For Froebel man's potential derived purely from his origin:

'Nature and man have their origin in one and the same eternal Being, and . . . their development takes place in accordance with the same laws, only at different stages' (2).

It is interesting to note that Froebel's view of God was not that of some static, unchanging, inert Being, nor yet of One who from time to time made incursions into man's natural realm of things. God was a dynamic Being who contributed to man's own dynamism by aiding man's spontaneity not only for the development of rich social relationships and adaptation to life, but also for changing life and society itself and for creating conditions for his own betterment as well as for changing himself in the process.

In all this Froebel recognized certain principles and needs—the need for a balanced sort of personal life as well as a balanced society; the need for proportion and harmony in all life and activity; and the need for a sound concept of individual as well as social purpose and function. Froebel was not a devotee of the crystal ball; he was a man with a vision of what might be, and what could be, if human beings were sufficiently forward-looking, and his vision of the creation of a new society, with mankind living a fuller, freer and better life, was not an airy idealism: it was a vision which led to practical applications within the framework of education, which he saw—as many have done before and since—as the means of its materialization.

Froebel certainly was not ignorant of the 'psychological and sociological verity' of his thought and practice; for him the whole of education centred upon a sound view of the nature of children, and a belief that the only true education was a humane one which, at the same time, saw God at the beginning of the process, in the process, and as the goal of the process. This is not very popular in the present half-century, but at least it had the merit of providing grounds and reasons for its particular practices. If God's will is expressed in the whole of the material world he has created, it seemed reasonable to Froebel that the child should be trained to observe and perceive that will in nature, and to express it in and through his personal life. And if he mingled philosophy and theology with educational theory and practice it was because for him life was whole, undifferentiated, a unity—and he wanted children to see life with the same perspective of a *Weltanschauung*. We may not accept his particular *Weltanschauung*, but at least he had one.

C HIS EDUCATIONAL THEORY AND PRACTICE

Froebel was a basically religious man with a consciousness of an all-pervasive spiritual influence. God, or the eternal Divine Unity, was for him the essence of all things and all beings; hence, he regarded human nature as good in itself. Growth was a form of self-realization or self-fulfilment, and it is therefore not surprising that he saw in childhood growth, or development, both the problem of education and its key. The unity which he saw in all things had somehow to be developed positively within the growing child. As he remarks,

'The essential business of the school is not so much to communicate a variety and multiplicity of facts as to give prominence to the ever-living unity that is in all things' (3).

In this process of the elicitation of 'the ever-living unity' in all things, Froebel was very much concerned with the recollections of his own youthful days spent in the country, in the woods and forests. It was here that he found harmony and unity within nature and himself, and he saw the possibility of all other children doing the same. God could be revealed to the child through Nature, and so any study connected with Nature was of vital concern to him. The biological sciences provided a disciplined approach to the evolutionary study of life in all its infinite variety. This unity of life Froebel transferred to the various aspects of education that concerned him; the various stages of the development of the life of each individual child, for example, possessed a unity which defied such broad classifications as infancy, childhood, youth and manhood. At best such divisions were guide-lines only; at worst they presented obstacles to unity.

This preoccupation with the unity of all things also pervaded his views on the child's mental life and his subjects of study. The classical tripartite division of man into intellect, emotion and will was perhaps superficially useful, since we must perforce see and understand all things analytically. But Froebel insisted upon the unity of the child's mental life in each separate moment of his existence—the child, even as the adult, operated as a unity, and thought, feeling and volition were not separate faculties of being which were capable of discrete operation. The more we thought in these terms, the more we assisted in the disintegration of the child: the more we viewed him as a unity, the more we were likely to assist in integrating his personality.

Froebel considered that the division of the school timetable into 'subjects' contributed to disunity and disharmony within the child. As a student he had himself pursued a large number of interrelated disciplines and interests, and he regretted the tendency to perpetuate somewhat artificial divisions of study and over-specialization. Had it not been for this 'total' view of life he might have achieved 'better' academic qualifications —but certainly narrower ones. He saw unity between the various subjects of study and he felt that this unity was such a vital one that it could be mediated to his pupils only through a curriculum which largely ignored a timetable system of school and class control. With our 'modern' concepts of integrated study, interdisciplinary enquiries, and so forth we are quite used to such concepts of unity—but this was in the early nineteenth century. Nor was this, for Froebel, a merely artificial integration of the subjects—it was the unity of the child that concerned him. Hence *educational play* involved the child not merely in playing in the popular sense but also in feeling, observing, perception of form, size, space, time and movement, so that the child's participation was total and perpetually concerned with life's dimensions and its unities. Hence, the 'gifts' which were offered to children, such as a sphere, a cube, or a cylinder, were utilized to evoke an awareness of life's harmonies.

Froebel's *The Education of Man*, which appeared in 1826, saw education as a process which consisted in

'leading man, as a thinking, intelligent being, growing into self-consciousness, to a pure unsullied, conscious and free representation of the inner law of Divine Unity, and in teaching him ways and means thereto' (4).

Man's development was a natural one, and there was a certain Rousseauesque naïveté about Froebel's belief that man's natural state was a harmonious one in unity with the Eternal and the Divine. All that was required of education was to provide a free *milieu* for the unfolding of this harmony, and the right sort of programmed or designed nourishment for its full development. Yet Froebel was certainly aware of the many conflicting interests along the road to such development. Much of his use of the Hegelian dialectic in relation to such things as the 'gifts' offered to children is nothing short of nonsensical, but his application of the dialectic in other spheres is a deeper reflection of his own personal commitment to idealist philosophy. Thus, for example, he clearly saw individual interests and group interests as being frequently in conflict. This did not cause him to view society in the way that Rousseau did. Rather he saw the need for a deeper synthesis and reconciliation of these opposing interests. It was through education that such a synthesis could be effected; for education, properly conceived, could provide the occasion and situation for individual activities and group projects.

Froebel was convinced that harmony and unity could be achieved because they were already potentially there. Something of Leibnitz's 'pre-established harmony' was intrinsic in Froebel's philosophy; the patterns were already implicit, they simply had to be made explicit in the development of the child. God was the ground of all things, animate and inanimate—and it was man's purpose to express God, the ground, in his own unfolding or development. For this reason alone there was strictly no end to education—the goal itself was so limitless that education became a continuous process ever seeking to express God in the individual and in the harmony of social interaction. The term pantheism is used all too loosely to epitomize philosophies which defy more precise categorization, or to express a pejorative attitude towards a particular philosophy. Froebel's religious philosophy has been described as 'a sort of pantheism' because he regarded God as 'the All'. Certainly he saw an external uniformity manifest throughout the entire universe which he attributed to the being of God; and he saw a development in the natural world parallel to that in the spiritual world. There was a sense in which the human race as a whole was an organ of the Cosmic Consciousness, or God. And as such man's education involved a maximizing of this Consciousness within his own being and within his society.

H. G. Good claims that Froebel 'had caught the grand vision of a unified people in a harmonious commonwealth' (5), so that education became a great social undertaking whatever means it employed. But it must be noted at the same time that for Froebel this social education, or education for a harmonious society, did not involve utilitarian and vocational education as an end. Froebel thought, lived and taught at the spiritual level, which he regarded as being also the natural level, because of the unity of the two worlds of spirit and nature.

Rejecting as he did purely utilitarian considerations in education, Froebel saw some of the deeper principles of life enacted in forms of activity and play from the earliest ages on. The very game of life was to be viewed in the play of the child right at its inception. Play, in a sense, was a very serious business, and therefore had to be carefully planned to develop the right unities and principles for full being. Nothing was further from

Froebel's mind than some of the free, unregulated play and activity sometimes seen in 'progressive' schools. Through play, educative play, regulated play, the individual developed a disciplined view of life, its complexities and responsibilities.

Thus the kindergarten was essentially a school for life, not the nursery playground which so many educators have seen in it. It was a place where the child could begin that natural unfolding of his essential being which was to go on throughout his entire life. It is not surprising, therefore, that Froebel saw the possibilities of an educational centre which would take in a whole range of schools from the nursery to the technical and the mothers' school. This latter he regarded as vital because of the child's tendency to imitate—a tendency which should be most carefully cultivated and with the best models and examples in mind. Hence mothers needed educating as well as their children. The gardeners (teachers and parents) had to be cultivated themselves before they could cultivate the plants (children) in their gardens.

But a garden which involved harmony, unity and beauty was not something that could be allowed to develop in any haphazard sort of way. The best horticultural productions, in Froebel's view, were those which were planted with considerable thought and awareness of the structural and aesthetic content as well as of the methods to be employed to encourage growth and development. He believed, with Rousseau, that any view of the child as 'a little man' could wreck the whole process of development. The child was a growing organism, and growth followed certain rules; there was nothing arbitrary, for example, about his introduction of certain 'gifts'—they appeared in the child's natural development at certain specific and calculated intervals, as the child was assisted through the progressive stages of his evolution. Here Froebel tended to follow Recapitulatory theory.

The purposive activities (*Darstellungen*) of children helped to provide knowledge and experience. Such activities included story-telling, play-acting, miming, writing, speaking, painting, building, inventing and so forth. Through such creative activity the child educated himself, provided certain general lines of direction were given. Without such control and direction much of the child's energy would be simply and uncreatively dissipated. To some extent Froebel foreshadowed the psychodrama of Moreno—the living out of what demands utterance as an essential feature of self-liberation and fulfilment. The senses which were being awakened in the child were encouraged and channelled by deliberately devised play-way methods.

Even a cursory reading of some of Froebel's educational ideas would make one seriously wonder whether there was the possibility of anything new in the realm of method, apart from the development of mechanical aids and the stream-lining of the process of direction through programming. R. H. Quick has said that practically all the best tendencies of modern thought on education 'culminate in what was said by Friedrich Froebel' (6). Much of it is certainly there *in embryo*, although many would argue for some of his methods on slightly different grounds. His methods and ideas also suffered the fate of those of all the great educationists: what begins in a methodical, yet unformalized way, tends to become formalized and stereotyped. The 'object lessons' of Froebel were designed basically to be the spontaneous acquisition of knowledge from nature's prodigal presentation of interesting and informative material. Methodologists, however, had to classify and categorize, and finally reduce the material to an inert exhibition of formal lessons following a precise, well-defined pattern; and some of the museum pieces that still remain in our libraries of lesson notes for tired teachers exemplify the final fossilization into formalism of something that began in a very lively and mind-teasing manner. But this is saying no more than could be said of any philosophy, theology or educational theory that has ever been produced: a thinker's worst enemies in the long run tend to be his devotees who reduce his thought to a system, a creed or a method which is finally self-stultifying.

Froebel, however, cannot be excused altogether from involvement in the formalizing process. The presentation of play materials on the basis of an interpretation of Hegelian dialectic was something that begged to be parodied as only serious followers know how to parody. And to insist that play is educative and purposive, and so should be controlled and directed, may eventually result in the sort of regimentation of play-activity which is neither recreation nor education, but a 'drill' lacking spontaneity and often enjoyment. Froebel's insistence upon play as something organized and based upon 'whole interests', as distinct from the 'elements of experience' of Pestalozzi, needs to be seen in the light of the work of more recent theorists on play, such as George Herbert Mead. Formalized play, whatever the theory behind it, can be deadly dull, whether in the primary school, the secondary school, or anywhere else.

Froebel, though not a professional psychologist, saw the necessity of understanding as completely as possible the psychological development of the child as he grew into boyhood and eventually adulthood. Whilst he accepted certain broad stages of development—infancy, childhood, boyhood and youth—Froebel made no detailed analysis, such as that of the Piagetian school, of the intellectual development of the child. The unfolding of the essence of the child's nature was seen by Froebel more in philosophical than in purely psychological terms. But in so far as his educational theory has a psychological basis, it is a psychology of activism: man unfolds himself by continuous participation, by doing, by creativity. Learning was always regarded by Froebel as secondary to doing; in fact, learning should not (and true learning could not) occur *in vacuo*. It could happen only through active experience and expressive activity.

In Froebel's educational concept, home, school and society possessed a basic unity which education reinforced, and all educational problems had to be seen in the larger context of society, much as Plato insisted that justice could be fully appreciated and understood only in the context of the larger letters of the Republic. School was not a teaching shop nor an instrument for learning inert ideas: it was a vital nexus between the individual and the group, between the home and society, between man and God, between the potential and the real, between the actual and the ideal.

Like Rousseau, Froebel had a very optimistic view of man's inherent nature. Man has to live largely by a series of fictions. Schiller somewhere remarked: 'Know this, a mind sublime puts greatness into life, yet seeks it not therein.' In opposition to theological dogmas of Original Sin, Froebel saw in the child a sort of primeval innocence, and he put into all life a divine unity and harmony which pervaded the personality of the developing child. How far Froebel really sought such sublimity and greatness in the children he educated it is difficult to say, but perhaps, like Schiller, he was content to posit such principles, and then to work furiously to make his fiction reality. It is always interesting to note how the pendulum swings and how events come full circle. The reaction against the religious dogma of Original Sin has been considerable, but the fiction dies hard, and has returned in our own time in more genetic and psychological terms, such as: 'All men are born criminals', and it is the work of education to socialize them into conveniently obedient citizens. Froebel saw the purpose of education as that of helping natural growth, and this growth was a purpose of unifying the outer and the inner. Herbert Spencer spoke of human development and evolution as the adjustment of internal relations to external relations, and of external relations to internal relations. Today we speak of socialization and internalization. But all these processes are, in themselves, neutral; it is the sort of society to which we are becoming socialized that matters: it is the principles we internalize that are important. And here Froebel had at least a philosophy to offer—a cosmic unity however remote and undemonstrable—and certain values which he considered worthy of internalization.

Moreover, Froebel felt that any educational system should make for unity without destroying individuality and diversity. In a sense he stated the modern dilemma of a Welfare State seeking to set up a 'comprehensive' system, in which all are promised equality of opportunity, but in which natural talent must be fully recognized and able to develop. There must be sufficient unity of aims and purposes to provide a stable society: but there must at the same time be sufficient individual, personal and diverse development to ensure a virile, mobile and progressive society. Froebel certainly aimed at social cohesion, through the harmonizing of conflicting interests and reconciliation of contrasts; and in his concern for the individual development of each child he also thought in terms of natural growth. He believed that the all-pervasive Divine Unity would be sufficient to adjust any resultant discord.

REFERENCES

1 Meyer, A. E., *An Educational History of the Western World* (McGraw-Hill, 1965), p. 371.
2 Froebel, F., *The Education of Man* (Tr. W. N. Hailman) (New York, Appleton-Century-Crofts Inc., 1911), pp. 160–1.
3 Ibid., p. 134.
4 Ibid., p. 2.
5 Good, H. G., *A History of Western Education* (Macmillan, 1966), p. 279.
6 Quick, R. H., *Essays on Educational Reformers* (Longman, 1904), p. 384.

BIBLIOGRAPHY

Blow, S. E., *Symbolic Education: a Commentary on Froebel's 'Mother Play'* (Appleton and Co., 1894).
Blow, S. E., *Letters to a Mother on the Philosophy of Froebel* (Appleton and Co., 1899).
Blow, S. E., *Educational Issues in the Kindergarten* (Appleton and Co., 1908).
Bowen, H. C., *Froebel and Education by Self-Activity* (Scribner, 1899).
Cole, P. R., *Herbart and Froebel: an attempt at Synthesis* (Columbia University Press, 1907).
Curtis, S. J. and Boultwood, M. E. A., *A Short History of Educational Ideas* (University Tutorial Press, 4th ed., 1965), Chapter XIV.
Fletcher, S. S. and Welton, J., *Froebel's Chief Writings on Education* (Longman, 1912).
Franks, F., *The Kindergarten System* (S. Sonnenschein, 1897).
Froebel, F., *Autobiography* (Tr. by E. Michaelis and H. K. Moore) (Allen and Unwin, 12th ed., 1915).
Froebel, F., *Letters on the Kindergarten* (London, 1890).
Froebel, F., *The Education of Man* (Tr. by W. N. Hailmann) (Appleton and Co., 1906).
Froebel, F., *Pedagogies of the Kindergarten* (Tr. by J. Jarvis) (New York, 1895).
Froebel, F., *Education by Development* (Tr. by J. Jarvis) 1899.
Froebel, F., *Mother's Songs, Games and Stories* (Tr. by F. and E. Lord) (London, 1885).
Good, H. G., *A History of Western Education* (Macmillan, 1966), Chapter 12.
Hailmann, W. N., *Kindergarten Culture* (Wilson and Co., 1873).
Hayward, F. H., *Pestalozzi and Froebel* (R. Holland, 1905).
Heinemann, A. H., *Froebel Letters* (Boston, Lee and Shepard, 1893).
Jarvis, J., *Froebel's Education by Development* (Appleton and Co., 1900).
Jebb, E. M., *The Significance of Froebel's Ethical Teaching for Education Today* (Liberal Jewish Synagogue, London, 1954).
Judges, A. V., *Freedom, Froebel's Vision and our Reality* (N.F.F., 1953).

Kilpatrick, W. H., *Froebel's Kindergarten Principles Critically Examined* (Macmillan, 1916).

Lawrence, E. (ed.): *Friedrich Froebel and English Education* (N.F.F., 1952).

Murray, E. R., *Froebel as a Pioneer of Modern Psychology* (Philips).

Priestman, O. B., *Froebel Education Today* (University of London Press, 1952).

Quick, R. H., *Essays on Educational Reformers* (Longman, 3rd ed., 1904).

Rusk, R. R., *The Doctrines of the Great Educators* (Macmillan, 3rd ed., 1965), Chapter XI.

Shirreff, E., *Short Life of Froebel* (London, 1887).

Shirreff, E., *The Kindergarten* (S. Sonnenschein, 1880).

Snider, D. J., *The Life of Frederick Froebel* (Sigma Publishing Company, 1900).

White J., *Educational Ideas of Froebel* (London, 1905).

Chapter 13

Froebelianism and Montessori

A FROEBELIANISM AND SLOYD

The second half of the nineteenth century saw a variety of developments of the ideas and practices of Friedrich Froebel throughout Europe and England. This was important not merely in the realm of educational practice, but also in relation to political attitudes towards the educational system. There are some methods, for example, which are not amenable to the more orthodox and conservative forms of examination, and so new attitudes and assessments have to be formulated. English infant school methods owe a great deal to Froebelianism.

In Europe the disciples of Froebel were spreading his teaching, or various aspects of it, throughout such countries as Finland and Sweden. In Finland, Uno Cygnaeus (1810–88) did his utmost to permeate the elementary schools with Froebelian principles, and in 1886 'sloyd' (*slöjd*) entered Finnish schools as a compulsory subject or occupation. This was a form of manual training which saw in the utilization of the knife, or penknife, a means of creativity. The word 'sloyd' meant the process of slicing or slashing, and the process derived from the fact that much of normal life involved the creation of useful, as well as beautiful, objects by use of the knife. Cygnaeus found that this manual form of activity was pragmatic in many ways; there is something therapeutic about cutting up in order to create since it combines two of man's diametrically opposed tendencies, namely, to destroy and to build. Europe generally was going through a period in which many of the old home industries were on the decline, and 'sloyd' at least provided children with the necessary skill to create as a hobby even if the total effect did little to arrest the general decline. Moreover, of course, educational ideas are amongst the most infectious in the world, however mangled and mismanaged they become in the process of transportation.

The Swede, Otto Salomon (1849–1907), was also painfully aware of the culturally destructive influences of industrialization. As a teacher he had been affected by the theories of Froebel and some of their practical consequences; and he had also visited Cygnaeus. In many ways he understood 'sloyd' better than the latter, for whom it was largely a nostalgic regress into the dying vocations in a progressive industrial age. For

Salomon there was an intrinsic value in craft activity even though the pupil never afterwards used it as a means of livelihood, or for that matter as a hobby. To him it was not an extra subject on the curriculum but an essential part of the whole process of total education and development. 'Action' and 'activity' were becoming as commonplace terms in the latter part of the last century as they are overworked catchwords and slogans in the present. In 'sloyd' there was both a development of individual skill and also a sense of personal achievement and fulfilment.

With these general concepts in mind, Salomon in 1875 held at Naas a summer training school to which were invited any teachers from foreign countries who were interested in teaching not so much from the vocational point of view as from the purely educational. To Salomon learning was not simply a cognitive process but a process involving the whole personality in the co-ordination of both thought and action. There was, he felt, far too much verbalization in the work of the schools; too much dependence upon rote-learning and memorizing of data generally, and too little creative thought processed into novel production. It is true that 'sloyd' used wood mainly as its medium to begin with, but the principle did not preclude the use of any media which might be of creative value. It is equally true that, initially, there was a utilitarian slant to 'sloyd'; pupils were trained to use their skills in the creation of useful, practical objects. But, again, this did not preclude the manufacture of what was at the same time aesthetic. Mind and body joined to create in a skilful, harmonious way something of value to society as well as to the individual.

Salomon felt that certain attitudes and qualities would be instilled into, or evoked from, the pupil through such training. A child who had worked with his hands, and had come to understand and fully to appreciate the skills in such manual activity, would never be tempted to despise or disregard those who worked with their hands for the benefit and running of society. We know, from experience in our own society, that a continued deprivation of some classes in the realm of manual skills, leads not only to an almost total incapacity of many individuals to perform sometimes even the simplest manual operations; but it tends also to inculcate an attitude of superiority towards those who 'work with their hands', however skilfully. Salomon realized full well the pride in a sense of personal achievement which children have when they have hewn out of a formless mass of wood an object which they can use in the home, and which they can regard as an extension of themselves and their personalities. Through such activities there would develop a healthy respect for nature in the raw, for the tools which man had devised, for the skills innate in most, if not all, individuals, and for the work and life-styles of other people whose roles, though not identical with our own, were as vitally important to the larger society as those which we ourselves had adopted.

One of the keynotes of such activity was enjoyment. Salomon recognized that much of the academic learning at schools was not enjoyed by the pupils and presented a repetitive chore for many teachers. True education was to be achieved by enjoyment through consciously organized activity—not through activity for activity's sake. A child learned to trust his own judgment through exercising it in creativity, and this in turn led to independence and self-reliance. The whole self was involved in an exercise of production, and in participation and involvement in the product from its mental concept to its detailed construction and completion. In this process, mind, muscle and nerve all collaborated in harmonious co-ordination to produce an artefact with which the child had complete identification. In so far as this was achieved the craft work not only had 'cultural value', it was in fact the extension of culture itself in the mind and activity of the child. Much of modern 'activity' seems to be activity for activity's sake, without any philosophy of culture extension or total participation—it is often just a way of 'learning' things.

But the philosophy behind Salomon's work was much more radical and searching. Much of what he did and hoped to achieve was naturally misunderstood because we all adopt practices which seem successful without a deeper inquiry into the underlying principles. Salomon's principles, whether right or wrong, were nothing if not thoroughgoing. The habits he sought to instil were those of industry, indeed a love of work, orderliness, neatness, exactness and cleanliness. With Salomon perfection was the goal to be aimed at and nothing less, and the teacher's function was to give every assistance to achieve this. The child was never completely alone, although he was encouraged to use fully his initiative, his imagination and his industry; but this did not mean the acceptance of work half-completed, ill-proportioned or inexact. To achieve the goal the child had to develop considerable patience and perseverance, for involvement was not *just* a question of busyness or undirected activity; it was a question of the cultivation of full attention on the work in hand as well as the goal set. Independence and self-reliance were not achieved by just leaving the child alone; he had to be given tasks which, with help and guidance, he could satisfactorily achieve and still be able to say, 'I did this', 'this is my work', 'this is my production'. How reminiscent this is of the Taoist leader and teacher:

'A leader is best
When people barely know that he exists . . .
Of a good leader, who talks little,
When his work is done, his aim fulfilled,
They will all say, "We did this ourselves" ' (1).

Salomon was concerned that the child should not only develop skill in his particular manual activities and productions, but that he should also have some appreciation of form through the perpetual training of the child in visual perception. It was precisely here that he saw the projection of the individual personality into the world of both nature and artefacts. Harmony with the natural forms which he perceived around him would assist the child in the development of the sense of form in his own production. And as he saw the perfection of the one so he would not be content until he had produced perfection in the other.

Teachers from both England and America were impressed with Salomon's work even if many of them missed the point of the principles behind it. We know only too well that preoccupation with methodology frequently leads to a complete misrepresentation of some of the most soundly based principles. Woodwork was often introduced as an extra subject, particularly for the less academically minded; to this was added some metalwork and other forms of handwork. Moreover, Salomon's emphasis on the completion of the work, and on the perfection of its execution, was frequently omitted or neglected; many felt that insistence on the sort of thoroughness which Salomon envisaged could result only in frustration and despair. In consequence, many of his basic principles were ignored, and too often children became involved in mechanical manual exercises with neither the vision nor the reality of finished articles.

Whilst Salomon was developing his 'sloyd', and disciples abroad were adapting it to their own particular requirements and ideas, more direct Froebelian links were being made in England through some of Froebel's European devotees. In the year 1854 the kindergarten movement began in England largely through the efforts of Baroness von Marenholtz Bülow from Germany, whilst two other women disciples, Madame Ronge and Madame Kraus Boelte were responsible for establishing the first kindergarten in Bloomsbury. This, and other schools developing along similar lines, sought to employ the 'activity method', although using the more natural energies of children in their spontaneous play. By 1874 there were kindergarten associations in various parts of England, and also in Dublin; and largely through such interested women as Emily Shirreff, Maria Grey and Madame Michaelis the English Froebel Society was eventually founded. Madame Michaelis was responsible for the inauguration of a kindergarten and preparatory school attached to the Girls' High School, Croydon, and several other schools associated with the Girls' Public Day Schools Company.

It soon became clear that the special concepts of education involved in Froebelianism required special teachers, and this led to at least two separate teacher-training activities. The London School Board appointed lecturers to lecture on the kindergarten concept to the infant school teachers employed in its area, whilst the British and Foreign School Society set up the first training college at Stockwell to train infant school teachers in Froebelian principles. The kindergartens tended to exist largely for the children of the middle and upper classes, although many Froebelian devotees denied this at the time. The mere fact, however, that they were attached to girls' public schools as a preparatory element tended to set the 'private school' seal upon them. And where the progressive influence of Froebel's teaching attached itself to the infant departments of public elementary schools, Froebelianism, like Salomon's 'sloyd' tended to be regarded as an extra 'subject' to be fitted into their timetables. It was all very akin to the attitude of some modern, 'enlightened', secondary schools which run a normal curriculum of subjects, but dotted here and there on the timetable are special periods for 'integrated studies'. It is not surprising that J. W. Adamson remarks that:

'throughout the nineteenth century Froebelianism remained a misunderstood exotic in the "infant departments" of our elementary schools. Whereas its author designed it as a systematic education of young children, those schools persisted in regarding the "kindergarten" as one "subject" amongst others; they saw no absurdity in time-tables which confined it to two specific school times in each week. . . . A better understanding of Froebel was not attained or applied in these schools before the twentieth century, when a few unofficial enthusiasts opened "free kindergartens" in Scotland and in this country' (2).

In 1887 the National Froebel Union was constituted to ensure that teachers were adequately trained in Froebelian ideas and principles, and knew how to apply them in a wholehearted way—where they were applied at all. Such teachers were tested by special examinations and awarded Froebel Certificates.

B MARIA MONTESSORI (1870–1952)

Like Dewey Maria Montessori bestrides both centuries, and indeed she died in the same year as Dewey. Montessori would certainly have been distinguished whatever she had taken up. As it was, she was the first woman to be awarded the degree of Doctor of Medicine of Rome University, where she worked in a psychiatric clinic and became the director of a special school which sought to help handicapped children. She was a deeply religious woman, a Catholic, who sought always to see life whole. Her interest in psychiatry led to studies in experimental psychology, whilst her concern for children who were handicapped in various ways directed her to an interest in anthropological pedagogy. She sought in every conceivable way to qualify herself for the varied and many tasks which she took upon herself, initially perhaps out of a sense of duty, but ultimately because she saw the care, development and education of children as her life's work.

It was only natural that she should become interested in the environmental factors in education when one considers some of the shocking conditions she experienced in Rome as the background to the children she was seeking to help. The dirt and squalor of the city's tenement buildings were something she sought to combat not simply through schemes of rehousing or reconditioning, but through re-education—or, at least, through the proper education of the new generation growing up. This she saw as a programme of teaching children, however small and young, the requisite standards of cleanliness and hygiene. To this end she began, in 1907, to establish infant schools in which children were trained to live a healthy, normal life wherein they could feel at home in their own world and not live as midgets in an adult world. The original *Casa dei Bambini*, or Children's House, was designed to allow children to develop in an improved physical as well as social environment. With everything adapted to their size, and special equipment which they could use and freely manipulate, coupled with a garden leading directly out of the house in which they could not only play but, during the fine weather, live an almost completely open-air life, Montessori felt that the children would inevitably improve in their educational development.

Montessori tackled all her ideas with scientific interest and rigour, and supported her theories and methods at the psychological level. She had discovered that certain methods were successful with abnormal and handicapped children, and she felt that what had succeeded with the abnormal might well prove successful with the normal. This was justified at the sensory level of training, and it is interesting to note that in order to improve the tactual sense she advocated reducing other senses and their activities to a minimum. This will be discussed in greater detail presently: it is mentioned here merely to indicate that her educational practice followed largely her experiments with children who were deficient in one sense or another.

There was, from the beginning, a certain suspicion of Maria Montessori and her work. Politically she was a democrat and she was seen as something of a contradiction—her many cultural and scientific interests, her reforming spirit, her desire to lead in a man's world, her freedom from authoritarianism (although not authority) in a close-knit Catholic society, her individualism—all these facts combined to arouse antagonism as well as jealousy from various quarters. Even her successful Children's Houses were seen by many as an affront to good order and social discipline; although, in fact, in all of her groups members were expected to conform to certain rules and standards of behaviour, neatness, and cleanliness for the benefit of the community.

Montessori argued, as Rousseau had done, that education should be pedocentric. The child had to be central in all our considerations of curriculum and timetable. Moreover, the child had to be treated as a child and not as a little man: Rousseau, too, had said that 'Nature wants children to be children before they are men' (3). Education was the means whereby, and the framework in which, the child was helped to develop in a normal way and to enlarge his awareness of the external world. Both the system, or organization, and the teacher existed simply to help the child as and when he felt the need of such assistance: but such help was to be unobtrusive. The teacher was not strictly such; she was a 'directress', providing the right direction when the child called for guidance. The essential thing was for the individual to gain experience through spontaneous self-expression and activity, and for this the child needed the right environment and time—time fully to express itself and exhaust its enquiry. The Hadow Report, in relation to the primary school, accepted some of this, at least in principle, in 1931, when it stated that

'the curriculum is to be thought of in terms of activity and experience rather than of knowledge to be acquired and facts to be stored' (4).

This statement at this time is perhaps doubly interesting when one recalls that it was during the thirties that Hitler dissolved the German Montessori Society and banned its schools, and that Mussolini also closed Montessorian schools in Italy.

Montessori strongly supported the concept of 'readiness' in the intellectual and general educational development of the child. According to her the free, spontaneous joy of discovery, and even the very means for further development, would be destroyed if the child were helped too early or given information prematurely. The child needed freedom, the perfect freedom which derives from the laws of its own nature. There was something of the flavour of Rousseau's 'discipline of natural consequences' about this; Rousseau honestly believed that the seeds of happiness were within us, and that given the right environment for the evocation of liberty we should find our happiness. Montessori accepted this too. Rewards and punishments of an artificial nature were quite unnecessary in the child's development—there was something self-correcting about a natural education.

In her philosophy of education Montessori produced a strange amalgam of idealism, naturalism and realism. Her idealism sprang from her acceptance of spiritual ideas and her religious, Catholic background. Her naturalism derived from the environmental situation of the children she dealt with in Rome, and a recognition of their need to live a full, free, healthy life without the restrictive influences of generations of social decay and conditions which lacked even the elements of sanitation, cleanliness and hygiene. But truth and knowledge she felt could be reached only through immediate, physical, sensuous environmental 'realities'. So that, whilst emphasizing the value of religion, morality, music, art and poetry she underlined also the vital importance of things and the child's relationship with them. Her philosophy was not so much consciously syncretic as unconsciously synthetic. There was, in all her thinking, a happy union of the ideal, the natural and the real.

Children had to be trained to look after themselves and to be essentially independent of others, whilst at the same time able to combine with others when the situation demanded it. In the training of the senses Montessori believed that one should isolate them whenever it was possible. If children were being trained for acuity of hearing then visual perception was minimized and the exercises were applied in both darkness and silence; similarly, the development of the tactile sense was accomplished by blindfolding the subjects and presenting only tactual stimuli. These were methods which Montessori had applied to the handicapped and deficient, and she argued that they could equally work for normal subjects. In her development of this theme she found that she could devise particular objects and materials (just as Froebel devised certain 'gifts') which would assist in sense-discrimination, such as perception of form, and size and weight, acuity of hearing, sight and touch, and a nice discrimination of colour. Coupled with this realistic, practical sensory training was mental training in association, recognition of objects, and recall of names corresponding with objects.

Much of Montessori's method seems to smack of faculty psychology and a doctrine of formal training which further implies transfer. Some of this she owed, no doubt, to the physiological approach of Séguin. Where a child was completely or partially deficient in a particular sense many of her methods seemed to have validity, but it is questionable whether such methods can be applied *in toto* to normal children. R. R. Rusk further questioned 'the value of a specific training of the sensory powers for their own sake', and argued that it was even doubtful whether the effects of a sensory training in any specific sphere could be transferred to other sensory spheres. As Rusk points out, however, much of the criticism of Montessori's sensory training disappears once the errors of faculty psychology are cleared away.

'What Montessori designates sensory training should have been termed perceptual training, involving as it does judgment and comparison' (5).

In this way the whole personality of the child becomes involved in and through perception; and the discrimination and acuity, to which Montessori so frequently refers, apply to the total self and not simply to discrete elements, whether physical or mental. But Montessori would seem to have had this totality in mind even though there was a concentration upon individual senses, for sense-discrimination implies a judgment, a discernment, a 'sifting' of possibilities, which is inevitably a mental process. One might attack her methods, perhaps, rather than her theory, for the 'gagging' of one sense in order to increase the acuity of another was anything but natural method. In play children are using all their senses in a co-ordinated way without the self-consciousness that the shutting off of certain senses must inevitably produce. Of course children must learn to discriminate; but in a modern world replete with perpetual, unremitting sounds, sights and smells it might even be deleterious to make them hypersensitive to their environment.

Montessori believed that in the more didactic processes writing ought to precede reading. This again was based largely on a physiological approach which saw in writing the involvement of the child mainly in muscular activity. Reading, on the other hand, involved more than the muscular movement of the eyes, it required some interpretation of the signs presented to the eyes, which was a mental activity, and the management of the voice. In writing Montessori sought to provide facility and skill in letter production without involving the child's mind initially in meaning. To hold and manipulate a pen freely as an instrument was in itself a skill requiring considerable concentration and adaptability; and the formation of letters was reduced to a piece of sheer mechanism, or mechanical copying. The next stage was to produce writing which expressed ideas, and then finally writing from dictation through the analysis phonetically of the spoken word. Thus, when the child reached the stage of reading it was not a question simply of an effort to produce certain accurate sounds, but rather an immediate response to meaning, to the ideas within the context of the words read. Montessori was opposed to the sort of reading where the child may eventually read a sentence correctly, without hesitation, but still have no understanding of its meaning. Reading was already prepared for in the process of writing.

When it came to number Montessori emphasized again the importance of the part played by the senses, and the value of actually handling things in order to evaluate their weight, length and size. She also made use of rods of different lengths and colour, as well as blocks, which might be used in play, but in an educational and functional sort of way. Judgment was trained by comparing size, shape and relationships in real things; so that training in number was never an academic exercise on paper divorced from the realities of life—it arose out of the manipulation of the child's environment. Today we have such structural materials as Stern Rods, Dienes Multi-base Arithmetic Blocks, Cuisenaire Rods, Lowenfeld Poleidoblocs, Algebraical Experience Material and so forth. All these, like the Montessori materials, have their value, but as L. G. W. Sealey and V. Gibbon have remarked,

'Structural material which attracts children and which, in time, can communicate its inherent properties to them, will have some place in the infant school. It might supplement the more common objects of the environment and the everyday situations through which children gain understanding of number and relations. It should never *replace* them' (6).

Montessori was at first influenced by the currently popular doctrine of recapitulation in human development. G. Stanley Hall (1846–1924), who pioneered child study in America, accepted that just as man had evolved physically, so he had gone through certain stages in his social and psychological development which paralleled, or virtually recapitulated, the history of the human race. In particular, he saw in children's play a recapitulation of the cultural epochs of man. In her provisions for free play Montessori had this idea very much in mind—the child had to work out, almost dramatize, in its play its own racial history. Montessori, however, had given up this view by about 1917, although she retained free activity or play. With Froebel she believed that through their play children became creative and expressive, and provided the 'directress' offered the right sort of material in the environment the child would learn in a self-directed way. This freedom was never viewed as something anarchical; it was a means of developing self-organization and self-discipline. Unfortunately, it very often happens that an imitation of the method, without any fundamental understanding of the philosophical and psychological principles behind it, results in a purposeless display of noisy non-events. The methods of Maria Montessori have often proved highly successful in small, selective groups of children with properly trained Montessorian 'directresses'; and equally unsuccessful in crowded, ill-directed classes presided over by uncomprehending teachers, often not too well disciplined themselves.

To Montessori the teacher may be an 'observer', but she has, nevertheless, to be a highly-trained observer; she may be an 'organizer of the environment', but she has to be a good organizer, and has to be sensitively aware of the sort of environment the child needs; she may be a guide, but we all know what happens when the blind guide the blind. Montessori's system makes great demands upon the teacher as a person, as a human being, as one of discrimination, experience and sound judgment, as a being who has great concern for the individual:

'instead of facility of speech she has to acquire the power of silence; instead of teaching she has to observe; instead of the proud dignity of one who claims to be infallible she assumes the vesture of humility' (7).

REFERENCES

1 Lao Tzu, *Tao Te Ching*, Book One, XVII.
2 Adamson, J. W., *English Education: 1789–1902* (C.U.P., 1930, reprinted 1964), p. 340.
3 Rousseau, J-J, *Emile* (J. M. Dent) (Everyman Library), p. 54.
4 Hadow Report, *The Primary School*, 1931 (reprinted 1946), p. 83.
5 Rusk, R. R., *Doctrines of the Great Educators* (Macmillan, 1965, 3rd ed.), p. 295.
6 Sealey, L. G. W. and Gibbon, V., *Communication and Learning in the Primary School* (B. Blackwell, 1962, reprinted 1964), p. 157.
7 Montessori, M., *The Advanced Montessori Method* (Heinemann, 1917), Vol. 1, p. 128.

BIBLIOGRAPHY

Adams, J., *Modern Developments in Educational Practice* (University of London Press, 1922).
Adamson, J. W., *English Education, 1789–1902* (C.U.P., 1930, reprinted 1964).
Boyd, W., *From Locke to Montessori* (Harrap, 1917).
Culverwell, E. P., *Montessori Principles and Practice* (Bell, 1913).
Curtis, S. J., *History of Education in Great Britain* (University Tutorial Press, 1963), Chapters VIII–X.
Curtis, S. J. and Boultwood, M. E. A., *A Short History of Educational Ideas* (University Tutorial Press, 1965), Chapters XIV and XVIII.
Curtis, S. J. and Boultwood, M. E. A., *An Introductory History of English Education Since 1800* (University Tutorial Press, 1964), Chapter X.
Holman, H., *Séguin and His Physiological Method* (Pitman, 1914).
Kilpatrick, W. H., *Montessori Examined* (Constable, 1915).
Lawrence, E. (ed.), *Friedrich Froebel and English Education* (University of London Press, 1952).
McMillan, M., *The Nursery School* (Dent, 1919, revised ed. 1930).
McMillan, M., *Education through the Imagination* (S. Sonnenschein, 1904).
Montessori, M., *The Montessori Method* (Heinemann, 1912, 2nd ed. 1920).
Montessori, M., *The Advanced Montessori Method* (Heinemann, 1917).
Montessori, M., *The Secret of Childhood* (Longman, 1936).
Rusk, R. R., *A History of Infant Education* (University of London Press, 1933).
Rusk, R. R., *Doctrines of the Great Educators* (Macmillan, 1965, 3rd ed.).
Salomon, O., *Theory of Educational Sloyd* (George Philip, 1892).
Smith, F., *A History of English Elementary Education* (*1760–1902*) (University of London Press, 1931).
Standing, E. M., *Maria Montessori: Her Life and Work* (Hollis and Carter, 1957).
Standing, E. M., *The Montessori Method: A Revolution in Education* (Fresno, Academy Guild Press, 1962).
Tozier, J., *An Educational Wonder-Worker: The Methods of Maria Montessori* (The House of Childhood Inc., N.Y., 1912).

Chapter 14

John Dewey
(1859–1952)

A HIS LIFE AND WORK

John Dewey grew up in Vermont, a New England State, where his father kept a shop in a small village. He soon became aware, from village gossip and from the seclusion of rural life, that such a society provided a strong group consciousness. As he grew older he came to feel that the current methods of education were sterile, and that it was through everyday human contact that real learning situations were provided. Dewey graduated at the University of Vermont in 1879, and then went on to read history, philosophy and psychology at Johns Hopkins University where, in 1882, he received his Ph.D. He then accepted a lectureship in philosophy at the University of Michigan. He was a man of wide interests, involved in all current problems, and was soon invited to become Professor of Philosophy at Minnesota University, and soon after at the University of Michigan.

In 1894 he became Chairman of the Department of Philosophy, Psychology and Pedagogy at the University of Chicago, and two years later he founded the University Laboratory School, hoping thereby to provide the raw material for experimentation. Dewey had noted that the old simple village life and village community were fast breaking up, and that, whilst other social institutions were undergoing rapid transformation, the institutions of the school and the church were providing little to make the average child aware of the new society. The town child was at a disadvantage since he was making use of amenities he had never seen constructed and was never really competent to internalize. He wore clothing—but knew nothing of how it was made; and he used gas light—but knew nothing of how gas was prepared.

In his experimental school Dewey sought to involve the child entirely in this new environment, and to experiment in new ideas and methods. Specially trained teachers were put in charge of groups of about ten pupils each, and the groups ranged between the ages of four and fourteen. The school was to Dewey largely an exercise in fulfilling Froebelian aims, and its purpose was to promote a spirit of social co-operation and mutual aid. Hence he sought by every available means to provide within the classroom living situations calculated to evoke such co-operation.

In *The School and Society*, published at the turn of the century, Dewey asked four specific questions which he considered any sound educational system should be able to answer:

1 What can be done to bring the school in closer relation to the home and neighbourhood life?
2 What can be done in the way of introducing subject-matter in history and science and art that shall have a positive value and real significance in the child's own life?
3 How can instruction in reading, writing and arithmetic, the formal subjects, be carried on with everyday experience and occupation as the background, and made interesting by relating them to other studies of more inherent content?
4 How can adequate attention be paid to individual powers and needs? (1).

Dewey considered that the school must be a second home: a good home in which the feeling of community and a sense of common interest, pursuits and ambitions could find a place. All pupils were encouraged to participate in practical activity, manual skills and creative work in the school shop; they were all taught to weave, to sew and to cook. In fact, the school was a community or society *in embryo*, and all the practical work the children did must be conceived as 'methods of living and learning, not as distinct studies' (2).

Dewey had thought deeply about the problems of educational content and method before he developed his Laboratory School, but he had no precisely conceived plans which must at all costs succeed. The school was experimental and he sought to discover what was, in the long run, in the interests of the child. It was not, however, a policy of *laissez-faire*: it was not suggested that his pupils should not do things unless they wanted to, or unless it had first occurred to them. As a microsociety the school required direction, leadership and control. Nothing was neglected, and the basic skills, such as the three Rs, would find double acceptance because pupils would appreciate their necessity for the living of a full communal life, and for the natural development of their other work.

In 1904 he became Professor of Philosophy at Columbia University, New York, a position which he held until, at the age of seventy-one, he retired in 1930. Nineteen years later he was still assisting in the writing of books. His prolific works ranged the fields of education, philosophy, ethics, aesthetics, psychology, history and politics; and he was no ivory-tower philosopher. He concerned himself with the public and its problems, with nature and experience, with characters and events, with man's search for knowledge and quest for certainty, and with social action.

B HIS PHILOSOPHY OF PRAGMATISM

The term 'pragmatism' is usually associated with John Dewey himself and with the American psychologist and philosopher, William James (1842–1910); but in its technical and philosophical sense it was first employed by the logician and mathematician, C. S. Peirce (1839–1914). For Peirce 'pragmatism' was a logical *method* for ascertaining the meaning of a particular formula or abstract idea. Peirce was more immediately concerned with applied mathematics and the experimental sciences than with any overall philosophical approach to life itself.

The word 'pragmatism' is itself derived from the Greek word 'pragma', meaning 'an act or deed done, or fit and right to be done'. James, a realist and pluralist philosophically, seized on the word, and in his *Pragmatism* he defined the pragmatic method as

'primarily a method of settling metaphysical disputes that might otherwise be interminable—to try to interpret each notion by tracing its respective practical consequences' (3).

James claimed that ideas *become* true in so far as they assist us to get into a satisfactory relation with all other parts of our personal experience. There was, he considered, a general *pragmatic test* which could be applied to all our so-called truths. If we could assimilate, validate, corroborate and verify our ideas, they were true: if we could not, they were false.

Peirce rejected this interpretation of his own use of the term; he had an intellectual and analytical approach to problems and this 'pragmatic' principle of James seemed to him thoroughly anti-intellectual—if not positively irrational. James appeared to give to the coherence theory of truth a very personal and individual interpretation; so individual that, in the final analysis, what might be 'true' in the experience of one individual could well be 'untrue' in the experience of another. Consequently, Peirce surrendered to James the right to use the term 'pragmatism' for his particular philosophy, and he coined the term 'pragmaticism' for his own original principle (4).

Dewey was particularly interested in the teachings of C. S. Peirce and William James. It was the business of living and the solution of practical problems that enthused him throughout his long career. Moreover, he saw the possibility of defending in rational terms many opposing metaphysical theories, which could in time be resolved by means of a pragmatic solution. The Hegelianism and its dualisms remained with Dewey to the end; and Hegel's synthesis was Dewey's pragmatic resolution.

Dewey began, in his thinking, to abolish the distinction between ends and means. The 'end' was simply a name which we gave to a series of acts taken collectively: the 'means' was a name which we gave to the same series regarded distributively. It was not the 'end' which mattered, since in absolute terms it could never be attained; and in relative terms each 'means' was equally an 'end'. Everything depended upon the point of view. In any event, however, it was not some distinct and distant end that mattered but the practical effects along the way in which we were immediately involved.

Dewey accepted no absolute Truths or Realm of Ends; for him there was the exciting possibility of universal growth and evolution. But, although nothing was ultimate and all was provisional, there was nothing inconsequential in his relativist view. It had its dangers as well as its exciting possibilities: it could well lead to a popular *laissez-faire* in thought and behaviour. And in 1910 he uttered a warning to the effect that the increased control of, and power over, means did not in itself guarantee ultimate or even present happiness. Each means had to be carefully examined and weighed, because the means was an end-in-itself. Life was not shallow or more carefree because the Realm of Ends had been dismissed; on the contrary, there should be greater involvement in all we do and a deeper consideration of the value of the means we employ.

Thus Dewey emphasized the personal and variable element in things; and the truth or falsity of human inquiry depended upon its success or failure, upon its results for the individual himself. Dewey's theory of truth is usually referred to as Instrumentalism, since knowledge, or truth, is never an end-in-itself, but a means or instrument; it is a personal matter, and each individual uses it for the purpose of adapting himself to new problems and situations. The meaning of any concept depends upon its relationship to the individual, and so the latter uses concepts, thoughts, and 'truths' in order to discover personal solutions to his daily problems.

Dewey appears to have reduced all 'truths' to the scientific level of causation: a thing is 'true' if it 'furthers our purpose', that is, if it causes or brings about the consequence that we desire. But we certainly don't always know the consequences of our actions, whether immediately or mediately, and we certainly cannot know them finally: so the pragmatic test seems to depend upon something further and outside itself; it is not in itself a sufficient criterion.

Dewey accepted in broad terms the general theory of evolution, of mutation, change and development. He saw no final end to the possibilities and potentialities of such a process, or to the influence and interrelations of environment and the individual. Dewey saw things 'whole'.

'Dewey's reference to a "unified whole" is an instance of his concern for the oneness of the world. If it dared be said that he had an aim, it was to see the world become a more organic, smoothly-functioning whole' (5).

Any vision of the possibilities of the future by an educational philosopher must, in some sense, be regarded as an aim; and Dewey saw his own philosophy as a basis for a *progressive* form of education. Education was for him a realistic training in the breaking down of existing social barriers and in the developing of ever new links within the whole framework of society. The *function* of education, if not its aim, was like that of inquiry generally to act as a process of reconciliation of opposites, whether in the make-up of the individual or in that of the group, the community or the macrosociety.

In his *Reconstruction in Philosophy* Dewey stated that the time had arrived

'for a pragmatism which shall be emphatically idealistic, proclaiming the essential connection of intelligence with the unachieved future' (6).

There is an implicit perfectionism about this that even Dewey himself could not deny. The evolution of man was not merely a *process*; by the application of his intelligence to his living in the present, by refining his works, by maturing and perfecting, he could achieve *progress* for the future. Dewey undoubtedly wanted 'the best' in life, whatever the best might be, and he wanted to maximize each moment of living. With Rousseau he believed that education was a natural development, a steady growth through experience and experiment, and it is perhaps noteworthy that the first chapter of *Schools of Tomorrow* is largely a series of quotations from Rousseau's *Emile*. Dewey saw schools as institutions which took the accumulated learning of adults (material quite unrelated, he considered, to the exigencies of growth), and then proceeded to force it upon children, instead of attempting to determine what these children needed as they went along.

C HIS PSYCHOLOGY

Dewey studied psychology under the tutelage of G. Stanley Hall (1846–1924), who was particularly interested in the study of the child, and who produced his outstanding work on *Adolescence* in 1904 (7). Through the work of Hall and his colleagues the scientific study of the child mind had become a serious and essential part of educational activity. In *The School and Society* (8) Dewey made the following points about the psychology of elementary education. He stated that earlier psychology had regarded mind as a purely individual affair in direct and naked contact with an external world; educational practice had exhibited an unconscious adaptation to and harmony with the prevailing psychology; the older psychology was a psychology of intellect and knowledge; and finally, the modern conception of mind was essentially one of a *process of growth*, not a fixed thing.

Thus Dewey took up the theme of G. Stanley Hall and developed it. In the process of evolution man has gradually acquired a brain, a mind and an intelligence which are all superior to those of other animals. Gradually man has evolved through adjustment to environment, and through the adjustment of the environment to himself, and he has acquired a measure of intelligent control over his own evolution. Dewey opposed the mechanistic psychology of behaviour and accepted that all persons had basic individual differences. The problems and difficulties he observed in the various children of his experimental school demanded some special help and attention, and he found part of the solution in the psycho-analytic methods of Freud. He did not reject the then current tendency

'to conceive individual mind as a function of social life, as not capable of operating by itself, but as requiring continuous stimulus from social agencies and finding its nutrition in social supplies' (9).

Mind was, it is true, essentially social, but children, according to Dewey, were still very much individuals and should be allowed to develop and grow in an atmosphere of freedom. This did not mean, however, that he supported the more *popular* interpretation of Freudian psychology, namely, that no restraint whatsoever should at any time be used in children's upbringing and education. Indeed, in this respect, Dewey appeared to change very little in his views, for as early as 1900 he had said that a really sympathetic teacher was likely to know much more clearly than the child himself what his own instincts were and meant, and that the teacher was there to suggest and direct the child who might not consciously know what his needs were. Thirty-eight years later he protested that there were some teachers who appeared afraid even to make suggestions to the members of a group as to what they should do; there were instances where children were surrounded with objects and materials and then left absolutely to themselves, lest their 'freedom be infringed upon' (10).

In his discussion of 'The Psychology of Elementary Education' Dewey gave an outline of elementary school life on a psychological basis (11). There are, he suggests, three main types of growth: from four to eight years of age, from eight to twelve, and from twelve onwards. Briefly, the first period, from four to eight years, is one of *play*, in which the child has left the narrowness and the limitations of the home and begins to make his first contacts with the social world beyond. In this new atmosphere, in which ends and means are not distinguished, he is untroubled by problems. The main concern of his first studies is the life and occupations of the home, followed by the larger social activities upon which the home itself is dependent—in Dewey's example, mainly farm life. Finally the child learns about the development of various occupations and vital inventions through an experimental reconstruction of the various phases of human evolution and life. Reading and writing are now introduced, and a systematic approach to geography is embarked upon.

The second period, from eight to twelve years, is one of *spontaneous attention* and the development of technique. The child is now able and ready to acquire skills because he is becoming increasingly aware of the possibility of objective results which may also be permanent. In ordinary affairs and in the solution of practical problems, the child begins to develop the ability to analyze details, and to act according to general rules of behaviour and thought. Because of these developments in the child there is a need for changes both in matter and in method of school pursuits. Special studies now find a place in the curriculum quite independent of one another.

The third period, from twelve years onwards, is one of *reflective attention* in which the child has mastered the methods of activity, inquiry and thought appropriate to the various phases of experience, in order to be able to specialize in particular studies for technical and intellectual aims. Dewey seems to admit that in this stage there is a sense of more remote ends, and the child is able to raise problems and look for solutions.

Like Herbart, Dewey emphasized very strongly the place of interest in school work and of learning through interest (12). To Dewey, an interest was 'an outgoing of the self' which was 'imperiously demanded' if the individual were to develop his natural growth. But 'imperious' or not, it was not just 'interests' as such which were important, but the organization and canalizing of interests. Dewey argued that it was essential to decide between really important and trivial interests: between helpful and harmful interests: between transitory and exciting interests and those which are enduring and permanently influential. What Dewey regards as important is the control and direction of interests, and when we somewhat loosely talk about 'arousing interest' in our teaching, it would be well to consider whether it is the right sort of interest that we are arousing, and whether it can be permanently related to something of value.

In his *Democracy and Education* Dewey considered education as a formal discipline. Older views of psychology had held that the mind possessed, or comprised, a series of faculties concerned with certain mental operations, such as memory, judgment, influence and so forth. Some of these were 'keyed-in' as it were at a later stage than others, though memory was considered to operate from the beginning. There were, of course, quantitative differences between individuals, and between the individual as child and the individual as adult. Dewey's belief in evolutionary growth would not permit him to accept this view of the mind, nor the view that education was the training of faculties. He stated that the theory, however influential it might be, was defective (13).

D DEWEY AND EDUCATION

Dewey held that philosophy might be defined as the general theory of education, or as the theory of education in its most general phases. His philosophical position was that of pragmatism, and his educational principles were pragmatic. The establishment of the Laboratory School at Chicago in 1896 was an attempt to show that he had the courage of his convictions. Of course, he had ideal conditions, and it is true that he left it all after eight years to become Professor of Philosophy at Columbia University, but H. H. Horne's criticism of Dewey, to the effect that he used the literary and dialectic methods which he decried rather than the experimental method which he praised, in advocating his own views, is a trifle harsh. Dewey *did* go into the laboratory and experiment, and continually made use of the experimental method. But it is a trifle naïve to argue that one cannot afterwards write about it even dialectically, or, for that matter, outline the experiment before the laboratory is entered.

Dewey obviously owed a great deal to Froebel, who saw the problems of education in their social setting, and he visualized the school as a nursery for the citizens of the future. His central theme for all child education was *Darstellung*—a concept of creative self-expression, in which children lived out their experiences in all their activities. In *The School and Society*, Dewey summarized the main educational principles of Froebel in the following terms (14):

1 The primary business of the school is to train children in co-operative and mutually helpful living; to foster in them the consciousness of mutual interdependence, and to help them practically in making the adjustments that will carry this spirit into overt deeds.

2 The primary root of all educative activity is in the instinctive, impulsive attitudes and activities of the child, and not in the presentation and application of external material, whether through the ideas of others or through the senses—the spontaneous activities of children are capable of educational use.

3 These individual tendencies and activities are organized and directed through the uses made of them in keeping up the co-operative living already spoken of, taking advantage of them to reproduce on the child's plane the typical doings and occupations of the larger, maturer, society into which he is finally to go forth.

The sort of school envisaged by Dewey was one capable of producing people for complete living in the world of today; and he regarded the ideal home as the model for the ideal school, which was a large family, a living community involved in a variety of pursuits which were of intense interest to the pupils, and which made them fully alive to the fact that they were all partners in a common effort. Each had something of importance to contribute to the success of the whole.

The Discipline of Experience and Experimentalism: For Dewey the school was a place for living, working citizens; it was a place where each individual could learn to discipline himself through experience, and in consequence there must be room to experiment. For example, Dewey saw history as dynamic and moving:

'The question of how human beings live, indeed, represents the dominant interest with which the child approaches historic material' (15).

To him the whole history of mankind could be concentrated into the evolution of flax, cotton and wool fibres into clothing, and into the 're-invention' of both materials and machines. In this way, from the examination and manipulation of raw materials to the construction of machines, and the final production of clothing, the child was able to recapitulate the history of his race and its culture epochs, and to participate in its discoveries and manufactures.

Such a method, of course, has its limitations. We can, in practice, import only to a very limited extent the economic life and conditions of the macrocosm of society into the microcosm of the school. Moreover, as Dewey himself admitted, experience *per se* is not necessarily educative; it depends upon the sort of quality of the experience, and the ability of the experiencer to apprehend his experience, and to make the right eduction of relations and correlates. Some experiences, indeed, may be termed *miseducative*. And again, despite Dewey's denial of ends, the Deweyan teacher has a great responsibility for helping the young to *evaluate* experience, and to see the direction in which their experience is leading them (16).

Dewey accepted the need for a teacher fully to understand his individual pupils so that he might be in a position to provide the right suggestion at the right time. He must also realize that the influences and contacts experienced by a child are all-important. Dewey has said that meaning arises through communication; if children are to apprehend the meaning of experience they must be able to communicate, and he suggests that the teacher should engineer situations and arrange experiences wherein such communication is possible, so that there may be continuity, expansion, development, progress and growth. Dewey saw, further, that within the context of the relative freedom of the atmosphere of experimentalism there was also the need for the discipline of group experience. All human life is lived in groups, and an essential part of individual development is the acceptance of social controls, and the intellectual and disciplined participation in the creation and formulation of such controls as may be both acceptable and socially desirable.

The Five General Features of Reflective Experience: Dewey has frequently been represented in the more popular mind as the initiator of 'progressive' forms of education, with children milling around engaged in noisy and messy projects without purpose or completion. It is, however, a sobering corrective to look at his steps in the thinking process, which he applied to the educational process. These are frequently compared with the famous Herbartian 'Five Formal Steps' of preparation, presentation, association, generalization and application. In *How We Think* (17) Dewey posed the question, 'How does a child get to know his world?' And he answers, 'Through reflective experience'. In all experience there exists a cause-effect relation, and the causal *nexus* is made by thought or reflection. Dewey states that there are five stages in the thinking process:

1 The first stage is a state of confusion, doubt and perplexity owing to the fact that the individual is involved in an incomplete situation whose full nature and significance have not yet been ascertained. In terms of education, the pupil must have a *problem*, which should be his own.

2 The second stage is an attempt at a conjecture, a tentative interpretation of the given data, attributing to them a tendency to produce certain consequences. In terms of the pupil, his problem must be a *real* one, that is, real to himself, and a *stimulus* to further thought.

3 The third stage is a careful examination, exploration, survey and analysis of every available consideration that would help to clarify and define further the problem under consideration. Here the pupil must have the necessary *information* and make the *observations* required to deal with the problem.

4 This stage is an elaboration of the hypothesis in order to make it more precise and more consistent as it begins to square with a wider range of available elements and data. Here the pupil is in the position of the *researcher*, developing his ideas and seeking his own solution.

5 Lastly, the hypothesis is tested; one takes a stand upon the projected hypothesis as an organized plan of action to be applied to the existing state of affairs. The pupil must be allowed to try out and *test the validity* of his own conclusions.

This, said Dewey, is how we think when faced with the solving of a problem; this is the Problem Method.

The Child and the Curriculum: Pedocentricism: Dewey strongly objected to the subject-based curriculum as the logical summary of the experience of the adult. He held that subjects were simply the summaries of human activities, and so children should reach them by making a summary of their own experiences. For adults all these subjects were useful compartments for the convenient storage of knowledge, but young children were not yet ready for this analytical approach to their world. The sort of abstractions made by geography and history, for example, in terms of space and time were not meaningful to them. Out of this belief Dewey developed his pedocentric view of education and the curriculum, and the influence which his ideas have had upon our modern school curriculum has been considerable. The child is the starting-point; he is the centre, and he is the end; his development and growth are, in fact, the only 'ideal' that Dewey will allow; these are the considerations that furnish the standard (18).

Dewey goes on to say that we should begin with the child's present experience before entering that represented by the organized bodies of truth which we refer to as 'studies'. The present world of the child is a total, integral one—for him: to us it may seem narrow, limited and small, but it is his personal world. There is a unity about this world of the child; an almost complete lack of differentiation which leads to a wholehearted interest in all things—from worms to cloud-formations—without any specialization or divisions of the curriculum. And because, in this pedocentric approach the subject-matter is always related to the child's personal experience, it leads ultimately to an enrichment of the subject-matter itself. In this view the task of the teacher is to organize learning situations and contexts of experience. But experiences have no final value—they are of passing value only and are specifically related to the growth of the child at some particular time and place. As early as 1906 Dewey argued that,

'it is the danger of the "new education" that it regards the child's present powers and interests as something finally significant in themselves' (19).

It would appear that the pragmatic test, as applied by Dewey, does not validate any experience *in vacuo*, nor in any final or absolute sense. The child's experience is useful, significant, satisfactory, even 'true', only contextually. There are no absolutes; and there are no external ends, whether immediate or remote; the educational process has no end beyond itself. It is its own end, and it is a process of continual reorganization, reconstruction and transformation. Education is growth, universal growth, and its purpose is to encourage growth—mental, moral and physical. And so, theoretically and philosophically, Dewey denies the existence of ultimate or eternal values; practically, he rejects ends and anything in the way of ready-made solutions. Subject divisions are an attempt to present such a solution, and therefore subjects, as such, should not—at least at first—appear on the curriculum.

Moral and Religious Aspects of Education: Although Dewey was strongly influenced in his early years by Hegel's philosophy, he gradually divorced himself from idealism and the realm of absolute values. In this he also rejected any idea that morals should be regarded as a special department of education requiring special lessons. Morality was not a fixed or final achievement, but a continuing process. Indeed, it was all one with growth itself: morals were, in fact, education. Dewey strongly disapproved of the separation of moral or religious education from any other form of educational experience; for him morality grew out of specific empirical facts, it was social. Thus, in the realms of morality and religion, experience and empirical facts must be the real teacher; the teacher as a person may be a guide, counsellor and friend, but he may do no more than indicate short cuts to his pupils, and encourage them to spare themselves miseducative adventures. Ultimately, however, the moral significance of a personal, disciplined and organized life can come only through the free and purposive judgment of each individual. This is the way that human progress is made and that communication is assured between people.

Dewey considered that youth must become the regenerating force in our future society, since education itself was a process of reconstruction or reconstitution of experience. It was the innate desire for increased *efficiency* which eventually led to discipline. But self-discipline and group-discipline develop through the will of the pupils themselves in order that their progress may be attained with the absolute minimum of disorganization or obstruction. Morality and discipline are thus seen as utilitarian and as promoting general 'efficiency', and in so far as they achieve this they possess pragmatic sanction. In all this the educator's part is to achieve and furnish the type of environment which will stimulate responses and direct the learner's course, for

'In the last analysis, *all* that the educator can do is to modify stimuli so that response will surely result in the formation of desirable intellectual and emotional dispositions' (20).

It is clear from the foregoing that Dewey means by 'desirable' that which '*ought* to be desired'; and we are entitled to ask what dispositions of an intellectual and emotional nature *ought* to be desired, why they ought to be desired, and on whose authority. And this brings us back once more to a criterion which is outside the purely pragmatic one—and this leads us to a realm of values and ends.

E SOME DEVELOPMENTS OF DEWEYISM

The Project Method: The methods employed by Dewey in his Laboratory School grew quite naturally out of his pragmatic philosophy and his psychological theories. In *The School and Society* he discusses the psychology of occupations (21), and he states that the fundamental point in the psychology of an occupation is that it maintains a balance between the practical and the intellectual phases of experience. Dewey was concerned with the processes involved in all human activity, particularly those involving man's basic needs for food, clothing and reasonable comfort. He, therefore, set about 're-inventing' and rediscovering the means for the fulfilment of these needs. This involved the posing of certain 'problems' which arose naturally in the pupils' minds, and others which were cunningly contrived by the teacher so that they appeared to originate from the children. This was known as the Problem Method.

Whilst Dewey does not appear to have invented the term 'Project Method' he was certainly largely responsible for the idea, and in Chapter XV ('Play and Work in the Curriculum') of *Democracy and Education* he refers to 'projects'. It was Professor W. H. Kilpatrick of Columbia University who developed the Project Method from about 1918 onwards, and in 1925 he published an account of it in his *Foundations of Method* (22). Kilpatrick regarded the project as wholehearted and purposeful activity proceeding in a social environment. He held that pupils must propose what they actually wished to do; that they should be permitted to do only those things which would build up certain attitudes; that all learning should be done only if it were necessary for what the pupils had actually proposed; and that what pupils were allowed to do should be guided so as to enrich the subsequent stream of experience. Kilpatrick's detailed analysis of the different types of project—producer, consumer, problem and drill—may be read in Chapter XXI of his *Foundations of Method*.

The Dalton Plan: The 'Contract Plan', which Helen Parkhurst developed at Dalton in Massachusetts, has been described by her in *Education on the Dalton Plan*. The Plan was a 'contract' between the pupils and the teacher to allow the independence of the pupil to work at his own rate on this particular assignment, and to permit the teacher to serve in a consultative capacity. The Dalton Laboratory Plan emphasized in particular the value of the *heuristic* method—a method of 'finding out' by the pupil, but not on any haphazard basis. The assignment was fully organized and planned in collaboration with the teacher, and procedures were to some extent programmed; then the pupil was allowed to go off to his 'cubicle' to search for the solutions, and the teacher was always available to give guidance when necessary. The hall-marks of the Plan were freedom and co-operation. The restrictions of timetables, curricula, syllabuses, bells and so forth are often incredibly frustrating to the teacher and pupil alike: the Dalton Plan sought to eliminate all these as formal limitations. But the Plan was not a 'free for all'; there must exist freedom within the necessity of co-operation. The Plan laid emphasis on the importance of the pupil's living whilst he did his work, and on the manner in which he acted as a member of society rather than on the subjects of the curriculum. His character and knowledge were determined by the sum-total of these experiences.

The Play Way: In *Democracy and Education* Dewey emphasized that play and work were not mutually exclusive, and that plays, games, and constructive 'occupations' were not merely agreeable diversions. Play is not. amusement or aimlessness, nor is work necessarily arduous and lacking enjoyment. Indeed, work which remains 'permeated with the play attitude is art—in quality if not in conventional designation' (23). In 1917 Caldwell Cook maintained in *The Play Way* that play methods were simply an active way of learning, not a relaxation or diversion from real study. Many schools, and many individual teachers, make use today, of course, of various aspects of the pragmatic approach, including problem and project methods, assignments and play methods, without seeing the necessity to discard a more formal framework as the general setting and organization of the work.

REFERENCES

1 Dewey, J., *The School and Society* (University of Chicago Press, 1900), p. 116.
2 Ibid., p. 11.
3 James, W., *Pragmatism* (Longman, 1907), pp. 45–6.
4 Gallie, W. B., *Peirce and Pragmatism* (Penguin Books, 1952), p. 22.
5 Curtis, S. J. and Boultwood, M. E. A., *A Short History of Educational Ideas* (University Tutorial Press, 4th ed., 1965), p. 473.
6 Dewey, J., *Reconstruction in Philosophy* (Holt, 1920), p. 177.
7 Hall, G. S., *Adolescence* (Appleton, 1904).
8 Op. cit., Chapter IV *passim*.
9 Ibid., p. 90.
10 Dewey, J., *Experience and Education* (Macmillan, 1938), p. 84.
11 *The School and Society*, Chapter IV.
12 Ibid., Chapter VI and VII.
13 Dewey, J., *Democracy and Education* (Macmillan, 1916, reprinted 1955), p. 80.
14 Op. cit., Chapter V.
15 *The School and Society*, p. 157.
16 *Experience and Education*, pp. 84–5.
17 Dewey, J., *How We Think* (Harrap, 1910, revised ed., 1933).
18 Dewey, J., *The School and the Child* (Blackie, 1906), pp. 22 f.
19 Ibid., p. 29.
20 *Democracy and Education*, p. 212.
21 Op. cit., Chapter VI.
22 Kilpatrick, W. H., *Foundations of Method* (Macmillan, 1925).
23 Parkhurst, H., *The Dalton Plan* (Bell, 1922), p. 12.

BIBLIOGRAPHY: (A) BOOKS BY JOHN DEWEY

The School and Society (University of Chicago Press, 1900).

The Child and the Curriculum (University of Chicago Press, 1902).
The School and the Child (Blackie, 1906).
How We Think (Harrap, 1910).
Democracy and Education (Macmillan, 1916, reprinted 1955).
Essays in Experimental Logic (University of Chicago Press, 1916).
Creative Intelligence (Holt, 1917).
Reconstruction in Philosophy (Holt, 1920).
Human Nature and Conduct (Holt, 1922).
The Public and Its Problems (Holt, 1927).
Experience and Nature (Allen and Unwin, 1929).
The Quest for Certainty (Minton, Balch, N.Y., 1929).
Sources of a Science of Education (H. Liveright, 1929).
Art and Education (Barnes Foundation Press, 1929).
Characters and Events (Holt, 1929).
Individualism, Old and New (Minton, Balch, N.Y., 1930).
Philosophy and Civilization (Minton, Balch, N.Y., 1931).
The Way out of Educational Confusion (Harvard University Press, 1931).
A Common Faith (Yale University Press, 1934).
Art as Experience (Minton, Balch, N.Y., 1934).
Logic: The Theory of Inquiry (Holt, 1938).
Experience and Education (Macmillan, 1938, 19th printing, 1955).
Liberalism and Social Action (Putnam, 1939).
Freedom and Culture (Allen and Unwin, 1940).
Education Today (Putnam, 1940).
Problems of Men, (N.Y. Philos. Lib., 1946).

Dewey, J., and Dewey, E., *Schools of Tomorrow* (Dent, 1915).
Dewey, J. and Bentley, A. P., *Knowing and the Known* (Beacon Press, 1949).
Dewey, J. and Tufts, J. M., *Ethics* (Holt, 1932).

BIBLIOGRAPHY: (B) OTHER BOOKS FOR REFERENCE

Baker, M. C., *Foundations of John Dewey's Educational Theory* (Columbia University Press, 1956).
Blewett, J. (ed.), *John Dewey: His Thoughts and Influence* (Fordham University Press, 1960).
Cook, Caldwell, *The Play Way* (Heinemann, 1917).
Curtis, S. J., *An Introduction to the Philosophy of Education* (University Tutorial Press, 1958), *passim*.
Curtis, S. J. and Boultwood, M. E. A., *A Short History of Educational Ideas* (University Tutorial Press, 4th ed., 1965), Chapters XVII and XX.
Dewey, E., *The Dalton Laboratory Plan* (Dent, 1922).
Edman, I., *John Dewey: His Contribution to the American Tradition* (Bobbs-Merrill, 1955).
Gallie, W. B., *Peirce and Pragmatism* (Penguin Books, 1952).
Geiger, G. R., *John Dewey in Perspective* (O.U.P., 1958).
Gull, H. K. F., *Projects in the Education of Young Children* (McDougall, 1926).
Halsey, M. and Schneider, H. W., *John Dewey: A Centennial Bibliography* (University of Chicago Press, 1962).
Handlin, O., *John Dewey's Challenge to Education* (Harper, 1959).
Hook, S., *John Dewey: An Intellectual Portrait* (John Day, 1939).
Horne, H. H., *The Democratic Philosophy of Education* (Macmillan, 1932).

James, W., *Pragmatism* (Longman, 1907).

Kilpatrick, W. H., *Foundations of Method* (Macmillan, 1925).

Kilpatrick, W. H., *Education for a Changing Civilization* (Macmillan, 1926).

Nathanson, J., *John Dewey, The Reconstruction of a Democratic Life* (Scribner, 1951).

Neff, F. C., *Philosophy and American Education* (C.A.R.E. Inc., N.Y., 1967).

Parkhurst, H., *Education on the Dalton Plan* (Bell, 1930).

Ratner, J. (ed.), *Intelligence and the Modern World, John Dewey's Philosophy* (New York, Modern Library, 1939).

Roth, R. J., *John Dewey and Self-Realization* (Prentice-Hall, 1962).

Rusk, R. R., *Doctrines of the Great Educators* (Macmillan, 3rd ed., 1965). Chapter XII.

Schilpp, P. A., *The Philosophy of John Dewey* (Evanston, Northwestern University Press, 1939).

Thayer, H. S., *The Logic of Pragmatism: An Examination of John Dewey's Logic* (Routledge, 1952).

Thomson, G. H., *A Modern Philosophy of Education* (Allen and Unwin, 1929), Chapter V.

White, M. G., *The Origin of Dewey's Instrumentalism* (Columbia University Press, 1943).

Wynne, J. P., *Theories of Education* (Harper and Row, 1963), Chapter 6.

Conclusion

Little has been said in this book of the welfare services that have helped to provide children with milk, cheap or free meals, dental treatment, medical examination and attention, psychological treatment and special education for a variety of handicaps. These are all vitally important in the development of education during the period under consideration, and in the gradual establishment of the principle of 'equality of opportunity'. Nor has justice been done to the gradual emancipation of girls and women in the various levels of education, or to the many thinkers and teachers who have helped to change both educational theory and practice—some from their more remote 'ivory towers', others in the more vigorous activity of the classrooms. For these, and other very important themes, the student must refer to the many books mentioned in the bibliographies.

A careful reading of the innumerable reports, papers and circulars issued by the Board or Ministry of Education in the past will reveal to the student that most of our 'modern' ideas have occurred to many educationists and administrators of the past, even though they were not perhaps implemented. There is little or nothing new under the sun. Perhaps the most recent elements in our various branches of education are bigness and busyness; in education we are all involved with large numbers of people—pupils, students and staff; and we are all enveloped in a restless round of continuous activity, discussion, talk, tasks and assessment. It is not without significance that Martin Buber warns, in *Between Man and Man*:

'The life of dialogue is not one in which you have much to do with men, but one in which you really have to do with those with whom you have to do.'

GENERAL BIBLIOGRAPHY

Adamson, J. W., *English Education, 1789–1902* (C.U.P., 1930, reprinted 1964).
Archer, R. L., *Secondary Education in the Nineteenth Century* (C.U.P., 1932).
Argles, M., *South Kensington to Robbins (1851–1963)* (Longmans, 1964).
Armfelt, R., *The Structure of English Education* (Cohen and West, 1961).
Barnard, H. C., *A History of English Education: From 1760* (University of London Press, 1961, 2nd ed.).
Birchenough, C., *History of Elementary Education in England and Wales from 1800 to the Present Day* (University Tutorial Press, 1938, 2nd ed.).

Blishen, E., *Education Today* (B.B.C., 1964).

Boyd, W., *The History of Western Education* (A. and C. Black, 1964, 7th ed.).

Curtis, S. J., *History of Education in Great Britain* (University Tutorial Press, 1963, 5th ed.).

Curtis, S. J. and Boultwood, M. E. A., *An Introductory History of English Education Since 1800* (University Tutorial Press, 1964, 3rd ed.).

Curtis, S. J. and Boultwood, M. E. A., *A Short History of Educational Ideas* (University Tutorial Press, 1965, 4th ed.).

Dent, H. C., *Growth in English Education: 1946–1952* (Routledge, 1954).

Eaglesham, E. J. R., *The Foundations of 20th-Century Education in England* (Routledge, 1967).

Eaglesham, E. J. R., *From School Board to Local Authority* (Routledge, 1956).

Good, H. G., *A History of Western Education* (Macmillan, 1966, 7th printing).

Jarman, T. L., *Landmarks in the History of Education* (Murray, 1963, 2nd ed.).

Lowndes, G. A. N., *The Silent Social Revolution* (O.U.P., 1948).

Maclure, J. S., *Educational Documents—England and Wales: 1816–1967* (Methuen, 1968).

Meyer, A. E., *An Educational History of the Western World* (McGraw-Hill, 1965).

Peterson, A. D. C., *A Hundred Years of Education* (Duckworth, 1952).

Raymont, T., *A History of the Education of Young Children* (Longman, 1937).

Rusk, R. R., *A History of Infant Education* (University of London Press, 1933).

Rusk, R. R., *The Doctrines of the Great Educators* (Macmillan, 1965, 3rd ed.).

Simon, B., *Studies in the History of Education, 1780–1870* (Lawrence and Wishart, 1960).

Smith, F., *A History of English Elementary Education, 1760–1902* (University of London Press, 1931).

Taylor, G. and Saunders, J. B., *The New Law of Education* (Butterworths, 1965, 6th ed.).

Wynne, J. P., *Theories of Education* (Harper and Row, 1963).

NAME INDEX

NAME INDEX

SUBJECT INDEX